# Always Emilie

# Always Emilie

Alyson Root

**ISBN-13:** 9798390809181
**Imprint:** Independently published

Cover design by: Cath Grace @cathgracedesigns

# Dedication

For all those who got their second chance.

# Table of Contents

# Chapter 1

"Holymotherfuckingshitballs," Charlie growled through gritted teeth. Her arm was on fire. Hours of having her skin scraped by the mechanical needle were taking its toll on her pain threshold.

"I'm adding another tenner to your bill for that one." Max laughed as he sprayed her arm with water before wiping the excess ink off with some kitchen roll.

"Ten quid, are you taking the piss?"

"Eleven now. You really need to get a grip on your swearing, lady."

Charlie had a few more choice words she wanted to throw at him at that moment, but the pain on her arm stopped her from unloading.

"There, done, all finished." Max rolled his chair back, tilting his head as he looked at his work.

Charlie let out a breath she'd been holding. Why did she do this to herself? She knew why. She'd wanted tattoos since she was a kid. It had taken her until her thirtieth birthday before she'd summoned the courage to get her first one.

"Take a look," Max urged.

This was Charlie's favourite part. Gripping the arm of the chair, she hoisted herself up. Her legs were dead from sitting for so long. Her arse was tingling with pins and needles.

The tattoo studio was small. It only had enough space for two tattoo artists, a piercing station and a small reception area. Across from the piercing station was a floor-to-ceiling mirror. Making her way across the room Charlie let her gaze wander over her new ink. Tears welled in her eyes. Max had captured her vision perfectly.

"So, what d'ya think?" He knew what she thought. His wide smile said it all.

"Max, you nailed it."

"Yeah, I did." He laughed as he began breaking down his station. "You know the procedure by now, so I won't go over it again. Look after those beauties. I worked hard on them."

Max really was a master artist. He was unlike any tattooist Charlie had ever met, though. His skin was completely devoid of any ink. Max was a haemophiliac. His blood's inability to clot prevented him from getting tattoos. Well, it was strongly discouraged by medical professionals, and Max had heeded those warnings. Thankfully, his husband Ben was more than happy to let Max use his body as a canvas for all the tattoos that Max wanted but couldn't have.

Max also ran his tattoo studio like a high end boutique. Gentle music played from the stereo system. The space was immaculate — as a tattoo studio should be. The reception area offered a plush sofa with a glass coffee table in front. Opposite was a coffee station with every coffee flavour known to man. The reception desk was made from solid oak and it served to separate the front of house from the tattooists as well as welcoming clients. The walls were cream with tastefully selected photographs of Max's work which ran from one end of the wall to the other. The photographs were fabulous — well they would be–Charlie had taken them after all. At the back of the shop was a full bathroom and kitchen area for Max and Ben.

2

Charlie had been friends with Max for twenty-five years. They'd grown up living next door to each other but hadn't spent all their time together as children. Max had gone to a different school and Charlie was painfully shy, so she never sought him out on her own. They had the odd afternoon playing together when Charlie's parents needed her out of their way.

Over the years, they'd kept in touch and it was only about eight years ago that they reconnected properly. It hadn't taken them long to form a strong friendship, and Max was the one to give Charlie the confidence to get her first tattoo. The rest is history, as they say. Charlie wouldn't go anywhere else now.

Max's forte was hyperrealism. It was as if the art he created came alive on the skin. Charlie could attest to it. Her body was proof.

"Shall we get a video of the whole thing now it's done?" Max enquired. Throughout the entire process they'd taken pictures, but now Max wanted to do a 360° video of the finished piece.

Unlike her childhood years, Charlie was no longer shy. It had taken a lot of time and help to gain the confidence she had now, but she'd done it. Her body was beautiful, she was worth loving. How sad that she had to repeat that sentence in her head to function. Her therapist had spent hours helping her and so had her best friend, Sam. All those insecurities because she had shitty parents who never gave a damn. Charlie rolled her eyes at herself. It did no good feeling sorry for herself. Especially not today. Today she was finally at the end of her tattoo journey and she couldn't wait to see the complete result.

"Yeah, let's do it. You got the camera ready, Benny boy?"

"Yeah, all set up in the back room."

Charlie followed Max and Ben. The back room was actually a very large storage space that had been cleared out and had a white drop sheet installed for the photographs Charlie took of Max's work.

"Get your kit off then," Max shouted from behind the drop cloth.

"You're a real charmer Max, I see why Ben fell over backwards to be with you," Charlie smirked. Max had spent three years trying to win over Ben, who was having none of it. Ben had been hurt badly in his last relationship and wanted nothing to do with men ever again. Until Max swept in and vowed to win his love. Inevitably Ben caved, and it was a good job he did. Those two men were made for each other.

"He couldn't resist me," Max laughed.

"Er, I think I resisted you for quite some time there, handsome," Ben chuckled, rolling his eyes at his husband.

"No way, you were just playing a little hard to get. You were always mine." Max wrapped his arms around Ben and kissed his cheek.

"Oh, Jesus, you two make me sick." Charlie mock gagged. Stripping off her top and bra, she stood in front of the camera.

"Oh, I got a new toy to play with for this," Ben hollered, rummaging through a box that sat next to the door. He produced something that looked like a bulletproof vest. "Look at this beauty. You attach the camera to the front. Obviously, you wear it like a vest. The little thingy here stabilises the camera so I can walk around you without the video being jittery."

"That's awesome," Charlie stated, because it really was. She was a massive tech nerd and could spend the day talking about it with Ben, who was equally nerdy.

"Alright you pair, before I lose you to the world of geek, can we get this video done?"

Charlie stood back in the middle of the room. Max passed her a hair tie to move her long mane out of the way. "Okay, Char,

4

just stand straight and look forwards, I'll do all the work," Ben said, manoeuvering himself into position. Charlie stood tall, looking at a spot on the wall as Ben circled her. The task only took a few minutes, but the end result was phenomenal. Ben loaded the footage onto his laptop.

All of Charlie's tattoos had been meticulously planned. Charlie wanted her ink to represent everything she held dear in her life. Max had taken those ideas and made them into reality.

Her back—well, the middle column—was adorned with a creeping rose bush. It was so realistic it felt like each flower could be plucked right off her skin. The thorny stems intertwined with each other growing up her spine. In between the thorns and flowers, Max had filled the spaces with individual memories. From afar only the roses and thorns were visible but up close greyscale pictures emerged.

The roses were an homage to her grandmother. Estelle Munroe was the only woman in Charlie's childhood that gave a damn. The problem was Estelle had been rather old when she'd had Charlie's mum, so by the time Charlie needed her, Estelle was too fragile. Their time together had been mostly spent in Estelle's nursing home. Charlie would take herself there as often as possible.

Charlie's most vivid memories were of Estelle tending to her rose bushes in the communal garden. The colours of those flowers had always mesmerised Charlie. The petals were so soft and she loved running her fingers over them as she listened to her grandmother talk. Sadly, Estelle passed away the week before Charlie's twelfth birthday. That was the start of Charlie's most lonely period.

Tears pooled in her eyes as she watched the video. Max had got the colour of the roses spot on. The image catapulted her back to those wonderful afternoons with Estelle. That was the reason she wanted these tattoos, to remind herself of all the love she had and not the love she was denied by her parents.

The camera panned round her left arm. Roses flowed seamlessly over her shoulder and down to her elbow. The pattern mirrored on her right arm. The rose buds were smaller on her arms compared to her back, they were also a myriad of different colour shades. Estelle had always had a variety of roses that she cared for.

Charlie's left arm went from that deep velvet red which covered her back to pink and orange flowers. Her right arm had blue and lavender petals. Each colour represented something that Charlie held close to her heart. The red roses were love, the love for her grandmother. Orange was for enthusiasm and passion, which Charlie felt for her work and her business. The light blue represented sensitivity and feeling. They were for her best friend Sam and, lastly, the lavender, which meant love at first sight. Only Charlie knew who those roses were dedicated to.

"Oh, Max." Charlie's voice was saturated with so much emotion she could hardly talk.

"Honey, you are a master," Ben added.

"It's been one of the most rewarding projects I've done, so thank you, Char, for trusting me with it."

"I wouldn't go anywhere else, you know that."

"Do you mind if I put this on the website?" Ben asked.

"Not at all."

"Sure? Your Tatty Bojangles are on show," he laughed.

"Tatty Bo... are you ten?" Charlie laughed along with them, shaking her head. "No, I don't care, anyway they advertise your piercings, so that's a bonus." Charlie had both nipples pierced, too.

"Excellent. I'll get editing and upload it then." Ben clapped with enthusiasm before burying himself in the video editing software he'd already loaded.

"Let's have a coffee, get some sugar in you and then you can get off," Max said, passing Charlie and heading out the door. Two sugary coffees and a digestive biscuit later, Charlie stepped out onto the street.

Oxford Street was rammed as per usual, and the thought of trying to fight her way through to the Underground sat as well as getting a tonsillectomy. The cab fare to get home was astronomical, but she could afford it. Her business with Sam was a raging success.

S. C. Photography had been their brainchild for the last four years. Charlie had originally started as an employee. She was happy doing the work without the responsibility. However, it hadn't taken Sam long to convince her to become a full business partner. Their careers had taken them around the world, which is why a lot of Charlie's filler tattoos were of different places around the globe.

The door to her home and the main HQ of S. C. Photography creaked open. Bowman Manor was a property that had been in her family for generations. Charlie came from old money, but she knew better than anyone that all the money in the world couldn't guarantee happiness.

Bowman Manor had been the last place that Estelle had lived. When Estelle moved into the retirement home, Charlie's parents moved them in. It was the only home she could remember well. Although she used the term *home* loosely. Charlie's parents, Kevin and Lucile Baxter, spent the bare minimum of time in the manor. Charlie was effectively raised by part-time nannies. That was until she reached an age where she could fend for herself, then she was on her own.

The lower half of the mansion was used for Charlie and Sam's business. The top floor was all Charlie's. Her parents had leased the building to them to begin with. Last year, however, Charlie had been surprised to find out that they'd signed Bowman Manor over to her completely. Apparently, it's what Estelle had originally requested. Why it took them over twenty years to oblige was anyone's guess.

As soon as the ink on the contract was dry, Charlie had used a tiny portion of her very large trust fund to completely redesign the top floor. Instead of there being several stuffy rooms, the upper floor was now one large, open plan apartment. Her trust fund had always made her feel queasy, and she'd never taken a pound out of it until the overhaul of the manor. Estelle would have wanted her to use the money for that.

Normally, the only thing she associated with the bulging bank account was disappointment and pain. Her mum had commented several times that what she lacked in love she made up in money. Lucile was a real piece of work sometimes.

Carol sat at her desk in the main reception area. Charlie hired her two years ago when things were really getting busy. Sam Lived in France and ran the French portion of the business, which was a lot smaller. Charlie had gotten overwhelmed with the organisation side of things and eventually conceded she needed help.

Carol was sixty-five and as sharp as a knife. She never suffered fools, and she had a fierce protective streak when it came to those she loved. Sometimes Charlie didn't know how she'd managed without the old girl for so long. "Old girl" was Charlie's favourite nickname for Carol because it wound her up to no end. They had a wonderful working and private relationship.

8

"Hello, Stretch, tats all done?" Stretch was Carol's nickname for Charlie. No surprise why. Charlie stood at 5'8" whereas Carol was a petite 4'9" at best.

"Ah, there's my favourite old girl. How's the hip?"

"Well, I'm about to stand up and kick you up the arse, so let's find out."

Charlie barked out laughing. "Max has done a beautiful job. I couldn't be any happier."

"Well, that's marvelous, love. I've been thinking of getting one, you know. My Sarah thinks I would look good with one on my foot or something." Sarah was Carol's youngest and wildest child.

"Deffo, go for it. Let me know if you really want to and I'll book it with Max."

"You pay me well, Stretch, but not Oxford Street well," Carol scoffed mockingly.

"One second." Charlie held up her finger and withdrew her phone. After a few brief minutes of tapping, she put it away again. "Right, done. Max is ready when you are and the bill is taken care of."

"Charlie Baxter," Carol boomed, "you can't... I never.."

"Too late, it's already done and if you refuse, you'll hurt my delicate feelings."

Carol drew in her eyebrows and scowled, causing Charlie to laugh again. "You're too good, young lady."

"No, I'm lucky to have you, Carol. Now any messages? Or have you been sitting around knitting all morning?"

"Oh, you cheeky bugger. Here, a couple of letters, but that's all."

Charlie took the letters and kissed Carol on her cheek. "I'll be upstairs for a little while. I don't have anything booked for the day, so I'm gonna chill. You get off early if you want."

"Alright, love, call if you need me, though. I'm going to stick around for the next hour or two. Your two minions should be back by then, and I want to make sure they've seen their updated calendars."

Charlie grinned. Carol had called Charlie's two apprentices *minions* because their names were Stuart and Bob — well, Bobby, but that was neither here nor there. The names stuck, and they found it funny. So much so, they both came dressed as minions for Halloween.

"Okay, just ring if you need me." With that, Charlie took the stairs up to her floor. The brick walls had been left exposed. The floor was hardwood and ran throughout the entire apartment. After the work had been completed, everyone who visited was stunned. It was a mix of old and new. Estelle would have loved it.

As she walked through the double doors at the top of the stairs, Charlie's phone vibrated. There had to be a mistake. Why on earth was Mr Eccleton calling her? "Hello?" This should be interesting. Mr Eccleton was her form tutor from Pickerton Academy. A private school that she was shipped off to at the age of fifteen.

"Ms Munroe?" Jesus, he still had that monotone voice that put her into a coma after thirty seconds.

"It's Ms Baxter now." She hadn't used her stage name in a very long time and she wasn't going to start now.

"My apologies, Ms Baxter. I hope you don't mind, I got your number off of the school's donor website. Is this a good time to talk?" No, it wasn't a good time, it was never a good time. She had solid plans to veg on the sofa with her PS4 for the rest of the day.

"I have a few minutes." *Way to stand your ground, Char!*

"Excellent. I'm ringing to make sure you received your formal invitation to the Pickerton Annual Christmas Ball." *Crap.* Yes, she received it, she got the bloody thing every sodding year.

"Oh, um, I'm not sure." Lies, lies, lies. The invitation was currently in her recycling bin.

"Well, I'll email you another. This year is extremely important. We're celebrating twenty years of our outreach programme 'Drama 4 All' and we have planned a splendid event. Nearly all the alumni will attend and I'd hoped you would be included, Ms Baxter. Between you and me, we hoped you would join your old bandmates again and do a little performance for us. Show the current students the quality that Pickerton can produce."

Oh, hell no, no fucking way, not on your nelly! "I would be happy to donate some more money if that helps, but I don't feel it's possible to attend. Christmas is by far my busiest time, and my calendar is completely booked."

"Oh, I do hope you'll reconsider, Ms Baxter. You were one of the brightest pianists I ever had the honour of teaching. Plus, and I'm sorry that this will seem like I'm trying to manipulate you, but we have a young girl attending who, well, who has had a rather rough time of it lately. Her parents were killed in a car accident six months ago. She was due to start with us this year but had to pull out. She has to move to be with her closest kin and, well, this ball is the only bit of Pickerton she will get to experience. Grace was so looking forward to seeing our best and brightest play."

Right. Poor unfortunate kid who's just lost her parents. Fan-fucking-tastic. How could she say no now?

Charlie cleared her throat. "Send me the invite and I'll add it to my calendar."

"Oh, Ms Baxter, that's wonderful." A thought struck her as she was about to hang up. If the band was coming back together, did that mean *everyone*?

"Just out of interest. Who in the band has agreed?"

"Everyone. I must dash. See you in a few weeks." The phone went dead. Shit, she didn't get the answer she was looking for. But surely he couldn't mean everyone right. Anyway, Emilie Martin would be far too busy to attend a school ball, right? Oh God, what if she turned up?

On the *very* slim chance that Emilie would be there, Charlie was not going to be alone, no sir. Seventeen-year-old Charlie was in the past. Gone were the pimples, greasy hair and chronic shyness. If she had to see Emilie again, it would be with a beautiful woman on her arm. Emilie would see that what she'd done to Charlie back then had no effect on her whatsoever.

The phone rang and rang. Eventually a breathless Sam picked up. "Dude, this better be important."

"I need your wife." Silence. Okay, she probably could have phrased that a tad better.

"Care to elaborate on that, mate?"

"Yes, I need Anna. Put her on the phone."

There were several muffled noises before Anna spoke. "I hear you want me," she laughed.

"I need you, desperately."

"For?"

"A school Christmas Ball."

"A what?" Sam bellowed. Of course, she was on speaker.

"Look, I need to borrow Anna for the night. I need a date and I need it to be with someone I'm comfortable with." That should be sufficient, right? No need to go into detail.

"Nice try, buddy. How about you explain fully before I lend you my wife?"

"*Lend me*, Sam. I'm not cattle. I'll decide who gets me and who doesn't thank you very much."

"Of course, my love, you know what I mean."

"Good job I do."

"I love you."

"Hello, I'm still here, you know," Charlie called in frustration.

"Sorry, Charlie," Anna replied. "Listen, come over this weekend and we'll talk. You can explain why you need an escort and we can see our very best friend. It's been a while."

"Alright, I'll book a ticket. See you this weekend."

"That's it, we're just leaving the conversation there?" Sam huffed.

"Yes, *mon amour*, it's clear that Charlie doesn't feel comfortable telling us right now so it can be saved for the weekend. Everything is better face to face, anyway."

Charlie smiled, she loved how understanding Anna could be. "See you both soon. Love you."

"Love you," they called in unison.

Okay, she had a plan. Sam was going to be pissed once Charlie explained everything. Although Sam and Charlie had been best friends since the first week of university, Charlie had omitted some things from her middle school years.

Sam was going to be hurt that she'd kept such a big part of her life a secret. The moment she left for university, Charlie had put the academy and all the bullshit that went with it in her rearview mirror. Ideally, that's where it should stay forever, but with the ball on the horizon, Charlie knew she was on borrowed time. Pickerton was calling and Charlie would have to answer.

# Chapter 2

Decades may have passed, but the same melody still ran through Emilie's head. Her pre-show ritual was sacrosanct, and everyone in her crew knew better than to interrupt her. Sitting cross-legged on her dressing room floor, she let the sound of her favorite musical piece play. To anyone else, the room was silent, but for Emilie, it was filled with music. The notes floated across her eyes as the music played on. No one knew what Emilie thought of or what she heard when she took time to ready herself. The ritual was hers and hers alone. The piece ended and with it her prep time. Opening her eyes, she took a deep lungful of air through her nose and let it out through her mouth. She was ready.

As usual, her guitar stood next to her dressing table. Emilie smiled as she perused her new instrument. Her name was big enough that guitar makers around the globe fought to have her play one of their instruments. For Emilie, though, she always stuck to what she knew.

Her very first guitar had been a hand-me-down from her grandfather when she was six. A beat up old Fender. That guitar had been with her for nearly thirty years. Now it sat in its custom-made case on her touring bus. She only played it privately.

For shows, she would take her newly gifted American Acoustasonic Jazzmaster on stage. It was a thing of beauty, and the sound it produced still sent shivers up her spine.

"Five minutes, Em." Jack's voice was muffled through the closed door.

"Got it," she called back. In five minutes, she would stand in front of twenty thousand people screaming her name. Adrenaline pumped. This was her favourite part. Even after twenty years of performing under her belt, she always felt the rush. It wasn't something she would ever get used to, and it was wondrous.

Her outfit had become a little disheveled. Wardrobe was going to kick her ass again. It was bound to happen, though. Emilie couldn't just lounge around, she had to be moving, doing something to curb her excitement. Normally, she would write songs or she'd pace with her guitar, playing random music to occupy herself. All that moving around left her trousers wrinkled and her shirt askew. Nothing that a quick pull here and there couldn't fix.

"Em, it's time." Jack again. He was a taskmaster sometimes, but as her manager and friend, she cut him some slack. He worked hard and had been loyal to her for nearly two decades. She picked up her guitar and made her way to the stage. The rest of the band would already be congregated, waiting for her. "You ready?" Jack always asked her that.

"Of course." Never in all her years as a performer had she *not* been ready, it's what she lived for. They turned the corner and headed to the small group of people waiting in the wings.

"Let's bring it in, people." The night might be about her, but Emilie was under no illusion. None of it would be possible without her bandmates. Jess Hill was one of her original band members. She was 5'4" with short black hair and was one of the best drummers on the planet. They'd met at fifteen and had formed a close bond quickly.

Back then, it was difficult to know if kids wanted to be Emilie's friend because they liked her or because they wanted to jump on the Emilie Martin bandwagon. Emilie had been in the spotlight since she was fourteen. Her voice had thrust her into the big leagues quickly, which at the time had seemed like a dream come true, but in reality, it left her unprepared to deal with what her change of status would bring. Fans, yes. Money grabbers, definitely. Brandon, her uncle, had done everything in his power to help her navigate the world of fame and fortune and for the most part he'd succeeded, but there were still a few times that the wrong people had got close to her.

By the time she was closing in on her sixteenth birthday, she'd learned her lesson and was notoriously picky about the people she surrounded herself with. Jess had proved trustworthy and loyal, and she was one of Emilie's oldest friends.

Lance Bishop was her bass player. He'd joined her ten years ago after Billy, her original bassist, passed away from a heart attack. Lance was a few years older than Emilie's thirty-six years. He wore his hair long and unbrushed, which drove Emilie a little insane. Thankfully, he wasn't allowed to wear his Hawaiian shirts on stage. The man exuded beach hippie, but he was a talented bass player, and that's all that mattered.

Last but not least, Liz Roper. Liz was a different kettle of fish entirely. Stupidly, Emilie had slept with her after a drunk night out and now things were all kinds of awkward. The world population knew that Emilie was gay. That wasn't the problem. It was because Emilie was usually so strict about crew members hooking up. Liz had been cool about it. They continued to play

16

well together, but now there seemed to be an expectation that they would sleep together again. An expectation that Emilie had been shockingly bad at rebuffing. Hell, she got lonely sometimes and if Liz could keep it casual, then maybe they could be friends with benefits. Maybe.

Liz cracked her knuckles as they gathered round in a circle. Was it healthy for a pianist to crack her hands like that? *Get your head in the game!*

"Okay, gather round my lovelies. It's the last show of the tour. Let's go out there and give them everything we've got." They wrapped their arms around each other, spurring each other on. The tour had been long and tiring and even though Emilie loved what she did, she was ready for some downtime. But first, one last show.

The rest of the band took to the stage first, revving up the crowd. Emilie donned her award-winning smile and stepped out of the shadows. The noise hit her like a wall. Twenty thousand people screamed at the top of their lungs for her. The stage lights made it difficult to see out, but it didn't matter. The sheer force of the crowd's energy pulsed through the air.

"Well, hello everyone." The crowd roared louder. Emilie enjoyed conversing with the audience, it made them feel like they were a part of the show and it made Emilie feel connected to them. "Shall we get this show on the road? I think I'll start with my favourite number."

Emilie swung her guitar round from where it had been hanging off her back. The microphone was already adjusted perfectly. Her lips brushed the metal of the mic head. She strummed the opening chord to "Losing My Head Over You," which was the first song Emilie had written at sixteen. The song had been an instant hit. The single had gone to the top of the charts worldwide.

17

Emilie smiled as the words poured from her soul. She tuned out the sound of the crowd. This ballad was one of the purest things she'd ever written because she felt the words in her very being. When the song came to a close, she took a beat to breathe. Singing "Losing My Head Over You" left her a little drained because of how much energy she put into it. Not physically, but emotionally. The chanting crowd overwhelmed her as she brought herself back to the present. With another giant smile, she launched into the next song.

By the end of the show, sweat was dripping down her cheeks. The tendrils of hair that she'd left down stuck to her face and neck. Thankfully, her signature messy bun was still in place.

The band had given it there all, and the crowd had been fantastic. With two encores done, Emilie headed back to her dressing room to decompress. Just like her pre-show ritual, she had an end of show one, too. Make-up and hair got sorted first. There was nothing like feeling her hair being literally let down. Next, she showered and changed into comfy jeans and a t-shirt, then she meditated for twenty minutes.

A show like that left everyone buzzing, and it was difficult to come down. Meditation had proved helpful over the years and allowed her to go celebrating with the crew without being ridiculous. Sure, they would dance and drink, but for Emilie, the soothing effect of meditation left her tired a lot quicker than everyone else. She felt no shame bowing out early to get some sleep.

"Ready to go?" Liz stood in the doorway to her dressing room. She looked good and Emilie wondered if she'd made a special effort just for her.

"Sure, but it won't be a late one for me. I'm done, it's been a long few months." Liz looked at her with a curious look. "What?"

"Nothing, just wondering if you'd like some company, you know, for your early night?" Emilie studied Liz. Was she stupid to even consider sleeping with her again? Probably, but, hell, a woman has needs.

"Sure, let's get out of here."

\* \* \*

The sun was just beginning to peep over the horizon. Emilie sat with her legs curled into her chest. It wasn't the first time she'd stayed at Shangrila-La The Shard and it wouldn't be the last, it was one of her favourite hotels. The views were spectacular.

Her entourage always stayed with her, so the hotel usually gave them an entire floor. There was only one requisite, and that was that Emilie got the Deluxe Suite. The plush seat by one of the many windows was her favourite spot. She loved sitting with a steaming cup of coffee, peering down over London.

That's where she found herself this morning, although she couldn't quite focus on the view because the other person in her room was distracting. Not in a good way distracting, more of a "why the hell did you do that again?" kind of distracting.

As usual, all the crew had headed to a club to let off some steam. Emilie and Liz had joined them, but only for two drinks. They'd said their farewells and headed straight to Emilie's suite, where they'd fucked for a few hours.

An unease settled over Emilie as she studied Liz's naked form sprawled across her bed. Sure, the sex had been fun, but that was all it was. Just like every other sexual encounter Emilie had experienced over the past decade. Fun, light and temporary, always temporary.

Damn it. This thing with Liz was going to become complicated. She could feel it. Even if Liz said she was okay with it just being a bit of fun, Emilie knew better. She caught movement from the corner of her eye. Liz was stirring. "Morning," she mumbled.

"Hey."

"You okay?" Liz shifted herself into a sitting position.

"Yeah, good. Really looking forward to some downtime." The air was rife with tension. Emilie wanted Liz to leave but didn't know how to say it without sounding rude, and Liz clearly wanted to have some sort of discussion, probably about their casual hookups turning into something more. Emilie could see it on Liz's face as they looked at each other.

"Emil-"

"Last night was fun, Liz. Probably best if we leave it at that. We need to work together and neither of us can afford complicated." *Was that too harsh?*

Liz studied her face for an extra beat before nodding. "Yeah, of course. It was fun. I'm going to grab my stuff and get back to my room. Everyone is meeting for brunch. I'll see you there." Liz wasted no time slipping out of bed, collecting her clothes that were scattered across the suite and leaving the room.

Emilie's time alone was short-lived as per usual. Jack sauntered in without knocking, gabbing about her itinerary for the day. Emilie suppressed her eye roll. The one major downside to her lifestyle was the lack of privacy. She loved Jack, but sometimes she just wanted some time alone.

"Okay, brunch at ten-thirty. Radio 2 interview at one."

"Okay."

"Oh, and here's the guest list you requested for that godforsaken school thing you decided to do. Without my approval, I might add."

"Watch yourself, Jack." Jack was an excellent manager, but he sometimes forgot who signed his checks. "I don't need your approval. This is something personal that I'm looking forward to. You didn't need to be consulted."

"You have a full calendar, Em, dropping unscheduled events is difficult to manage."

"And yet you rearrange my schedule with little fuss when you see dollar signs. The event is in my downtime, which I'm going to take full advantage of. On that note, I do *not* want any events scheduled within that time unless I request it."

Nearly every year, Emilie had worked over her break. Jack was a fabulous manager, but sometimes too eager and a little too greedy. He had to understand that she wasn't a money-making machine, her breaks were essential.

"Not even the—"

"No, nothing, not this time Jack, do I make myself clear?"

His face blushed red. He wasn't embarrassed, he was pissed at being scolded. "Fine." It came out almost as a growl. Emilie raised her eyebrows. Now he blushed with embarrassment. "I'll meet you downstairs," he added, scuttling out of the room.

Emilie puffed out her cheeks and sighed. Her irritation ebbed when her eye caught the guest list for the Pickerton annual event. This would be the first year she would attend. Her celebrity status meant that she couldn't turn up to things off the cuff. She was mobbed wherever she went and she had planned to turn the invitation down. That was until Mr Eccleton had mentioned that everyone from her year was attending. Everyone!

Scanning the list, Emilie frowned. Her name was at the top—quelle surprise—but it was the lack of one name that gave her pause. The only name she wanted to see. Charlotte Munroe. There was a Charlotte Smith, no idea who that was. A Charlotte Bott. A year below Emilie, if memory served, and then there was Charlie Baxter. Not a name she recognised. Shit, had old

Eccleton lied to her? Maybe Charlotte Munroe just hadn't sent her confirmation in yet.

There was only one way to find out, and that was to go. The publicity for the school would be worth it, anyway. Emilie had loved every second of her time at Pickerton until the last week. She closed her eyes and tried with everything she had to shove that memory away. For years, guilt ate away at her and no matter what good she did to override it, that feeling never abated.

* * *

The BBC Radio 2 station was only a thirty-minute drive, thank god. All Emilie wanted to do was crash, but this was her last engagement before her time was truly her own.

This would be her fifth time as a guest for the BBC in three years. It was a testament to her popularity that they clamoured to get her on anytime she was in the UK.

As usual, Jack had everything down to the millisecond. The moment her car arrived, she was whisked off directly to the studio and fitted with headphones. No waiting around, which was great. She could kiss her manager for his efficiency.

"Emilie, great to see you again, it's been a while." Emma Jones, host of the morning show, said. Having people suck up to her was the norm now, but she genuinely liked Emma and knew that she was being sincere in her greeting.

"Emma, you look wonderful. How's little Teddy? He must be, what? Six now?"

"Oh, it's sweet of you to ask. He's doing just great. He *has* just turned six, so he's a handful, but an adorable one."

Emilie had met little Teddy the last time she was here. Emma's sitter had let her down, and was mortified that she'd had no choice but to bring her son to work. She was nearly catatonic when Teddy spilled juice over Emilie's cashmere top. Emilie had found the whole thing funny. She loved kids, and Teddy really was a little sweetheart. The incident got her and Emma talking. They followed each other on social media, but today was the first time they'd seen each other in person since.

"Please give him a squeeze from me. That little tux you bought him was excellent, he looked so cute." Emilie had done a little squeal when she'd seen the picture on Emma's Instagram of Teddy dressed to the nines.

"Ha, it lasted about an hour before he was pulling it off. He's a pyjamas kind of boy." Emma's face lit up as she spoke about her son. A light flashed in the corner of the room.

"Okay, Emilie, we're up in thirty seconds." Emilie gave a thumbs up and waited to be introduced. She took a long drink from the coffee that had magically appeared in front of her. Jack strikes again. There was no need to get a PA, not when Jack filled the role. Well, he was paid an exorbitant amount of money, so she wasn't going to feel bad that he took on additional jobs.

"Let's welcome to the show, everyone's favourite French Canadian and singing superstar, Emilie Martin." Emma crowed delightfully.

"Thanks, Emma, it's great to be back."

"So, how have you been? It's been a few months since we last spoke and in that time it looks like you've been busy." Emma laughed. She knew how hard Emilie worked.

"Definitely, it's been nonstop with the world tour, but that finished last night so I get some time off now. And, may I say, what a great way to start my holiday by visiting you lovely people here at the BBC."

"We love having you. By all accounts, the tour has been one of your most successful. How does it make you feel after all these years to be still pulling in such high numbers?"

23

"Emma, honestly, it's the dream. My fans are the reason I do what I do. There is nothing as thrilling as standing on stage in front of all those awesome people."

"What's been the highlight of this tour?"

"The same as every tour I've done. Meeting the people. Being on the road so much can be tough, but when I see the fans singing along to my songs, it makes all the hard stuff worth it."

"There is a rumour that you're already writing another album. Can you tell us anything about it?"

Goddamn Jack. He'd been pushing her to begin another album halfway through the tour and she'd been emphatic that it wasn't going to happen, not until she'd taken a break. Once again, he'd undone his hard work by overstepping.

"Sorry to disappoint, but I'm not currently working on one just yet. I'll probably start looking at it next year. The past few years have been so full-on, I'm ready to take a step back. My music is my passion and I want it to always come from the heart. Rushing an album or forcing it isn't how I give the fans my best. I promise you'll be the first to know when I'm writing," she chuckled. *That's it. Keep it light, even though you want to strangle Jack.*

"We all need a holiday," Emma laughed in return. "So, what's on your relaxation agenda? Spa, skiing, hiking? What is it that Emilie Martin does to unwind?"

"Sleep will be the first thing I do," Emilie laughed even though it was absolutely true. "After that, I plan to hang around the UK for a couple of weeks and then I'll fly home. See family, hike and play with my dog."

"And when you say home, you mean Canada?"

"Yeah, Quebec, it seems like so long ago since I was home. I've had a blast on tour, but I'm ready to get back to my house."

"Sounds wonderful, Emilie. And thank you for coming to spend some time with us today. Let's remind everyone why you are a musical genius. You're listening to BBC Radio 2 with Emilie Martin and her latest release 'Back in your Arms'."

Emilie waited until she was given the signal that she was clear to leave. After a brief hug, she left Emma to get on with the show. Emilie had one goal, and that was to chew out Jack. By the look on his face as she approached, he had already guessed what was coming.

"Look before you get mad I—"

"In the car." Emilie barked. They were *not* having this discussion in the middle of a radio station. Jack stumbled along behind her as they climbed into Emilie's blacked-out SUV.

"Have I given you some sign that you run the show here, Jack? We work because you used to understand what I needed from you. Somewhere along that way, you seemed to have forgotten."

"Look, Em, I'm sorry, but it's just good business to get the next album written. You're hot right now and people want more."

"It doesn't matter what you think. I have told you *repeatedly* that I need a break. I've told you I wouldn't be starting the next album until next year. How could you put me in that position on live radio? What did you think, that I would fold and tell the nation I was writing something? What the hell were you thinking?"

"I'm just looking out for you, Em. You've been around a long time and it's not guaranteed that you will always have this level of success. You should milk it whilst you can."

"Milk it? Are you for real? I do this because I love it. If the fans fall away, that will suck, but it won't be the end of the world. I'm not burning myself out because you want to get richer than you are. Jesus, Jack, I don't know what to say to you right now." Where was this attitude coming from? Jack never focused on the money. He'd always understood that Emilie did her job for the love of music. "I think this break will be just as good for you as it will be for me. Get your priorities back in order or don't bother coming back. You, more than anyone, understand my position on money grabbers. I never thought in a million years you would be in that category. Shit, Jack, I don't speak to my own parents because of how they behaved."

"Hey now, no need to be dramatic. You know I am not like them. Sometimes I get carried away and push you. I'll back off. I'm still your guy."

For the first time in their friendship, Emilie doubted him. Something more was going on, but he wasn't going to give it up. "Jack, take some time anyway. I don't need you right now. Fly home, see the kids. I'll connect when I get back."

Clearly everyone needed some time and space from each other.

Things felt tense with Jack. He didn't look happy about leaving her to her own devices, which was bizarre. Hell, she couldn't think about that now. The Pickerton Ball was coming up, and that needed all her attention.

# Chapter 3

Charlie entered the code into the automatic keypad lock. Anna's and Sam's apartment in the 16th arrondissement was equipped with all the latest security. The lock gave a little beep as she pressed enter.

Pushing the door open, she covered her eyes with her hand. "I have entered the apartment, so you have thirty seconds to get dressed and put your toys away." It was a running joke in their friendship group that Sam and Anna went at it like rabbits. There was never a safe time to enter a room when they were in it. A shuffling sound drew her attention. Anna walked into the hallway in comfy looking pyjamas and boot slippers.

"We were not having sex." Anna laughed, drawing Charlie into a hug.

"I'll put money on you pair doing it before I arrived. Sam's got sex hair." Charlie pointed at her best friend, who had followed her wife into the hallway. She did, in fact, have sex hair. And the blush that crept over her creamy skin was a dead giveaway, too.

"That was like an hour ago," Sam mumbled.

Charlie burst out laughing. "Hey, I'm not criticising. I just don't think my innocent eyes can handle catching you two in the act again. My therapist had a field day after the last time. He even threw around the term 'PTSD', just sayin'."

"He did not, you drama queen, plus it was a lesson in knocking before entering. That was all on you." Sam was still bright red. It was highly amusing to Charlie how easy it was to get under her skin.

"Who the hell is shagging at half two on a Tuesday afternoon, and in the office, I might add?"

"She has a point *mon amour*," Anna stated. Sam rolled her eyes, then swept Charlie up into a bone-crushing hug.

"Hey, I missed you, lady," Sam whispered in her ear.

"Missed you, too."

Although Charlie flew out to visit them in Paris often, it was still difficult to be away from Sam for so long. Samantha Chambers was more than a friend to Charlie. They were like sisters. Sam and her mum Sandy had made Charlie a part of their family ever since they'd met at university.

When Sam packed up and moved to Paris, Charlie felt bittersweet. The year before Sam met Anna, she'd had a rough time of it, so when they got together and Sam finally found the happiness she deserved, Charlie was so thankful but after Sam had moved away, it highlighted how much Charlie relied on her friend.

There were times when Charlie felt extremely lonely. It was especially difficult when she felt that way in her own home. No matter how much she changed the interior of Bowman Manor, she could never quite escape the old feelings of being a small kid trapped in that gargantuan place all alone. Maybe she was a masochist. That would explain why she'd moved back into her childhood home that had always made her feel shitty.

"Hungry?" Anna asked, making her way to the kitchen. There was the most delicious smell wafting through the room.

28

Charlie's tummy growled loudly, causing everyone to laugh. "I made your favourite."

"You're too good to me. I'd marry you if you weren't already taken." The smell of melting cheese made her mouth water. Tartiflette was a calorific nightmare, but the tastiest thing Charlie had ever put in her mouth. Layers of potatoes, bacon and cheese mixed with a little cream. Who the hell wouldn't love that?

Sam and Charlie made their way to the table by the window in the living room. Plates, cutlery and glasses were already set, leaving them nothing to do but wait for Anna.

"So you gonna explain that call?" Sam quirked her eyebrow.

"Which call?" As if she didn't know which call Sam was talking about.

"The one where you asked to borrow my wife."

"Oh, that one, right, yeah, later. Let me eat first." Honestly, Charlie really wasn't looking forward to explaining her past to Sam. There was no one in her life now that knew about Pickerton and everything that went down. It was doubtful her parents would remember the name of the school they shipped her off to, let alone the resulting drama that occurred in her final year.

Thankfully, Sam was cut off from whatever she was going to say by Anna entering with a bubbling pot of orgasm-inducing food. Alright, maybe that was a tad dramatic on Charlie's end, but it really was tasty.

They sat in comfortable silence. Charlie watched Sam and Anna interact. Anna spooned out their food whilst Sam poured herself and Charlie some wine. Oddly, she poured Anna sparkling water. The fork that had been making its way to Charlie's mouth stilled mid way. Why was Anna not drinking?

She never missed out on excellent wine. Hell, she never missed out on wine full stop.

*No way, no fucking way…*

"Is there something *you two* would like to share?" Charlies eyes bored into her friends. Sam shifted and went red. She was so bad at hiding things. "Samantha?" Charlie knew using her full name would do the trick. Sam looked rapidly from Charlie to Anna. Anna squeezed Sam's hand and smiled, her entire body lighting up.

"There is one thing we wanted to tell you. That's the real reason we wanted you to visit." Sam's voice held a slight quiver.

"Say it," Charlie almost shouted. Her heart rate was through the roof.

"Anna's pregnant." That did it. Charlie couldn't hold it in any longer. She jumped from her seat and launched herself at the two of them. Anna laughed wildly as Charlie peppered her face with kisses.

"Oh, my fucking god, I'm so happy for you both. Shit, I can't believe we're having a baby!"

"We?" Sam laughed.

"If you think I'm not going to be a part of this every step of the way you're in for a rude awakening, mate. I'm gonna spoil the shit out of all of you. How far along are you? Do you know if it's a boy or girl or are you gonna let the kid determine its own identity? Will you stay in the apartment? Christ, have you told Sandy?" Charlie was running out of air.

"Jesus, Char, take a breath," Sam cackled.

"I'm four months, no idea about the sex, and we don't want to know. We will stay in the apartment. Our parents found out an hour ago, and, of course, you will be involved. I expect you to make sure Sam doesn't have a panic attack during the birth, because we both know she's going to be a mess."

"Hey," Sam protested, and then laughed. She knew damn well Anna was right.

"I just… I mean, wow." Charlie sat back in her seat, the food forgotten about. "I'm going to be an aunt."

"You're going to be the best aunt," Anna beamed.

The rest of the evening was lost to excited conversation about the baby. Charlie couldn't even muster any upset that they hadn't told her they had been trying for the past year. Actually, Sam keeping this from her could work in her favour! Sam couldn't get pissy about Charlie leaving out certain things from her past now. That would be hypercritical, right? *Ha, keep dreaming Char, she's going to throw a right fit.*

* * *

Charlie smooshed her face further into her pillow. She needed to ask Anna where she got this bedding from because it was stupidly comfortable. Her heart felt so light as she lay sprawled out, starfish style, thinking back to the night before. Wow, a baby! Charlie couldn't wait to be a mum. She had so much love to give a child. She just needed to find the right woman.

Her thoughts strayed to Pickerton. Nope, she had to shut that down right now. Pickerton and the girl that got away were a lifetime ago. They were firmly in the past and that's where they should stay. Attending the ball was going to stir it up again, though. Well, only if Emilie attended, which, let's be honest, was doubtful.

"Coffee." Charlie lifted her head at the sleepy voice. Sam shuffled into the room and climbed into bed next to her.

"Caffeinate me, woman." After propping herself up against the headboard, Charlie grabbed the coffee and inhaled deeply. Her body didn't function without at least two cups of the good stuff first thing in the morning. After a few silent minutes, Charlie studied Sam, who frankly looked harassed. "Mate, are you okay?"

"Hmm?" Sam wasn't even looking at Charlie. She was staring at the bedroom door.

"Now, I'll never be one to complain about you supplying me with my drug of choice." Charlie held up her coffee cup. "But why are you in here bringing me coffee? Where's Anna?"

"Shh, she's asleep." Sam looked at her, alarmed.

"Okay, why do you look so... I don't even know."

"Can I tell you something but you can't tell Anna?" Sam's head was pivoting from the door to Charlie.

"Obviously, you tool."

"I'm hiding from her." Sam was dead serious. Her eyes were the size of dinner plates. It was a very comical look.

"Right, any reason in particular?" Charlie was worrying. Why was Sam hiding from her pregnant wife? Was she regretting the baby? No, surely not.

"She never stops, Char. I'm so tired, but she's relentless."

"What on earth are you talking about, Sa—"

"Sex!" Sam shouted before panicking and lowering her voice. "Sex, Charlie, she wants it all the time. I don't know what's happened but suddenly she's become crazy about it. Every morning and then lunch, usually in the afternoons too and don't even get me started on evenings. I'm so tired, she's... she's insatiable."

Charlie had to take a second to suppress the laughter that was threatening to come out. "Mate—"

"Don't mate me! You don't know, I've become a sex slave since she got pregnant."

Okay, now Charlie couldn't stop her laughter bubbling up. Sam looked so serious, which made it so much funnier. "Sam, suck it up. That woman is going to be pushing a human out of a very small hole! If the one thing you can give her is

32

multiple orgasms to help her until then, that's what you're gonna do. Grab a Redbull and get yourself together. Woman up and give your baby's mother what she needs!"

"Charlie—"

"Nuh-uh, no excuses. She's giving her body up to create life. Her hormones are going to be going nuts. Yeah, you might be tired for a few months, but buckle up buttercup, coz that's going to be your life for the next eighteen years. And let's be honest here, buddy, is it really a hardship that you get to screw like bunnies? Think of all those poor bastards that have their pregnant partners rebuff them completely! Imagine Anna not wanting you anywhere near her."

"Sam?" Anna's voice carried through the apartment. "Babe, can you come here for a minute?"

Charlie punched Sam on the shoulder with a wide grin. "Show time. Give that woman what she needs. I'm gonna slip on my headphones and enjoy a bit of music for a while."

Sam slipped out of the bed, rolling her shoulders in preparation. After a couple of jumps and a shake of her head, she headed to the door. "Turn the music up. She's not quiet and honestly, she doesn't give a shit who hears anymore."

"Roger that. No pun intended." Charlie laughed harder at Sam's expression, who looked genuinely worried for her own health. With music blaring, Charlie pulled back the blinds so she could look out as she sipped her coffee. She couldn't help but giggle to herself. Poor Sammy.

An hour went by before Charlie dared remove her headphones. Her ears were ringing, and a headache was surfacing behind her eyes. That was probably due to scrolling through baby wear for too long. How the hell did anyone get anything done in life when there was so much cuteness available online? She'd spent a small fortune, which she was sure Anna

33

and Sam would balk at, but it was too late. They were going to get a shipment of all the coolest baby stuff available.

There was no noise, so Sam must have got the job done. Leaving her room, Charlie headed for the kitchen. The radio was playing softly. Anna danced to the music as she cooked pancakes.

"Mornin', mama, you sleep well?" Charlie gave Anna a quick hug before refilling her coffee cup.

"Like a log. I'm not feeling uncomfortable yet and Sam is wearing me out every night like a trooper."

Charlie barked with laughter at Anna's cheeky smile. "Speaking of the stud muffin, where is Sam?"

"Sleeping. She deserves a break."

"Bloody hell, Anna, don't feel too sorry for her. She's getting laid like four times a day!"

Anna laughed, clearly not phased that Sam had spoken to Charlie about their very full sex life. "Oh, I don't feel sorry for her, I just need her rested because in about —" Anna checked her watch " —two hours I'm going to be ready to go again. Sorry, Char, not great for you, right?"

"Hey, you do what you gotta do. Pregnant ladies should get to do anything they like in my book."

"I'll tell Sam you said that."

"I already did," Charlie grinned.

A beat passed as they looked at each other. Anna was great at waiting things out. She seemed to have infinite patience and understanding and she could read Charlie well. Sometimes too well.

"I have some stuff to explain to Sam, and I think she's going to be upset. I kept it from her." Charlie worried her lip.

"Sam will understand that you didn't feel ready to share it. Yes, she might be a little hotheaded sometimes, but she loves you more than anyone. Just talk to her."

A loud yawning sound caught their attention. Sam plonked herself down heavily at the breakfast bar. "Morning," she mumbled. Anna leaned over to give her a kiss. They were the vision of domestic bliss, and Charlie loved it.

"Okay, I need to tell you why I need to borrow Anna." Charlie just wanted to get it over with.

"Alright, shoot." Sam cradled her coffee like it was her lifeblood.

"Okay, no interrupting. Questions only at the end." Anna and Sam nodded. "As you know, my parents were pretty shit. They didn't want to give me their time, so they shipped me off to school as soon as they could. I told you that already. What I neglected to mention was that from the age of fifteen, I attended Pickerton Academy of Performance Art. I was accepted because of my talent as a pianist. In fact, I was well on my way to becoming one of the most successful pianists in the UK." Charlie cleared her throat. "I haven't always gone by Charlie Baxter. My name back then was Charlotte Munroe, you may or may not of heard that name. Anyway, I met and fell in love with a girl and to cut a very long and painful story short, she left me heartbroken beyond anything I could have ever imagined. I left Pickerton and the piano behind. I changed my degree to photography and dropped my stage name."

"You're Charlotte Munroe?" Anna blurted. Okay, she clearly had heard the name then. Charlie nodded.

"Hang on, let me get this all straight in my mind. Your name isn't really Charlie Baxter, and you're a famous pianist?" Sam was staring at her like she'd sprouted another head.

"My legal name *is* Charlie Baxter. Charlotte Munroe was my stage name that I went by back then and I was — past tense — a pianist. My grandmother's last name was Munroe. After what happened in my final year, I just wanted to forget. I wanted to be rid of all those arsehole stuck-up bitches that made my life

35

hell. I wanted to find friends that liked me for me and I did that in uni."

"Why didn't you tell me? We tell each other everything." Sam was hurt. Charlie could see it in her eyes.

"I just wanted to leave it in the past, mate. It wasn't anything against you. I had successfully left it behind until my old teacher called and roped me into doing a bloody charity ball. He laid it on thick this year and I felt bad. Plus, it's been nearly twenty years, so I really need to get the fuck over it."

"So that's what you need me for? To go to the ball?" Anna clarified.

"Precisely that," Charlie pointed at her.

"But why? Just take a date." Sam argued.

"No, I need someone who knows me, who I feel comfortable with and no offence, Sammy, but we don't come across as two people that would date, hence why I need Anna."

"Who do you need to convince?" Sam looked completely confused.

"Okay, so it's possible that the girl, or I should say woman, that carved out my heart and left me to rot all alone will be there."

"Wow, that was really visual." Sam chuckled nervously.

"Well, it's true. So now you know, will you be my date, Anna?"

Anna nodded as if there had never been a question that she would do it. "Of course, no problem. Although it's possible I'll be showing more by then. Is that a problem?"

"Not at all. I'm not going to lie to anyone. You'll be my date and that's all I'll say."

Sam scratched her head, still in a fog of sleep deprivation. "Who was the girl?"

"Okay, I'll tell you, but don't be daft about it."

Sam rolled her eyes. "Alright, Ms Dramatic. Who is it?"

"Emilie Martin." Charlie watched as Sam and Anna's features went from curious to utterly stunned.

"Emilie Martin, as in *the* Emilie Martin?" Sam shouted.

"As in the lesbian goddess of singing, Emilie Martin," Anna blurted, just as shocked as her wife.

"Err, yeah, that would be the one." In unison, they started shouting questions at her. Unsurprising really. How was anyone supposed to react when they heard their best friend had once been involved with the biggest singing sensation the world had seen in decades? Charlie sat back and let them ramble. Eventually, they came to a natural silence. "Finished?" They nodded. "Okay, look, when we met, she was only just starting out. She was just Em to me and everyone at school. But the problem is that she may well be at this ball and I need support if I'm going to see her again."

"Wow, she really did a number on you, hey?" Sam commented looking worried.

"Yeah, she did, but I don't really want to go over it if that's okay?"

"That's fine, sweetie," Anna smiled. A tension settled on Charlie's shoulders. She hated that something that happened two decades ago still affected her so much.

The call of the doorbell shattered the silence that had ascended upon the trio. "You expecting someone, babe?" Sam asked Anna.

"No." The bell cried again and again. Whoever was at the door was keen to be let in. Sam huffed as she left the kitchen to answer the door. Charlie looked at Anna before there came a gaggle of screams. Charlie and Anna shot out of the kitchen and ran to the door. In a mess of bodies and arms were Kim and Hélène, who were beaming with happiness.

"What are you doing here?" Anna screamed excitedly.

"We got home last night. We couldn't wait to see you. Get your gorgeous butt over here, mum-to-be." Kim scooped Anna up into a tight hug. Tears were raining down both their faces. Kim and Hélène had been sailing around the world for the past year. Kim was a Marine Biologist who was working with a foundation to research the decline in marine life around the world. Hélène, her fiancée and close friend of Sam's, was a professional Scuba Diver. They travelled together diving and working on their sailboat *Perfect Platinum*.

"Charlie," Kim cried once she'd let go of Anna. Charlie braced herself. Kim just made it to Charlie's shoulder, but that didn't stop her from squeezing Charlie to within an inch of her life.

"Hey there, little one." Charlie gave as good as she got, squeezing Kim back. After a good fifteen minutes of hugs and kisses, the group finally relaxed in the living room with coffee and pastries. Kim and Hélène filled them all in on their adventures. They'd just been stationed in Martinique and, by the way Hélène described it, they'd been in paradise.

"So, is this just a regular visit for you, Charlie?" Hélène asked. Balls! She was going to have to explain the real reason she was here. Nothing stayed hidden within the group for long. Wasting no time, Charlie filled in Kim and Hélène. She wanted to laugh at their stunned faces.

"Well, I wasn't expecting that," Kim laughed.

"Neither were we," Anna smiled.

"So will Emilie definitely be there?" Kim enquired. Her excitement was palpable. It wasn't a secret that Kim was a huge fan of Emilie's.

"I don't know for definite, but it's a strong possibility."

"In that case, I think it's only right that *all* your very best friends accompany you to the ball." Kim beamed.

Charlie laughed, shaking her head. "I only need one date."

"No, you need support and let's be honest, Anna is going to be wanting to go to bed by nine so—"

"Hey," Anna interjected.

"Am I wrong?" Kim cocked her eyebrow.

"No," Anna mumbled.

"There it's settled. Charlie, you can go to the ball with the reassurance that you will have a hoard of bad ass bitches who have your back." Kim winked.

Maybe going with *all* her best friends was the best thing. If she ran into Emilie, she wouldn't be alone, and if she didn't, well, she could just party with her peeps.

# Chapter 4

Silence, nothing but glorious silence. No cars with their loud engines and blaring horns. No people talking her ear off, wanting her attention and time. No, finally, after months of noise, Emilie had the peace and quiet she'd so desperately craved.

Once the Radio interview had finished and she had successfully put Jack in his place, Emilie drove the two hours to Pickerton. After leaving the academy, Emilie bought a rundown cottage that had been abandoned years ago by the old school caretaker. The property was one of the first buildings she'd acquired after making her first million. Nobody in the local village knew she was the owner. Emilie preferred it that way. The cottage was on the academy grounds, but tucked away at the far edge of the school field. It was surrounded by high conifers and a ten-foot wall that Emilie had installed, providing the property with all the privacy a superstar needed when taking a break.

Jess was the only person close to her that knew she'd bought the place. Emilie was sure that Jack would think she was nuts buying something so close to her old school, but that didn't matter. For Emilie, Pickerton Academy was where her life had really begun. It was where she met her best friends, where she'd made music and where she'd found her heart. No matter what had happened in the end, she would always be thankful for her time there.

Renovating the place had taken several years. Emilie had paid a small fortune to have the gardens secured and landscaped. The cottage itself had needed a new roof and all new plumbing and electrics. In the end though, the results were worth the time and money.

The front exterior of the building retained all its original design. From the driveway, it looked like a typical English cottage, but inside was a different story. Emilie had chosen an open plan layout. The kitchen, which boasted sleek lines and top of the line appliances, merged seamlessly with the dining room and lounge. Each area felt as if it had its own space, even though there were no walls separating them.

The back wall of the building that faced south had been ripped out and in its place floor-to-ceiling folding windows had been installed. In the summer, Emilie could open the entire back of the cottage, which lead to a large patio area. Maybe her favourite part of it though, was the heated pool.

Now English summers aren't exactly known for their consistency or predictability so to ensure that she could swim whatever the weather, a pergola had been built with a motorised roof and sides. With just a press of a button, the garden pool became an indoor one in a matter of minutes.

The last time she'd visited the cottage was nearly three years ago. There was nowhere on the planet—except her home in Quebec—that gave her the solitude and peace she needed. Sadly, her schedule didn't allow for impromptu visits, so when Mr Eccleton called to arrange her attendance at the ball, Emilie seized the opportunity to stay in the cottage for a couple of weeks.

Stretching her body, Emilie strained her ears to listen to the birds chirping in the cherry tree by her bedroom window. The cottage originally had the one and only bedroom attached to the living room. For the old caretaker, a small box room would have sufficed, but it wasn't overly practical for a modern woman who enjoyed space and comfort. Not wanting to diminish the size of the floor plan, Emilie had opted for a mezzanine style bedroom. From her bed, she could observe the dining area and kitchen.

There had been many times she'd fantasised about living in the cottage six months out of the year with a wife and dog. How they would enjoy hours of lovemaking beneath the skylight above the bed. Her wife would then make them breakfast in just a t-shirt, and Emilie would watch her from their bed. Music would play through the speakers that were wired all around the house.

That was the dream anyway. The reality was very different. Pickerton allowed her the privacy she wanted, but she was still there alone. Jess would stay over, but it wasn't the same. As the years went on, Emilie wanted a partner to share her life with. Touring was long, and even though she was surrounded by people, none of them could give her the intimacy and love she needed.

Her reverie was interrupted by the sound of car tyres on the gravel drive. The only person it could be was Jess. Hefting herself out of bed, she stretched again, steadying herself against the wall as she rode out the head rush she got from standing up too fast.

Jess came through the door just as Emilie flipped the switch on the kettle. Jess was a typical Englishwoman, meaning the first thing she wanted was a steaming cup of Builder's tea. Emilie had been mocked mercilessly by her friends at Pickerton when she first tried to make tea for her classmates. Now she could brew a pot of tea like a pro.

"Good morrow dear friend, sleep well?" Jess was overly chirpy in Emilie's opinion.

"I always do here." Emilie busied herself with the stove. A hearty breakfast of scrambled eggs and bacon would get her in the right headspace to face the day. Usually, it took her several days to recuperate from travelling before she was completely herself again.

"Did Jack get off okay? I presume he's gone back to Quebec?" Jess took on the job of opening up the folding windows. The sun was shining brightly, even though the temperatures weren't very high, Emilie appreciated the fresh air wafting through the house. Jess knew her too well. They'd spent so much time together on tour and in the studio over the years that Jess could read Emilie's moods and what she needed to get over them like no other.

"Yes, after I had words. The stunt he pulled at the radio station was way over the line."

"He's been doing that kind of thing a lot lately," Jess mused, tapping her finger to her chin.

"He has, hasn't he? Maybe it's the pressure of the tour. We all start acting strange in the end."

Being cooped up with the same people for months on end wasn't the easiest way to live. Still, Jack was being pushy lately and if Emilie thought about it, his behaviour changed *before* the world tour. She'd assess it when they got back from their break. Right now, all she wanted to do was relax, swim and plan for the Pickerton Ball.

"Have you heard from Eccleton?" Jess asked, sitting back at the kitchen island.

"He hasn't called. Why, have you?"

"Yeah, he's emailed us a schedule. We get a few hours to rehearse before the big day," she chuckled. It wasn't as if they needed it. "We have been given the last rehearsal slot. The ball is on the Saturday and we rehearse Friday evening. I think he's trying to keep us from being harassed. He's certainly trying to keep your appearance a secret. I spoke to Lydia, and she reckons that no one who RSVP'd has the foggiest we will be playing."

Lydia was one of Emilie and Jess's friends from Pickerton. She was one of the few people Emilie kept in touch with. Lydia had followed Emilie on tour for a while until her attempts to seduce Emilie failed. That was an awkward few weeks.

"When did you talk to Lydia?"

"About half an hour ago. She's planning on arriving early Friday morning before the main event."

Lydia Beecham was also a part of the original Pickerton band the group started in their first year. Reforming the band had given Emilie palpitations when Mr Eccleton had first suggested it. Over the years, Emilie had missed all the academy's Christmas events because she was either on the road or had other prior engagements. Jack had never liked the idea of her going and seemed to always schedule something that made it impossible.

This year though, was the twentieth anniversary of the academy's charity. *Drama 4 All* was dear to Emilie's heart. She'd donated tens of thousands for over a decade because she believed in it so deeply. Emilie was privileged, she knew that. Her start in life had been full of opportunity, which had made it easier for her to pursue her passion. It wasn't that easy for everyone though. *Drama 4 All* helped get kids involved in the arts and even though the name suggested it was just for acting, it covered all mediums of performance art.

Mr Eccleton had sealed the deal when he'd told her about the young girl who had lost her parents in a car crash and was having to move away, thus losing her place at the academy. If seeing Emilie and the band perform bought that poor girl some joy, then by god she was going to do it.

Jess cleared her throat, catching Emilie's attention. Her mind had drifted, and she'd stopped talking. "You okay?" Jess leaned over the counter squinting at her with concern.

"Fine, just tired, my mind zoned out. So anyway, how was Lydia?" Hopefully, they could put any awkwardness behind them and move on.

"She sounds good. Apparently, she's seeing someone, and it's pretty serious. Though she was cagey and didn't give details, so for all I know she's lying to save face with you." Emilie rolled her eyes. They weren't in school anymore, surely Lydia wouldn't play silly games like that. Especially when nothing actually happened between them.

In the last term of their senior year, Lydia had struck up the nerve to tell Emilie that she had a crush on her. As flattering as that was, Emilie was very much involved with Charlotte Munroe. There hadn't been any drama or teenage tantrums, Lydia had understood, and they'd remained friends. Years later, Lydia had reiterated that she still felt something towards Emilie. This time however, when Emilie let her down—gently, mind you—Lydia wasn't so understanding.

The thing that stopped Emilie from ever exploring things with Lydia after Pickerton was a gut feeling that Lydia was more enamoured with the lifestyle that Emilie could provide rather than genuine feelings. Charlotte was the only one who Emilie bared her soul to all those years ago. Lydia never came close to knowing Emilie like Charlotte and that didn't change later in their lives, either.

Lydia hung around for the after parties and the celebrities. She never took the time to get to know Emilie, even in a friendly way, so when she started declaring deep-rooted feelings for her, Emilie couldn't believe that they were genuine.

After Emilie had stood there watching Lydia scream and shout at her in front of her crew members after being let down, Emilie politely asked Lydia to go home. Her touring days were over. That had happened four years ago. Since then, Lydia had been in contact, apologised and hoped they could remain friends. Fine by Emilie as long as the friendship was long distance which it had been.

"Well, I suppose we'll see." Jess mused. "Hell, it could be new, and she doesn't want to jinx it." Jess didn't even convince herself with that statement.

"Hmmm. So what's your plans for the next couple of weeks?" Jess lived half an hour away, with most of her family dotted over the county.

"Visit the folks and my siblings, I suppose. The usual. I'll have two weeks of passive aggressive jibes from everyone and then I will attend the ball before happily buggering off home to Canada. You?"

Emilie laughed. Jess wasn't a family-oriented person. Neither were the rest of her clan, really. They could manage a few hours at a time together before the claws came out. Unfortunately, Jess was always the first to get picked on. Jealousy was an ugly mistress and her siblings had it in buckets.

"You don't actually have to see them, Jess. Hell, nip over for an hour today, get both visits out the way then come back here. We can have two glorious weeks of calm and cocktails by the pool. The weather is actually supposed to be alright, so if I stick the patio heaters on, we can spend our days lazing on the sofas outside." That sounded pretty perfect, actually. Emilie would do it even if Jess turned her down.

"You know what, sod it. I'll nip off now, get it done and I'll be back for dinner. I'll pick up Chinese."

46

"Yes. Do that!" Emilie laughed, pointing at her friend. Together, they lifted their cups and clinked.

* * *

When touring, days would blur together. Most of the time, Emilie had to check what day it was, sometimes what month. It was easy to become disorientated. One venue blended into the next, one town looked like the last, and it was frustrating, to say the least. Now, though, she was able to gather herself, concentrate on making each day memorable. Over the past two weeks, that's exactly what she'd done. Okay, so her days wouldn't usually pass as being "memorable" in the way others might expect. Reading copious amounts of lesbian romance, swimming daily, cooking and binge watching all the shows that she'd missed was what Emilie saw as memorable in her downtime. She'd been able to fully embrace each day, rested and relaxed.

Jess had spent her entire break at the cottage. Emilie was positive that her family would be spitting feathers. Emilie wasn't sure where their jealousy came from, but she knew they loved to bring Jess down a peg or two when she visited, so the fact that she'd snubbed them and was spending her time with Emilie wouldn't have gone down well. It didn't matter though, Jess worked just as hard as Emilie and it was nice that she wasn't going to be alone for once.

Friday rolled around faster than Emilie would have liked. Although she'd relaxed, her brain had kept a little anxiety filled thought in her mind's eye. Friday meant rehearsals for the ball, which meant she would see Charlotte. There was no guarantee that she would be in attendance, but there was a chance. After all, she was an original band member and Eccleton had said that the whole band was going to be there.

Emilie had to decide how to handle it. Nearly twenty years had passed, surely Charlotte would be over it, right? An icy wave washed over her as she recalled the last day of term. She shook her head violently, hoping to dislodge the memory and the stone of regret that had made its way to her stomach. If she still felt like this at the mere memory of what she'd done, how could she expect Charlotte to have forgotten?

"Hey, you about ready to go?" Jess threw her wallet and phone on the sofa as she donned her jacket. It really wasn't necessary for them to rehearse. Jess and Emilie were always in sync, but it had been a while since they'd played with people outside of her crew, so maybe having a few hours to play together was a good idea. She knew that Lydia still played the bass with a band part-time, but what about Charlotte?

Over the years Emilie had kept an eye out for Charlotte Munroe, pianist extraordinaire, but it was like she'd vanished off the face of the earth. Had she given it up? What a shame that would be. What shame *Emilie* would feel if Charlotte had given it up because of her.

"Ready as I'll ever be." The drive to the main entrance of Pickerton's was two minutes at the most, but it was quite a trek on foot. Even though her cottage was on the school grounds, the land was immense. From Emilie's house, she could just see the school building in the distance. Trudging over the field was the last thing she wanted to do.

Emilie's Mini Cooper crawled up the long driveway that led to a building akin to Downton Abbey. Okay, maybe not so ornate as that, but it was impressive, and it was old. Pickerton was in a very affluent area, only the brightest — and richest — students could attend. The building belonged to the Pickerton family, whose presence in the county went back centuries.

If records were correct, they were related to the royals. After Richard Pickerton died in 1926, he left the building and all his money to his niece Evelyn Pickerton. She was his only living relative. She was also an unmarried spinster who defied her advisors and opened the house up as an academy. If that wasn't bad enough, she dared to offer places to underprivileged children who would never otherwise have had the opportunity to better their circumstances through their education. Emilie, for one, was so thankful that Evelyn had opened up her home and offered people the chance to study their craft.

Though Emilie was already on the verge of stardom at fourteen, she had always wanted to attend school like a normal kid. Pickerton was the compromise she had come to with her uncle. Unsurprisingly, he'd pushed her to seek the limelight, but understood that she was still so young and needed some semblance of normality. The academy offered her the chance to still be a normal teenager and work on her music, too. Pickerton was the best of both worlds. Her heart always gave a little start when she saw the building, and she couldn't help but smile.

"Right, let's get this over with," Jess gruffed, flinging open the passenger door. It was clear that she didn't hold the school in such high regards as Emilie. A few cars dotted the front carpark, Emilie wondered if any of them belonged to Charlotte. Her stomach churned. She wished she'd eaten breakfast now, but the thought of food this morning was too much. It was a fact that as soon as Emilie felt stressed, her stomach was the first thing to protest.

Emilie wasn't past sticking the car in reverse and hightailing it back to the cottage. In fact, that's what her body was willing her to do. Jess caught on to her spinning thoughts before she lost the plot completely. "Hey come on, it's going to be fine." Jess tugged on her elbow and led her into the school.

Nothing, absolutely nothing, had changed since Emilie had last visited, which had been several years ago. The inside was a strange melange of old high class gentry and modern day practicality. Bulletin boards were mounted on elegant walls that had gold leaf crown mouldings. There were dozens of portraits dating back hundreds of years mixed in with posters of previous gala's charity balls. The only noise they could hear was the clattering of workmen setting up the auditorium.

Pupils had left for their Christmas break last week, which meant the school had an eerie silence to it, which Emilie loved. Over the course of her two years, Emilie had spent most of the holidays at Pickerton. Not every pupil boarded at the school, but several international students and wealthy kids did. Emilie had been one of those pupils.

It wasn't that she had nowhere else to go, it's just she didn't want to spend time with her money-grabbing parents, and her uncle couldn't look after her full time. So it was within these halls that Emilie enjoyed her Christmas and Easter breaks. It was in these halls that she met and fell in love with Charlotte Munroe.

Footsteps clacking down the hall brought her back to the present. Mr Eccleton was hurrying towards them with a smile as wide as London Bridge. Emilie smiled at him warmly. In twenty years, the only thing that looked different about him was his hair that still seemed to have a mind of its own but was now a shocking white. His nickname back then was Dr Emmett because he resembled the character from *Back to The Future* so much.

"Oh, Ms Martin, what a pleasure to see you again." He reached out and shook Emilie's hand enthusiastically.

"Mr Eccleton, how are you? It's been so long."

"I'm wonderful, thank you. Still alive and kicking. Oh and Ms Hill, what a wonderful thing it is to see you again too."

"Mr E." Jess smiled. She wasn't one for small talk, causing Emilie to roll her eyes.

"Is everything ready for tomorrow?" Emilie enquired. Obviously, she would have to be the one to make conversation.

"Yes, yes. We've had some students in this week rehearsing. You will be the showstopper, though. I've put you on last."

"Are Lydia and Charlotte already here?" Jess cut straight to the point.

"Ms Beecham is waiting for you in the hall and unfortunately it's just you three this evening. I have an alternative pianist for today."

Disappointment weighed on Emilie's shoulders. She'd really hoped that Charlotte would be here and they could clear the air. That way, it wouldn't be awkward in front of everyone. No such luck. Straightening her spine, she shook off her melancholic feelings and plastered a smile back on her face.

"Well, three out of four band members isn't bad. We can rehearse, and I'm sure Charlotte will be flawless tomorrow. Shall we get on?"

Mr Eccleton clapped excitedly at Emilie's words. Jess, on the other hand, gave her side eye, letting her know she understood Emilie wasn't completely okay. No point wasting time though, they had a rehearsal to do.

# Chapter 5

"Goddamn it!" Charlie yelled. Her fingers just weren't cooperating. She'd been practicing this bloody piece for three days and she still couldn't get it down. *Well, that's what happens when you don't practice for twenty years.* God, her internal voice was an arsehole. Mr Eccleton had passed along the list of music the band would be playing. None of the pieces were particularly difficult, but Charlie hadn't touched a piano in a long time. She certainly hadn't trained the way she used to. Her hands felt stiff, they struggled to reach, and it was pissing her off.

"Is it possible, love, that you're not playing well because you're so bloody stressed out?" Carol was leaning against the arm of the sofa, watching Charlie with sympathy. When Charlie returned from her weekend away in Paris, she'd sat Carol down and explained what was going on. Her actual parents couldn't give two monkeys, so she'd turned to the only person who even slightly resembled a parental figure (except for Sandy who was out of town).

"This is stupid. I'm calling Eccleton and telling him I can't go. I'm a busy woman and yet here I am spending my time fucking about on a piano. I have a million other things I could be doing and none of them make me feel like shit." This week, Charlie's mood had grown dark. As time counted down to the ball, the memories of that last day in school flooded her mind. She hadn't had a decent night's sleep in a week. Her dreams were a cinematic reel of all the shitty things that had happened.

"Calm down, Stretch. Can I suggest you go take a nap and then come back to it fresh? Nothing good is going to come out of a sleep-deprived Charlie Baxter." Her eyebrow rose, daring Charlie to argue back. Which she didn't. With great reluctance and irritation, she took herself to bed and collapsed. Her brain had had enough and within minutes she was passed out.

Thank god she hadn't dreamt, her subconscious had finally given her a break. The sky outside was considerably darker when she sat up in bed from her power nap. Her mood felt lighter, and she was buzzed to get practicing again. Her fists gripped the bedsheets. It had been years since she'd felt the urge, let alone the excitement to play.

Deep down she must have wanted to reconnect with it though, because her grand piano had been in storage since school. She could never bring herself to sell it. Now her prized piano sat in her living room by an arched window. It was the perfect spot to sit and play whilst gazing out onto the grounds.

Sam's voice echoing through the apartment snapped her back to reality. The ball was two days away so her friends had travelled over to stay with her this evening before they all drove to Pickerton in the morning.

"Hey, beautiful lady," Charlie called. Sam opened her arms to receive a hug. Charlie fucked with her a bit by walking straight past her, hugging Anna instead, who burst out laughing at Sam's dejected face.

"Hey, Char," Anna chuckled.

"Oh, hey Sam." Charlie spoke as if she'd only just noticed her best friend.

"You're an arsehole." Sam grumbled before smirking.

"Come here, grumpy knickers." They held each other tightly. More noise filtered through the room. Hélène and Kim bustled in with their bags. Kim let out a low whistle. It was the first time she had visited since the renovation.

"Wowzer, this is nice, Charlie."

"It's gorgeous," Hélène added, her eyes scanning the space feverishly.

"Thanks guys. Your bedrooms are just down the hall. Sorry you two —" she pointed at Hélène and Kim " —your room is next door to this pair. I hope you have earplugs." Everyone laughed. Sam went red.

"Hell, we might give them a run for their money. Do you know how hard it is to have proper sex on a boat? I mean, *Perfect Platinum* is spacious but when you want to branch out with some sexy moves, she's not all that convenient." Kim was so serious when she said it, Charlie burst out laughing because now Hélène was bright red, too. Out of the group, Sam and Hélène were the ones that embarrassed easily.

"Kim, for the love of... would you not tell everyone about our sex life?"

"Who else have I told? Anyway, it's not like it's a shock. You're the loud one. Tell her, Anna."

"No, no, no, no. Don't bring me into this, I already get enough stick from Charlie about our sex life."

"That's because you all *have* sex lives. I'm going to die a shrivelled old lady. I can't remember the last time someone made me scream out loud." Charlie said wistfully. It was frightfully depressing and accurate how long it had been for Charlie. The pubs and clubs didn't do it for her any longer. Maybe it was seeing her friends settle down? Whatever the

54

reason, that's what her heart wanted now. She wanted to fill Bowman Manor with love and laughter.

"What are you talking about? You're out every weekend." Sam scrunched her eyebrows in confusion. Okay, so Charlie may have led Sam to think she was still living a full bachelorette lifestyle, which included frivolous hookups but that wasn't the case at all. Now, she hadn't outright lied. She'd just stopped correcting Sam's assumption that she was clubbing every Saturday.

"Doesn't mean I get laid every weekend, though." Charlie could see that Sam was puzzling something out. She needed to pull attention away from herself. "Come on, let's get you all settled."

* * *

Their evening had been a blast. Catching up, laughing, drinking and eating. Four of Charlie's favourite things to do. It hadn't taken Kim very long to usher her over to the piano, though. Her friends were eager to get a glimpse of Charlotte Munroe.

"Just remember that I'm not the pianist I used to be, okay? I feel you're all going to be disappointed."

"Not a chance," Sam said, shaking her head. "Play something you love. Come on." Charlie sat for a second. There were two pieces of music she loved dearly and she had written them both. The first one that came to mind, she quickly dismissed. That one caused her too much pain, so she settled with the second. It was a piece she'd written in her first year at Pickerton.

Closing her eyes, she let her fingers brush the keys. She shuffled to get into position and then she let the emotion of the music overtake her. Her hands moved automatically, they knew what to do without her having to think. The room around her fell away. There was nothing but the music.

Every emotion that she'd felt when she'd written the piece flooded back. Charlie felt tears prick at the corner of her eyes. She played with everything she had until the last note. Her hands stilled. Eyes remaining shut, she took a few steadying breaths. Her heart hammered in her chest and she felt herself smile. Never again did she think she would get to feel the pure joy that playing the piano gave her all those years ago. Slowly, she opened her eyes and looked at her friends. Their faces were a wash of surprise, happiness and elation. Except for Sam. Sam's face was sadness and pain.

"Oh, Charlie," Anna breathed, her face streaked with tears.

"I can't find the words, Char, that was…" Kim began.

"Beautiful," Hélène supplied.

"Breathtaking," Anna sobbed. Charlie didn't know how to respond. Her eyes were still squarely on Sam. Her best friend tilted her head to Anna and whispered something in her ear. Anna gave a nod and ushered Kim and Hélène out of the room. Sam waited until they were alone and then sat on the bench next to her. They sat silently for a few moments. Charlie had no idea what was coming.

"How could you not tell me about this side of you, Char?" Sam's voice was almost a whisper. "I… I just don't understand. I've never seen you come so alive as I did just then. Never, and we've known each other for so long."

"It was too painful, Sam. Everything about the piano reminded me of a time that I just wanted to erase from my memory."

"What happened that made you walk away from something you clearly loved?"

56

Charlie rubbed her hands nervously up and down her thighs. She hadn't spoken to anyone about her last few days at Pickerton, but Sam deserved to know. There was no other person on the planet that loved her the way Sam did.

"I was a shy kid at school. I kept to myself most of the time. If I wasn't practising, I was in the library or in my room. That's where Emilie found me one day. She was looking for a book and I helped her. After that she started spending more time in the library, eventually we became friends which was astounding because I'm sure you can imagine how many people wanted to be her friend and she chose me.

"We talked like normal teens. I think she liked I wasn't starstruck. I enjoyed talking about books. We chatted about music, but not hers. She wanted to know what I wrote. As the months went on, we started writing together. She would hang around with me more and more." Charlie took a breath. "One night, we were sitting by the lake at the back of the school. Most other kids had gone home for the Christmas holiday, but Emilie stayed. We'd been getting close, and I already knew I was completely smitten with her. I never thought she would feel the same way. Fuck, Sam, I was this gangly shy nerd, and she was Emilie Martin. Anyway, we sat by the lake watching the water and the next thing I know, she kisses me."

"Wow, I bet that took you a minute to process," Sam laughed.

"Actually, no. It felt so right. Let's just say that night was a night of many firsts."

"You mean, she took your —"

"Yup. First kiss, first everything, and it was wonderful. Alright, a little messy." Charlie laughed at the memory of their fumbling hands and sloppy kisses. "But you know what they say, practice makes perfect, and, boy, did we practice!" Sam let out a bark of laughter. "Then it went wrong." Sam's face sobered instantly. "We'd been together for nearly two years by the time we came to graduating. They had been the best two years of my life. For once I felt *wanted*."

"So what happened?"

"Some really personal bits of information got leaked to the press. Things that Emilie said she'd only told me. I couldn't believe she would think that I would sell her out, not after everything we'd shared. The problem was, she had her so-called 'friends' whispering in her ear, convincing her I could be the only one that had sold her information.

"Before I knew it, other kids were whispering behind my back, defacing my locker with spray paint. I begged Emilie to believe me, but it was too late. She looked at me like I was dirt. Then on the last day of term, it all blew up. I tried one last time to talk to her, and she humiliated me in front of everyone." Charlie felt Sam's arm snake around her shoulders. "She took everything precious and destroyed it, including my love for piano. I had no one to turn to, so I did what I thought was best and walked away from that life because it was tainted and always would be."

"You never once thought about going back?"

"Nope, not once. I loved photography, and you gave me the stability I needed so badly. You and your mum." Charlie gave Sam a small smile.

"And now, how do you feel about it?"

"When Mr Eccleton called I was ready to tell him to sod off, the last thing I wanted was to reunite with Emilie or her gang of bitches, but then he talked about the little girl losing her parents and I couldn't say no. I remember being that young and loving music. I remember how therapeutic it could be and that girl needs some music therapy after what she's gone through, even if it is just one night."

"That's really nice, Char, I'm proud of you."

Charlie shrugged. "If it helps her, then it's worth my discomfort. I've been trying to practice for days, but until this evening I've struggled."

"Why?"

"Because I was disconnected. Music for me is more than simply sitting down and hitting some keys. I feel it, it flows through me when I play and I'd lost that. So when I was practicing I couldn't engage. But now, after playing for you guys I can, because, for the first time in a long time, the music spoke to me again."

"You play beautifully, mate. That little girl is going to light up when she hears you."

"I hope so. Now I just have to get through meeting up with Emilie and the others." That was more nerve-wracking than playing in front of an audience by a mile.

"Hey, we will be right there with you. I don't give a fuck who Emilie Martin is. She won't hurt you again, ever. As for her 'gang of bitches', they have nothing on your boss bitch friends. We're family, Charlie, always."

"Will you listen to the music I have to learn?" Having Sam, Anna, Kim, and Hélène by her side was more than enough to boost her confidence. Charlie might have been the shy gangly outcast twenty years ago, but she wasn't any more and she was going to show every single Pickerton prick exactly who Charlie Baxter was.

* * *

A car horn blaring from the driveway jolted Charlie. She'd been nursing her second cup of coffee, willing herself to stand up and move. The time had come. There was no escaping it now. Pickerton was calling.

59

"Char, let's hustle, everyone is waiting." Sam shouted from the large oak door leading outside. Grumbling, she took her cup to the sink. Today she was supposed to arrive in Pickerton and attend rehearsals at the school with the rest of the band. Her stomach rolled every time she thought of getting close to Emilie. There was no doubt in her mind now that Emilie would be there. Mr Eccleton made too much of a fuss for her not to be. She was leaning over the kitchen sink when she felt an arm curl around her waist. Expecting it to be Sam, she was surprised to see Hélène.

"You don't have to do this, Charlie, not if it's going to affect your mental health. Nothing is worth that." Her low voice was soothing to Charlie's raw nerves.

"I have to do it. It's been twenty years, I need to move on from it. I've just found music again."

"Okay, then let's go. You have us, all of us, by your side."

The drive took just over two and a half hours. It would have been less if they hadn't needed to stop for Anna every thirty minutes. Apparently, her bladder was *not* coping with pregnancy. Charlie had rented a three-bed cottage for their stay. It was only for two nights, so she didn't mind splurging. The cottage was located just outside the main village square.

They pulled up to the gate. Hélène had rented a ridiculously large Land Rover for their weekend away. Apparently, she felt they deserved to arrive in style. As if they were an entourage of celebrities. Which they weren't, not next to the likes of Emilie Martin, anyway.

In front of them stood a beautiful one-story cottage. It was a relatively new listing on Airbnb. Not surprising really. Pickerton was a picturesque village in the middle of the countryside. Walkers from all over the world would visit to traverse the different routes available. Charlie had done it herself a few times in her youth. Staying at school in the holidays left a lot to be desired. Sometimes Charlie had needed an escape and the surrounding area of Pickerton provided that in bucket loads.

They poured into the cottage laden with bags. Why they'd all packed as if they were away for a month was a mystery. The floor plan was an open concept. The walls were white with bold colours splashed about the place in the ornaments and art that hung on the walls. It was nice, but not entirely Charlie's cup of tea. It felt a little too modern. The owner had stripped the cottage of all of its originality.

"Right, everyone pick a room and get settled. I'll go grab some food for us all." Sam was already halfway out the door before anyone had a chance to reply. Charlie would put money on Sam going to the local Fish and Chip shop. It was one of her favourite meals. One she didn't get to indulge in often.

Hélène and Kim took the room that faced the front of the cottage. Anna collapsed in the bedroom next to theirs. That left the room on the opposite side of the cottage for Charlie. She wasn't going to complain. The last thing she wanted was to listen to them four at night. Good job she bought her headphones.

Sam was back twenty minutes later and the smell of fresh Fish and Chips engulfed the cottage, making everyone salivate. They sat in the living room, scarfing down their food in relative silence. Now and then Charlie would see her friends exchange looks. They were worried about her. It was sweet.

"Ladies, I'm fine. I've decided to skip rehearsals. I doubt it will harm the performance. I would feel better having you guys there when I meet everyone again."

"Of course," Anna smiled.

"No problems, Char," Sam nodded.

"Have you decided what to wear?" Kim asked.

"Not really. I brought several options. What about you guys?"

"Sexy cocktail dress for me," Kim winked.

"Same," chorused Hélène and Anna.

"Some nice trousers and a top," Sam commented, her focus was still on her plate of food.

"What did you bring with you?" Kim asked.

"Jeans, T-shirts, the usual."

"Charlie, you cannot attend a Ball in jeans and a t-shirt." Kim looks aghast that she'd even uttered the words. "Please tell me you brought something you could actually wear. The entire plan is to knock those Pickerton bitches on their asses." Charlie laughed at Kim's serious outburst. She was really taking this whole *We've got your back* thing to heart.

"Well, I brought some fitted black trousers and a waistcoat. Similar to what I wore at your wedding," she nodded toward Anna and Sam. Her suit for their wedding had been navy blue, but Charlie always preferred black.

"Yes," Kim shouted, making Anna jump.

"*Merde*, Kim, now I have to go to the toilet again. You can't make me jump anymore, I'll pee myself?

"Sorry," Kim laughed. The group waited for Anna to return. "Charlie, you will look phenomenal in trousers and a waistcoat. Forego the shirt underneath and let the world see your beautiful tattoos. Keep your hair down, add a bit of eye shadow and *bam* Emilie Martin will cream her pants."

"I don't want her creaming her pants, Kim," Charlie laughed.

"Yes, you do. You want all those motherfuckers to know that Charlie Baxter is a sexy ass woman and they are all lucky just to be in the same vicinity as you."

"All right, babe, calm down," Hélène said, chuckling.

"I will not calm down. Charlie has been carrying this hurt for nearly two decades. It's time she took back her power."

"Too fucking right," Sam chimed.

62

"Here, here," Anna called. Charlie could feel her face warming. Surely she was blushing.

"Thanks, guys." They clinked their glasses and settled down.

"We have to make a good entrance, too," Kim said. "What time do you need to get there?"

"Well, the first band starts at eight. We are on around nine-thirty I think. I should be there by half eight at the latest." If she could get away with showing up, walking on stage, playing and then leaving, she would, but, alas, she couldn't be that rude. Not even to Emilie.

"Eight-forty-five it is then—"

Charlie laughed, "I said eight-thirty, Kim."

"Yes, and we need to be stylishly late. I want all eyes on you, sugar, when you walk in that hall."

Charlie rolled her eyes. There was no point arguing. She would put herself in the hands of her friends, sit back and hope everything worked out.

# Chapter 6

The rehearsals had been fine. Nothing to write home about. It was a little difficult to really get it flowing without their pianist. Deep down, Emilie had hoped Charlotte would show, but it wasn't to be. Now she sat on her bed dressed to the nines in a long black ball gown, swallowing hard. Her nerves were out of control. Not for the ball or for their performance, but for Charlotte. Tonight was the night she would finally come face to face with Charlotte Munroe.

"The car is here," Jess bellowed unnecessarily. The cottage wasn't exactly gargantuan. She could hear her friend easily from anywhere in the building.

"On my way," Emilie replied in a normal voice.

The academy had sent her a stretch limo, which, in Emilie's opinion, was over the top. She understood that Mr Eccleton was happy she was attending and performing but she didn't deem it necessary to go through all the fanfare. For one night, she just wanted to be Em, not the famous Emilie Martin. *Think of the donations.* That's what really mattered. If she could boost their annual donations and help that little girl, then it would all be worth it.

Jess looked smart in a form-fitting black suit. Lydia had told them she would also be in black, more than likely a dress. Emilie took the champagne offered by Jess as she sat herself in the back of the car. Ridiculous really, they would arrive in two quick minutes. Oh well, she would have to down it.

The school had been completely decked out. Lights had been strung in the trees. Huge Pine trees adorned with hundreds of lights stood guard either side of the main entrance. Emilie had to smile. It was pretty magical after all.

The small silver watch on Emilie's left wrist told her it was seven. They'd arrived in time for the cocktails to be served in the auditorium. The large hall had been stripped of its usual chairs, and instead a dozen large round tables were perfectly placed about the room. The stage was kitted out with all the musical instruments needed.

Before Emilie could go over and investigate, she was surrounded by people. She and Jess had literally walked in thirty seconds ago and already they'd attracted a crowd. Time to put her game face on. Playing to an adoring crowd was what Emilie was known for. If she could keep thousands of fans happy, she wasn't going to sweat a hundred old classmates and their spouses.

"Oh, wow, Emilie, we can't believe you're here," some unknown woman gushed. Shit, maybe she should have studied her old class profile because she had no idea who half these people were.

"I wouldn't have missed it." *Smile and everything will be ok.* That's how the next hour and a half went, fake smiles, pleasantries and wondering who the hell she was talking to. The fact that some of these people talked to her as if they'd been wonderful friends back in the day grated on Emilie. This was why she was guarded around people. Everyone wanted something from her.

At around eight-forty, the attendees had calmed down a little. Emilie found it easier to stand and have a drink with Jess and a couple of women she remembered but didn't overly like.

The student bands had been playing for an hour, and Emilie was suitably impressed. Eventually, Lydia joined them.

"Hey, these kids are good," Lydia said, pointing to the stage.

"I've been impressed with all of them so far," Emilie replied.

"Did you see that pianist in the second band? I think she could give what's her name a run for her money." Celia, one of the women who Emilie barely liked, commented.

"What's her name?" Jess asked.

"Yeah, your weird bandmate. Oh, what was her name?" Celia asked.

Emilie bristled. She knew damn well that Celia could recall Charlotte's name, hell anyone in the music industry knew Charlotte's name.

"I wonder if she's still a goth?" Lydia laughed. Emilie kept quiet.

"God, she was awkward," Daniella — the other tolerated woman — added.

"Shouldn't she be here already?" Lydia said, noting the time. It was almost quarter to nine and ideally Charlotte should be here talking to her bandmates, preparing for their performance.

"She probably couldn't decide which T-shirt to wear with her baggy trousers," Celia laughed. It was true that back in their school days, when Charlotte wasn't in her uniform, she rarely strayed from wearing baggy T-shirts with even baggier jeans.

Suddenly, the air changed. It was as if an electric current zapped through the room. Emilie could hear murmurs and slight gasps. Turning towards the entrance to the auditorium she saw the crowd parting. Had Moses popped by? Why the hell was everyone gawping and moving out of the wa...

"Fuck me," Jess said, louder than she'd probably meant to. Emilie felt all the air in her lungs vanish. Walking towards them was Charlotte, surrounded by four absolutely gorgeous women, two of whom were hanging off Charlotte's arms.

As for Charlotte herself, Emilie was gobsmacked. Gone was any awkwardness. Striding towards her was an ethereal dark goddess. Emilie's eyes wandered from Charlotte's black patent leather heels to her form-fitting black trousers up to her waistcoat that was so snug Emilie was sure that Charlotte wouldn't be able to move much without her breasts spilling out.

Holy shit, she wasn't wearing a shirt underneath. Emilie blinked several times and clenched her thighs. She stared at the most beautiful tattoos she'd ever seen that covered Charlotte's upper arms. Jesus Christ, her cleavage was unbelievable. Emilie's eyes travelled farther up to Charlotte's face. Twenty years may have almost passed, but Charlotte's face hadn't changed at all. Her eyes were just as piercing as they were when she was a teen. Her skin had cleared up and was radiating warmth and softness. And that hair. Wow, she still had bum-length hair that looked like black silk.

Everyone in the hall was silent. Charlotte sure knew how to make an entrance. She wasn't hiding away, trying to slip into the background. No. This Charlotte was in your face and she fucking owned it. Emilie was entranced as the angel that was Charlotte Munroe, stopped in front of her. Celia, Danielle, Lydia and Jess were all gaping. Jess was looking Charlotte up and down like she was a meal.

Emilie felt an elbow in her side. Jess was nudging her. She cleared her throat, willing herself to get it together. They stared at each other for a moment. Emilie didn't know what the hell was happening when she saw Charlotte lean in. Then Charlotte's face was next to hers. She felt the kiss on her cheek and she almost keeled over.

67

Charlotte pulled back, "Hello, Em." Lord have mercy. Charlotte's voice was orgasm inducing, all low and husky.

"Char... Charlotte," Emilie stuttered. She was not winning any prizes for her smoothness this evening, that was for sure. Blinking again, she straightened her shoulders and got back into entertainer mode. It was the only way she was going to function like a sane person.

"It's Charlie now," Charlotte commented. "Charlie Baxter."

Well, that explained why Emilie had never been able to keep track of her. Charlotte Munroe didn't exist anymore.

"Charlie, it's great to see you." Did she sound convincing? She hoped so, everyone was still watching their interaction. Another wave of guilt rolled about in Emilie's stomach. People were watching because they probably remembered the last time Emilie and Charlotte — sorry Charlie — had spoken. Well, more like when Emilie had humiliated Charlie in front of everyone.

"You too, congrats on the success. Happy to see you got everything you wanted." That was a swipe at her if ever she heard it. "Let me introduce my companions." Charlie leaned to her left and kissed the stunning platinum blonde on the cheek. "This is Kimberley Richmond." She turned to the dirty blonde on her right and kissed her cheek next. "Hélène DuBois." Letting the two women go, she turned and ushered a glowing brunette forward. "Anna Holland." Next, she put her arm around a very fit looking redhead, "And Samantha Chambers. Ladies, may I introduce you to Emilie Martin. Also Jess and Lydia, who are the other members of the band." Charlotte then turned to Celia and Danielle. "Sorry, I don't recall you two." Emilie nearly choked on her tongue. Charlotte had just given them the proverbial finger. Everyone knew Celia and Danielle.

68

"It's lovely to meet you all," Emilie stuttered. Christ, she needed to do a better job than this, she was Emilie Martin, for god's sake.

"Wow, Charlie, you look... Just wow," Jess said, nearly drooling.

"Indeed, a lot has changed in the last two decades," Charlie smiled. That voice, wow, it was doing very inappropriate things to Emilie.

"Charlotte," Lydia said. Okay, she still wasn't a fan then.

"It's Charlie, sorry didn't you hear the first time?"

Lydia blushed. She wasn't used to Charlie calling her out on her shit. Lydia had been a bitch to — then Charlotte — every day. Emilie assumed it was because Charlie and she were together and Lydia was jealous.

"Sugar, I'm going to grab a drink with the girls. Bourbon?"

"Yeah, thanks, Kim, I'll be over shortly." Was Charlie sleeping with all these beautiful women?

"That's quite the entourage you have there," Celia mocked. Pissed off Celia was a nasty piece of work.

"Not an entourage, just close friends. Thought we might as well make a weekend of it whilst we're here." Charlie replied smoothly. "I apologise for being absent yesterday, but it was unavoidable. Did I miss anything important?"

"No, not at all. You got the set list?" Jess asked.

"Yeah, I can't see any of those pieces being an issue. Although I have to confess, it's been a while since I played."

"Really?" Emilie was desperate to know what Charlie had been doing all these years.

"Yes, I gave up the piano in university. I'm a photographer now."

"Hang on, you're Charlie Baxter. *The* Charlie Baxter of S. C. Photography?" Danielle asked, her tone disbelieving and a little starstruck. Emilie looked at Charlie, who smirked.

"That's me."

"Bloody hell," Celia choked. "Your work is... Well, it's beautiful."

"Thank you." Emilie made a note to immediately Google Charlie when she got back to the cottage.

"You stopped playing completely?" Jess asked.

"Yes, I thought it best to leave all that behind. The love was gone." Emilie felt that statement in her very soul. "Don't worry though, I'm sure I'll be fine this evening. Now, if you don't mind, I have a bourbon on the rocks waiting for me. I'll see you backstage later."

Emilie watched Charlie turn and walk away. Her eyes were glued to Charlie's ass, which looked delicious. "Hey, Em, you good?" Jess asked. Emilie was not good, she was shaken. A light pressure on her upper arm pulled her attention from the spot where she'd lost sight of Charlie. "Em?"

"Yeah, yeah, fine. I just need a second." The bathroom Emilie crashed into was thankfully empty. She gripped the edge of the sink and took some deep breaths. That had been harder than she thought.

\* \* \*

The third cocktail was probably a mistake, but Emilie drank it anyway. In two minutes, she was about to go onstage with Charlie again. The last time had been a couple of weeks before everything had turned to shit between them. Could Charlie still play?

Mr Eccleton introduced them. The crowd — now well inebriated — cheered wildly. Emilie peered over her shoulder as

70

she waited in the wings with the rest of the band. Jess looked bored. Lydia was glaring at Charlie, who was smirking back at Lydia. Jesus, it really *did* feel like they were back in school.

No time for all that now though. There was a show to perform. With a bright smile, Emilie walked on to the stage. The crowd that was no more than one hundred people bellowed and screamed. Emilie surveyed the room. Finally, she spotted the little girl that had lost her parents. She was sitting to the left of the stage on a stool. Next to her was a woman who had her hand on the girl's shoulder. Grandmother, perhaps? Emilie caught the girl's eye and gave her a wink.

"Good evening, everyone." The room erupted into more screams. Emilie looked back at the others. Jess had settled behind the drums. Lydia was pulling her bass strap over her head and Charlie, well Charlie, was looking at the piano like it was going to burn her. *Please don't freeze Charlie.* Emilie turned back to the room. If she could entertain them for a few more minutes, maybe it would give Charlie enough time to relax and settle.

"I am absolutely honoured to be here tonight. It's wonderful to see so many of my classmates again. And what a treat it is to reform our band." A couple of wolf whistles pierced the air. "Tonight we are going to play some of our greatest hits. I hope you remember them all. We played them often enough," she laughed. Considering their band was the only decent one in their year group, they ended up playing to the school a lot.

With a quick glance, Emilie saw that Charlie had sat behind the piano looking calmer. "Alright, ladies, let's do this." With that, Jess counted them in. They had five songs to play. Time flew by as they played. Emilie sang with all the love and devotion as if it were one of her own concerts.

"Okay, last song of the night, guys," Emilie announced, garnering protests all around, which made her laugh. This song was the one she was nervous about. It was her song, the one she wrote in school, the one that had become a hit. Usually she played the song with her guitar, but originally it had been written so that only a piano assisted her. The truth was, "Losing My Head Over You" wasn't just her song, it was hers and Charlie's. Emilie wondered if Charlie still saw it that way. Only one way to find out.

"I think you'll all recognise this last song. I'm sure it was on the radio at some point," she laughed. "Tonight though, I'd like to change it up. Charlie…" she called, looking over. She saw the look in Charlie's eyes. Yeah, she remembered all right. "Just you and me this time," Emilie finished.

Turning back to the crowd, she prayed Charlie would begin playing. Closing her eyes, she summoned all the energy required to sing the song. When the first note rang through the air, Emilie smiled. Charlie played the intro, and Emilie wanted to cry. She played just as beautifully as she did twenty years ago. Holding nothing back, Emilie sang. Tonight, she sang for her friend, for the girl she hurt all those years ago.

\* \* \*

"Well, I think that went well," Jess said, leaning against the bar with a beer in her hand. They'd finished the set half an hour ago, but Emilie had only just finished chatting to all the people that had rushed over once the last song had finished. It was all part of it, though. She'd spent some time talking to Grace, the young girl. It broke Emilie's heart hearing about her mum and dad. It was remarkable how strong Grace was.

"I'm pleased," Emilie commented, her eyes scanning the room. Charlie had zipped off stage as soon as she could and then disappeared into the crowd.

"If you're looking for Charlie, she just went to the bathroom." Emilie wasn't going to hide the fact that she had definitely been searching for Charlie. Jess knew their background and understood what a big deal tonight had been.

"Order me a martini. I'll be right back." The problem now was figuring out which bathroom she would have gone to. Pickerton had a lot. *Would she have gone to our bathroom?* A little ember glowed in her chest. Their bathroom was on the floor by the teachers' quarters. Students never used it because technically, it was supposed to be for faculty. That hadn't stopped Emilie and Charlie though, not when they found out the teachers usually used the bathroom closer to the teachers' lounge, leaving that one empty ninety percent of the time.

Surely Charlie wouldn't go there, though. Would it mean something if she did? Thinking no more about it, Emilie headed to the teachers' quarters. Every corridor reminded her of the good times she'd had here. Nearly all of them included Charlie.

Stopping briefly, she rolled her shoulders before pushing open the door. Standing at the sink with her head bent was Charlie. Emilie repressed the smile that wanted to bloom on her face. It looked as if she'd interrupted Charlie and she wasn't sure she was going to be welcomed. They had to talk, though, properly.

"Hi," Emilie said quietly. This part of the school was completely empty bar them. The silence was a little eerie, but that's how Emilie remembered it and liked it. Charlie raised her head. She gazed at Emilie through the mirror.

"Hi." Charlie straightened up and turned around so they were facing each other. Emilie took a tentative step forward.

"You played beautifully, Charlie." If nothing else, Emilie hoped Charlie would accept her compliment. Honestly, Charlie looked as if she wanted to sprint out of the room as fast as she could. As Charlie's green eyes bored into hers, Emilie had to remind herself to breathe.

73

"Thanks, you sang wonderfully. It's no surprise you're a megastar, Em." Em. She called her Em again. Most of her friends called her that, but it never sounded so sweet as it did when Charlie said it.

"I've been lucky." Emilie smiled, and Charlie nodded. Silence settled between them again. Emilie was going to have to take the plunge. "Charlie, I need to apologise—" she was interrupted when Charlie held up her hand.

"Stop, I don't need an apology. It was twenty years ago."

"Yes, and I'm twenty years late giving you the apology you deserved the moment I'd finished shouting at you."

"So, it's to assuage your own guilt?"

"No, Charlie, I'll live with that guilt for the rest of my life. You deserve my apology for you."

Charlie ran her hands through her long mane. God, Emilie wanted to touch her. "You know, it was never about the fact that you shouted at me in front of everyone. It was the fact you believed I would have done something so terrible to you in the first place. How could you have taken the word of those manipulative bitches over me, after everything we shared, after everything we talked about and planned?"

The pain in Charlie's eyes was unbearable. It was true though, back then Emilie had believed others over Charlie. And she'd done it so easily. "Charlie, I don't know what to say. It will just sound like an excuse, no matter what."

"Try me. Em, tell me why you blew up our lives."

"I was scared, Charlie. Fuck, when the press got hold of all that information, I spun out. It was all so personal, and I'd only divulged it to you. I wasn't thinking clearly at all. My uncle was going nuts. He was threatening to sue the academy. On top of that, I had my friends telling me it was only logical that you were the one to sell my information."

74

"Did you ever stop to think that I had zero reason to do that? Well, did you? I was wealthier than you back then, for fuck's sake. Regardless, you knew me well enough. I never wanted money. We were supposed to be in love. We'd made plans for a life together, Em."

"But you *were* the only one I told —"

"So even after two decades, you still believe it was me?" Charlie bellowed. Emilie hadn't meant for it to sound like another accusation. "Whether you like it or not, Em, we were never in private here. Christ, we shared the building with four hundred other girls. Even on holidays, it was never just you and me. And if I recall correctly, the day you told me all that stuff, we were in the locker room. Can you guarantee we were alone because I can't? But that's unreasonable, right? Much easier to think the girl who loved you more than life was the one to betray you to the fucking press."

Emilie had never seen Charlie so angry. *That's what twenty years of hurt will do to a person though*, she supposed. "Charlie, I'm so sorry."

"Me too, Em. I think you broke something precious. I suppose we'll never know for sure. It's been good seeing you again. Good luck with everything. Maybe we'll catch up in another twenty years." Charlie shook her head as she walked past Emilie and out of her life again.

# Chapter 7

Charlie weaved her way through the crowd and made it to the bar where everyone was waiting. There were shots lined up for them, all of which Charlie downed in quick succession. She'd order more for the girls. Right now though, she needed the alcohol.

All night she'd kept a lid on her feelings. From the moment she stepped into the room, and saw Emilie surrounded by her adoring bitchy friends. She'd managed it when talking to them. Hell, she'd managed it when Lydia glared at her backstage. All that time until she faced Emilie in *their* bathroom. Why had she gone there? Charlie knew she was playing with fire, visiting their old haunt.

"Hey, you good?" Sam asked.

"No." Another shot disappeared down her throat.

"Tell us what happened," Anna said calmly.

"I ran into Emilie in the bathroom. We ended up talking, and I said stuff." That was the Cliff Notes version of the conversation. Charlie couldn't believe she'd spewed all that out. But in that moment, listening to Emilie apologise and give weak arse excuses for how she treated Charlie, she couldn't keep quiet. For decades, she'd needed to know the answer to her question. Why had Emilie believed anyone over her?

Her body was enveloped. Kim, Hélène, Anna, and Sam had wrapped themselves around her. She smiled. "I'm okay, sorry, just got emotional in there."

"Hey, no apologising." Kim was the shortest of them all. She was wrapped around Charlie's waist like a koala bear.

"I suppose I should thank you all, really. I know you're fans of Emilie's and I'm sure you wanted to get a little starstruck, but you held out for me. I appreciate it." *Especially you, Kim.*

"Yeah, we're fans of hers, but we're bigger fans of you," Sam said, kissing her temple.

"You were truly amazing up there!" Anna gushed.

"And I think we need to discuss how fabulous that entrance was. I mean, seriously, every head in this room was turned," Hélène noted.

"Plus, I lost count of the amount of women giving you come-fuck-me-eyes," Kim chuckled.

"You're good for my ego." Charlie laughed.

"It's true. The woman standing by Emilie when we came in was eyeing you up like you were dessert," Sam said.

"Who? Jess? I don't think so." Charlie didn't dislike Jess. She wasn't one of the girls that had been awful to her, but she was a bystander. She never stood up for Charlie.

"Yes, Jess, in fact she's still looking at you that way," Hélène commented, raising her eyebrow and looking over Charlie's shoulder. There wasn't a subtle way for Charlie to turn and see, and, honestly, she didn't want to. No one from her past interested her. Well, no one but Emilie.

"How long does this shindig go on for?" Kim asked.

"Until half twelve, I think. It's my first time here, so I'll go by what the email said." Hopefully, Charlie wouldn't have to stay past the midnight mark. She'd much rather go back to the cottage and drink with the girls.

77

"Okay, so we have about an hour and a half left. Let's put everything aside and enjoy ourselves. You've done the hard part, Char, now you get to let loose with your besties." Kim was already handing her another shot. The effects of the previous ones were only now kicking in. She needed to pace herself. The last thing she wanted was to make a tit of herself, not after she'd handled everything so well.

All four of them raised their shots and necked them. Anna sipped on water. The live music had been replaced with the auditorium's sound system. There were plenty of people dancing on the makeshift dance floor. Kim grabbed Hélène and headed to the middle. Charlie loved watching Kim strut her stuff. She was phenomenal on those heels.

Charlie, Sam, and Anna followed close behind. Anna was looking fatigued, but she didn't say anything, and Charlie didn't want to piss off her pregnant friend by pointing out how tired she looked. Instead, she danced with them both. Eventually, all five of them ended up in a huddle in the centre of the floor.

Several times, Charlie found herself dancing with a beautiful woman. Maybe Kim was right? Maybe she had turned more heads than she thought. The music got more upbeat and the guests more inebriated. Charlie hadn't seen Emilie since the bathroom and she chided herself a few times when her eyes wandered around the room looking.

Six songs in and Charlie saw Emilie. She was dancing with Jess and Lydia, seemingly enjoying herself. Charlie allowed herself to look. Since she'd unloaded on Emilie in the bathroom, she felt mildly better. Getting it all off her chest was cathartic. Now though, as she watched Emilie dance, the hurt she'd felt when arriving had all but vanished. What was the point of holding on to it? Who did it help? Certainly not Charlie.

The last song was announced and surprisingly Charlie felt herself move towards Emilie. Her friends gave her a questioning look, which she ignored. Right now, she just wanted to be close to Emilie again. She would chalk it up to nostalgia. Whatever, it didn't matter. Emilie turned just as Charlie reached her side.

"Care to dance?" If Emilie was surprised by Charlie's invitation, she didn't let on.

"I'd love to." Once again, it felt like every head turned their way and watched as they manoeuvred into position. The song was a ballad, Elton John's "Your Song." Charlie took the lead, guiding Emilie's hand to her waist whilst grasping the other. They moved seamlessly together, just as they always had. Neither spoke. Their eye contact never faltered as they danced.

It had been a very long time since Charlie had felt… well, something that she couldn't put a name to. It was warm and safe. Looking into Emilie's eyes was like coming home. She still had that voice in her head reminding her of what Emilie had done, but right at that moment, she was lost to her first love.

The song ended, and the lights came up. Mr Eccleton tapped his glass informing everyone the ball was officially over. Charlie and Emilie hadn't shifted from their dance position, and they were still locked in a heated stare. Charlie had the overwhelming desire to kiss Emilie. Before she could do anything, Lydia sidled up to Emilie's side, breaking their moment.

"Em, you ready to go? We're heading back to your place, right?" Charlie looked from Lydia to Emilie. Jealousy surged through her system, especially when Lydia gave her a knowing smirk. Bitch.

Emilie looked to Lydia, "Yeah, I'm ready." And then she turned back to Charlie. "Do you and your friends want to come?"

Charlie answered before thinking it through. "Sure, that would be fun." Lydia's face at the surprise invitation alone was worth accepting. Even if the rest of the night turned out to be a disaster, Charlie would hold on to that.

* * *

Oh, lord, her head hurt. The afterparty must have been wild. Why couldn't she remember... Oh, shit. Charlie had a rush of memories flicker through her mind. There had been a lot of drinking. Plenty of laughing and a ton of chemistry between her and Emilie.

Charlie rolled over and felt the other body laying next to hers. She closed her eyes again, preparing herself for the person she was about to see. Turning her head, Charlie focused on the chocolate brown hair splayed across the pillow. Emilie looked so peaceful sleeping.

Another set of memories presented themselves. Emilie beneath Charlie, writhing, her body shaking. *Oh fuck, what have I done?* Propping herself up on her elbows, she looked around the room. They'd made it up to Emilie's bed at least. Peeking down into the main part of the house, Charlie could've cried with relief when she saw no other bodies. Her friends must have gone back to their cottage.

How should she play this? Was she sorry she'd slept with Emilie? Honestly, no. They'd been dancing around each other since they'd returned to Emilie's cottage. The more they drank, the more intense their connection felt until finally Charlie couldn't take it anymore. Drunk Charlie was a horny bitch at the best of times. Add a very sexy Emilie Martin to the mix, and she never stood a chance.

Taking a few deep breaths, Charlie decided to treat the morning as if it were any other. Emilie was softly snoring, which made her laugh. Slipping out of bed, she made her way down to the kitchen. After the coffee machine got going, she rooted around the fridge for breakfast. Only a combination of bacon and eggs would do.

The grease from the frying bacon made Charlie's stomach roll a little. She definitely had a hangover, but not the worst she'd ever suffered. A nice egg and bacon butty would sort her out. Placing a tray on the kitchen island, Charlie plated up Emilie's sandwich and coffee.

Climbing the steep stairs up to the bedroom wasn't the easiest of things. She wondered how they'd managed them last night without breaking their necks. Emilie was on her front with her head buried in her pillow. The familiarity of the sight caught Charlie by surprise.

The rooms at Pickerton were dormitory style, unless you were lucky enough to get a single. Charlie and Emilie were given their own rooms, which was fantastic. Yes, they weren't supposed to stay with each other overnight but that never stopped them. They were two teens who had just discovered sex. Nothing could have kept them apart. Charlie lost count of the amount of times she woke up to see Emilie in the very position she was now.

Setting the breakfast down, she climbed back into bed. Leaning over, she brushed Emilie's hair away from her face, smiled and then kissed her on the temple. A small groan was the only evidence Emilie had felt the soft kiss. Charlie chuckled to herself. "Em, wake up. Breakfast is ready." Emilie's eyes fluttered open. Charlie held her breath, waiting to see how Emilie was going to react. A broad smile crossed Emilie's face as she registered Charlie leaning over her.

"Morning," she said in a husky voice. It was adorable. Charlie always loved Emilie's sleep voice.

"Bacon and egg butty. Coffee as well."

"Oh my god, yes, that's exactly what I need right now. Probably a thousand litres of water and painkillers too."

"I can help with that." Charlie jumped out of bed and headed back downstairs. She heard Emilie shuffle about, probably sitting herself up. When she looked back up to the bedroom, she saw Emilie watching her. A tingle swept down her spine. Ignoring her building libido, Charlie filled a large jug with water, took a glass and painkillers that had been sitting on the kitchen counter back up to Emilie.

"You didn't have to do that," Emilie said in a soft voice.

"It's no biggie." Charlie propped herself up against the headboard close to Emilie and took a bite of her sandwich. "Careful, the egg yolk is soft," she muttered as she licked yolk off her hands.

Together they ate in silence, listening to the birds. Charlie could almost imagine herself living here with Emilie. Waking up and making breakfast for her on a weekend. It was painful to know it was just a fantasy. They might have slept together, but nothing had really changed between them.

When Charlie asked Emilie to dance at the ball, she'd allowed herself to let go of a lot of the hurt she still felt. Not being weighed down by those feelings felt good. Charlie wanted to forgive Emilie. It was better for both of them. Finally, they could both move on. Having sex had *not* been on her agenda, but maybe it was a good way for them to close the chapter.

Emilie was going back to Canada and then back to her superstar life. Charlie would go back to work. Now they could separate with no baggage. "When do you leave?" Charlie asked.

"I have a flight out tomorrow evening."

"Montreal right?"

"Closer to Quebec City, actually. I can't wait to get home. I need to cuddle my dog," Emilie laughed.

"What dog do you have?" This was a strange reality for Charlie, lying here in a bed with Emilie Martin making small talk.

"A Golden Retriever called Spud."

"Spud?" Charlotte laughed.

"Yeah, it's her spirit name. She sits on the sofa looking like a sack of potatoes. I didn't want to call her potato, and I remembered the English slang was spud so I called her that. Do you have any pets?"

"Nope, I'm away too much. I hope one day I will. Maybe when I'm more settled." Charlie wanted to say more, but she didn't. It was time to extricate herself from Emilie's bed before things got messy. "I... I'd better get going. Sam will wonder where I am."

"Oh, sure, okay." Emilie put her plate down and sat up straighter.

"It was good seeing you, Em."

"Yeah, you too. Um... could we keep in touch?" Was that a good idea? Surely a clean break would be better. The hope in Emilie's eyes was so clear though, Charlie couldn't say no.

"Sure. I'll leave a card on the counter downstairs." Not wanting to stretch out the situation, which was rapidly becoming awkward, Charlie got up and dressed. In her peripheral vision, she could see Emilie watching her.

Fastening her trousers, Charlie picked up her heels. "I'll see you around, Emilie Martin."

\* \* \*

"Well, look who it is!" Kim shouted as Charlie tried in vain to sneak into the cottage unseen.

"Ah, the walk of shame," Sam laughed. All four of her friends were sitting on the couch with coffee and croissants.

"No shame here," Charlie said, dropping into the small tub chair opposite her friends. "Sorry, I kind of ditched you all."

"No apology needed, Char. You were clearly enjoying yourself," Anna laughed. Thinking back to last night, Charlie couldn't remember her friends leaving. Honestly, once she'd started dancing with Emilie again in the living room, everything else sort of disappeared. It was just her and Emilie.

"When did you all leave?"

"Oh, right around the time you picked Emilie up, wrapped her legs around you and took her up those bloody steep as fuck stairs," Kim laughed.

"Oh shit, really?" Charlie was mortified.

"Absolutely. You both kind of just went for it, regardless of the fact we were all there. I had to practically drag that Lydia woman out kicking and screaming. Jess found it hilarious, even if she was a touch disappointed she didn't get to have a crack at you herself," Sam commented.

"Jesus!" Charlie groaned.

"How did you guys leave it?" Anna asked.

"Well, we didn't have a big heart-to-heart if that's what you're thinking."

"Okay, so what *did* you say?"

"Nothing really. I made her breakfast—"

"Breakfast, do you usually do that?" Sam quirked her eyebrow. She knew full well that Charlie wasn't the type to get domesticated with the women she slept with.

"Well, it didn't feel right just leaving, and I woke up before her. Em *never* did well at getting up," Charlie mused. Then she realised her mistake. Four sets of perfectly shaped eyebrows raised at her brief trip down memory lane. "Look, Em and I have history. But that's all it is. I think we did some healing, that's all. We were able to close that chapter in our lives. She asked to keep in contact, so I left my card, but I doubt she'll call. We have lives to go back to. Coming back to Pickerton was a good thing for both of us, I think. It was special, but now it's done."

"And that's what you want?" Sam asked.

"I think it's the right choice." Was there any other option, really? Surely she would set herself up for more heartache if she entertained the idea of allowing Emilie back into her life again.

"Hmm, not sure I agree," Sam stated, looking at Charlie with concern. Hélène, Kim, and Anna all exchanged a look. Charlie didn't like this at all.

"I think it's time to pack up, honey," Kim said to Hélène. Anna followed behind, stating she needed to go to the loo again and was going to pack her and Sam's belongings.

Sam shifted closer to Charlie. "Can we talk about this?"

"What's there to talk about? I've already told you how I feel."

"No, you haven't. You told us what you think is best. Char, you've been a mess because of Emilie for two fucking decades. Now you're suddenly okay and it's all over?"

"I don't want to hold on to it anymore, Sam. But I don't want to open myself up to her again either."

"Hey, I get that. I'm really surprised you slept with her though, Char."

"You and me both. I forgot how magnetising she is to me. It was the same as when we first met. I couldn't keep away from her. Especially after we had sex for the first time. Fuck, I think we hid away in her room for an entire week once."

"That's my point, Char. You had something really intense with Emilie. Do you really think you can just go back to the way it was before this weekend happened, before you got to speak and touch her again?"

"Shit, Sam, I don't know, but what's the alternative? Become friends? I can't see that working, can you?"

85

"No, I guess not. I just don't want you to regret anything, that's all."

"I know and I love you for your concern, Sammy, but I need to figure this out alone. However, right now I need to shower, pack my stuff and get home." Sam nodded and squeezed her knee.

Shuffling into her bedroom, Charlie sighed in frustration. Sam was right. Now she'd spoken to Emilie, felt her body, it was like she craved her all over again. The need for Emilie had never fully abated, but it had become manageable as the time passed. Now she felt as if she were back at square one.

This wasn't the time to figure it all out though. The weekend had been intense and stressful. The only thing that Charlie knew was that she had to get home. With all her things packed, she stowed her bag in the back of the car.

"Come on, let's go," Hélène said quietly in her ear. With one more look around, Charlie slinked into the Land Rover.

Hélène began winding down the country roads. Charlie let her head rest on the back of her seat, her mind returning to her time with Emilie last night. She could feel Emilie's soft skin on her fingertips. The touch of her lips as they travelled down Charlie's torso. The euphoria she experienced when Emilie brought her to climax so skilfully.

Being completely lost in her reverie, it took her a second to register the sharp tug of her seatbelt as Hélène slammed on the car's brakes. "*Putain mais c'est pas vrai!*" Hélène growled. Charlie peered through the gap between the two front seats. Beyond the windscreen, Charlie could see a Mini Cooper blocking their way. The door to the compact car opened and out climbed Emilie.

"What the...?" Charlie mumbled. Without questioning her actions, she climbed out and went to Emilie. "Em, what the hell?"

"I'm sorry, I really didn't mean to get in the way, well, not like that, I mean I wanted you to stop but not so quickly, is everyone okay?"

Immediately, Charlie thought of Anna. "Hey, is everyone okay?" she asked through the passenger side window.

"We're good," Anna replied. Charlie assessed her before going back to Emilie, who was wringing her hands together nervously.

"Right, we stopped, so what's up?" Charlie had no idea how to handle this situation at all.

"I want to hire you," Emilie rushed out.

"Hire me?"

"Yes, I want to hire you for the next few months."

Charlie stood looking at Emilie as if she'd lost her damn mind. "You could have just called, Em. I gave you my card."

"Yes, but it would have been too easy for you to blow me off." Yeah, Charlie would definitely have done that.

"Okay, so what job do you want to hire me for?"

"First, I'll be completely honest and tell you I'm flying by the seat of my pants here. After last night, I can't imagine you just vanishing from my life again, Charlie. So I thought that if I hired you, it would give us a chance to spend time together, get to know each other again."

"Em, last night was great, but do you really want to go there again? Open up old wounds, some that still feel raw?"

"If we don't, I think we will regret it, Charlie. Please, just think about it."

"Well, what will I be doing because it doesn't seem you've thought this through, Emilie? I can't just hang around for months on end."

"You'll be my private photographer. I'll pay your rate. Hell, I'll double it. Just say yes, please."

87

Charlie turned to look at Sam. What the hell should she do?

# Chapter 8

Emilie held her breath as Charlie made her way back to the Land Rover. What she'd asked of Charlie was a lot. Yes, she would be paying Charlie to do a job, but they both knew that wasn't why Emilie wanted Charlie with her for the next few months.

Dancing with Charlie, inviting her back to the cottage, and sleeping with her came as a complete shock. Never in her wildest dreams did Emilie think she would have the chance to be that close to Charlie again.

When Charlie had asked her to dance at the ball, Emilie was wary. Their heated discussion in the bathroom left her feeling as if there was no way back to any kind of relationship between them. First, she thought maybe Charlie was going to give her another scolding, but when she felt Charlie take her by the waist, so gently she knew it was going to be okay.

In that one moment, twenty years were erased. They were just two teenagers looking adoringly into each other's eyes as the world fell away. The song ended far too quickly for Emilie's liking. It was only when Lydia came over to see if she was ready to leave that the idea of inviting Charlie and her friends back to the cottage felt like the only option because she needed the night to continue. If one night was all she could have with Charlie Baxter, then she wanted it to stretch out for as long as possible.

Lydia had thrown a shit fit in the car. Raging on about it being a friend-only gathering. Lydia was the only one who had a problem. Jess was more than happy for the group to join. Emilie wasn't blind. She saw how Jess had looked at Charlie all night, and it sent acid shots through her stomach.

With music playing and drink aplenty, the after party had been a riot. Charlie's friends were hilarious, even if they were reserved around her. Emilie guessed Charlie had filled them in on their past and she could understand why they were being a little cool towards her. The short blonde woman, Kim, was a little terrifying, if she were being honest. Although after a couple of hours everyone seemed to thaw. Everyone bar Lydia.

The living room in Emilie's cottage was their dance floor, and every one of them gave it their all. At some point, Charlie and Emilie gravitated to each other. Emilie shouldn't have been surprised, it was always the case. They were naturally drawn to each other.

Whether it was the alcohol or just their raw magnetism, Emilie found herself pressed up against Charlie as their bodies wound around each other. They moved so well with each other, even after all this time.

It was around about *that* time that Emilie couldn't remember anything else about the party. She only had eyes for Charlie. The cottage could have been burning to the ground and she wouldn't have flinched. Emilie remembered Charlie's eyes turning into black pools of lust. The look stole Emilie's breath clean away.

The next thing she remembered with delicious clarity was Charlie's lips on hers. Those soft, plump lips that knew how to extract Emilie's desires in a second. The tongue that licked her bottom lip and then devoured her entirely. The sensation of every bit of blood rushing south. Her excitement soaking her thong. Charlie's hands lifting her so effortlessly. Her legs wrapping round Charlie's powerful body. The motion of them ascending the stairs. Charlie lowering Emilie to her bed and taking what they both needed.

Their very first time together having sex was clumsy. They did a lot of practicing and they got better. Hell, they spent every spare second they could locked away fucking. They were young and in love. Now, though, things were different. They'd both been with other women and it showed. Charlie used to be a quiet, almost timid lover. This Charlie, the Charlie now ripping off her underwear with her teeth, was *not* timid. This Charlie was confident, she was completely at ease with taking what she wanted and Emilie wanted her to take it all. Yes, she'd loved having sex with timid sweetheart Charlie, but she was elated to be having ravishing, ferocious sex with this version of her first love.

The first orgasm had been quick, Emilie had been so turned on she couldn't hold on. The second, third and fourth were coaxed out of her by skilled hands and tongue. She was a wreck by the time she told Charlie to give her a few minutes break. Had she ever experienced anything this carnal before? Nope, never.

Finally, Emilie was given the chance to reciprocate. Charlie didn't hesitate to tell her what she liked. Another thing that differed from her younger self. Emilie was more than pleased to follow instruction. Charlie wanted Emilie to eat her out? No problem! Charlie wanted to be taken from behind? Absolutely fantastic! Charlie wanted to ride Emilie's face? Go for it! Emilie was there for everything and boy did she deliver.

Waking up to Charlie gently kissing her head was surprising. The first threads of thought that danced through Emilie's head was that of uncertainty. How was Charlie going to feel about what they'd done? Would she freak out? Would she get angry? None of those thoughts were correct. Charlie seemed calm, happy to be there. She'd made breakfast for crying out loud.

Sleeping together had been more than a quick lay. Emilie felt she could speak for both of them when she said it had been restorative. Nothing erased the past, or her mistakes, but what they'd experienced that night paved a way for them to move on.

When Charlie had gone to fetch Emilie some painkillers, Emilie made the mistake of watching her go. It was a mistake because what she witnessed was her dream come to life. Her in bed watching the woman of her dreams potter around downstairs. It was just how she'd envisioned it, but, sadly, it wasn't the permanent life she so desperately wanted. No matter how much they'd healed last night, Charlie would leave again.

After Charlie had left to go back to her rental place, Emilie cried. The weekend had been so far from what she thought it would be. The emotions she'd experienced were so unexpected that the only way she could process everything was to let them out in the form of tears. Emilie knew there was no way she could let Charlie disappear again. Even if they could only salvage a friendship out of it, that would be enough.

With that in mind, it had taken her a split second to decide she would offer Charlie a job. If she could just get Charlie to spend some time with her, she knew things would work out. Driving like a Formula One racer down country lanes hadn't been the best idea, but she was so eager to get to Charlie before she left, Emilie hadn't taken care on the roads.

Watching the Land Rover careen towards her had been frightening. It would have totally been her fault if the cars had collided, but thank god that hadn't happened.

Now she was here standing waiting for Charlie to confer with her friends and give her an answer. Emilie sent silent prayers up to the universe that Charlie would agree. Time seemed to slow to a crawl as she watched Charlie talking to Sam.

After a few minutes, Charlie straightened herself and walked back over to Emilie. "Alright, I'll take the job."

"Really?"

"Yes, but hold on, I have some conditions." Emilie wasn't at all surprised that Charlie wanted to take control. "First, this is business, Em. Whatever happens between us can't get in the way. This is my job, and I have a reputation to protect."

"Of course."

"Second... well, I haven't really got anything after that," Charlie mumbled. Emilie had to stifle a laugh. Charlie was very cute.

"We'll play this any way you want, Charlie. All I want is the chance to get to know you again."

"Okay, but I'm not ready for anything more, Em." It was disappointing to hear and her heart ached, but she understood. They had a lot of time to make up for, and Emilie had to find a way to make up for her mistakes.

"Will you fly home with me tomorrow? I have a jet to take me back to Quebec at eight."

"Yes, alright. I need to go home first and collect my gear and pack."

"Right, so shall I meet you at the airport or..."

"Are you staying here until tomorrow?"

"That was the plan."

"You could come to my place. If you wanted. I have a spare room and it would be easier for us to get to the airport. We could discuss the job more, what you're expecting, etcetera."

Emilie's heart did a little happy dance. Not only was Charlie coming with her to Canada, she was about to spend another evening with her, hopefully alone. "That would be great. I just need to let Jess know. She'll be travelling with us, too."

"Oh, she can stay at mine as well. I have the room." Not what Emilie wanted, but whatever.

"That's really kind of you. I'm sure she will be happy with that."

"Okay, give me your number and I'll message you the address. I need to head back with these guys," Charlie said, motioning to her friends. "You can follow when you've got everything squared away here."

"Okay, great." They stood looking at each other for a moment.

Finally, Charlie broke the stare and smiled. "I'll see you later then." With that, she walked back to the Land Rover. Pleased with how everything was turning out, Emilie gave a little wave, climbed back into her Mini and reversed out of their way.

* * *

"Where the hell have you been?" Jess asked from somewhere in the cottage. It took Emilie a second to locate her friend, who was bending down, looking under the couch.

"What are you doing down there?"

"I can't find my sock." Jess mumbled as she reached under the furniture, searching. "Anyway, you didn't answer my question."

"I…" How was she going to explain that she had made a rash decision to ask Charlie along to Canada? It's not like she had anything to be ashamed of. She also didn't need to explain herself to anyone. Jess wasn't just anyone, though. She'd witnessed the relationship between Emilie and Charlie, and its subsequent breakdown. "I had to chat to Charlie."

"Ah, did it not end well after last night?" Emilie felt her face go red. What had her friends witnessed, exactly?

94

"No, no, everything is fine. I offered Charlie a job." Well, that got Jess from under the sofa.

"What do you mean? What job?"

"I've hired her to be my personal photographer."

"Why?

"Because I'm not ready to say goodbye yet. We have a lot to catch up on."

"Bloody hell, Em, it was only a shag. You don't need to be dragging all this up again. Wouldn't it be better to just leave it now?"

"Excuse me? Unless you were in bed with us last night, you have no business commenting on what it was or was not. You don't have to like it, Jess, that's up to you, but I've been carrying this with me for a long time. I've carried *her* with me. If I want a friendship with her, I'll damn well have one."

"Jack isn't going to be happy about it."

"What the fuck has Jack got to do with anything? Why are you being so negative right now?"

"I'm just looking out for you, Em. Don't forget that I've been around for all this bollocks. I don't want Charlie hurting you again."

"I hurt her! I took what we had and threw it away because I let other people get in my head. I won't do that again."

"Alright, alright, don't get your knickers in a wad. Just be careful alright. Jack's going to be pissed because he hates being out of the loop. You know he likes being the one to do the hiring and firing."

"This is personal. Jack is my manager, not my guardian."

"Sorry, Em, I'm not trying to bring you down. Honestly." Emilie wasn't sure she believed Jess, but what could she do? If Jess wanted to have a problem with it, then that was up to her. Emilie knew she'd done the right thing by inviting Charlie, and that's all that mattered.

"Let's move on. If you're agreeable, we're going to go to Charlie's tonight. Stay over and then go to the airport together."

"Sure, whatever you want." Jess resumed her search for the elusive sock. Emilie felt a pang of irritation, but she needed to let it go. Something good was about to happen and she wanted to be present for it.

* * *

The drive to Charlie's house was done in relative silence. Emilie still couldn't understand why Jess had acted so negatively towards the plan of hiring Charlie. Was it down to residual jealousy? Was Jess that upset that she'd not had the chance to seduce Charlie herself?

Emilie shoved all thoughts aside as they drove up to Charlie's house. No not house, mansion. Emilie herself owned several large homes, but none of them had the character and history like this one. Charlie had told Emilie about Bowman Manor many times over the course of their relationship. From what Emilie could remember, Charlie had never felt comfortable in the house, not after her grandmother had passed.

Looking up at the gargantuan building, Emilie could fully understand why little Charlie had felt so out of place. Emilie wasn't a stranger to loneliness, her own childhood had been plenty lonely. Charlie told Emilie many times that her parents were always gone. Imagining Charlie as a young kid, holed up in the house all alone, was heartbreaking. That's why Emilie found it strange that Charlie had stayed and made it her permanent home.

Pulling the car into a vacant space, Emilie settled her breathing before getting out. Jess, as usual, didn't seem affected and was out of the car in a flash, grabbing their bags. The great oak doors on the front of the house opened, spilling light out into the early evening shadows. Emilie strained to see who stood waiting for them. It wasn't Charlie, but an older woman. Emilie doubted it was Charlie's mother.

"Evening all, come on in," the woman called. Hauling her bag over her shoulder, Emilie proceeded into the house. "Stretch is expecting you. Go up the stairs. You'll see where you need to be."

"Thank you…"

"Carol."

"Thank you, Carol. It's lovely to meet you. I'm Emilie and this is Jess."

"Nice to meet you too, duck. Off you go, don't want to keep the lady of the house waiting. I think she's cooked." Emilie chuckled. She could see that Carol was someone fun to be around. She also gave off a warm, motherly vibe.

Taking the stairs slowly, Emilie let her gaze roam. From what she could see, the lower part of the manor had been turned into offices. It was definitely used for business. At the top of the stairs, Emilie saw that Charlie's door had been left open for them.

The open plan apartment was stunning. Emilie loved the modern feel with all the characteristics of the building's original design. It was very Charlie. Even though she didn't know adult Charlie well, Emilie could tell the space reflected her character perfectly.

"Oh, hey, you're here. How was the drive?" Emilie wasn't sure she would ever get used to the sight of Charlie again. There she was, standing in slouchy jogging bottoms and a white tank top that showed off all her glorious tattoos with her hair whipped up in a messy bun. Emilie remembered tracing that ink with her tongue and her teeth. *Down girl.* A twitchy clit was the last thing she needed right now.

"No problems at all."

"Hey, Jess." Charlie gave a little wave.

"Hi, Charlie, thanks for the invite." Jess was looking Charlie up and down. She was not being subtle, and that pissed Emilie off. Sure, Em didn't have any claim on Charlie, but she thought Jess was being a tad disrespectful. Her friend knew their history and what happened last night, yet here she was ogling Charlie, right in front of her.

"So, I have two spare rooms. Pick any one you want. I'm just making dinner. It's got about twenty minutes left, so take your time settling in. After that, I suppose we should iron out some details."

"Great, sounds wonderful," Emilie said, smiling through her irritation.

With her bag placed at the end of the bed, Emilie wasted no time returning to Charlie in the kitchen. Everything in the space screamed professional, from the oven to the block of knives. Charlie obviously enjoyed cooking. "You about ready to eat?"

"God, yes, I'm starved." Emilie's stomach rumbled on cue.

"Go sit at the table then and I'll ferry everything over."

"I can help, Charlie."

"Fine, grab the wine and some glasses from the rack." It was all very domesticated. They moved effortlessly around one another, setting the table and bringing over the food. Emilie smiled widely when she realised Charlie had made Shepherds Pie, Emilie's absolute favourite dish. Jess wandered out a few minutes later.

"This place is gorgeous, Charlie." Jess said, settling down at the table.

"Thanks, it was a labour of love. Worth it though."

"I was surprised you stayed here," Emilie said cautiously.

"Ah, you remember. Yeah, for a long time I left this place behind, but then my parents offered it up to me and Sam for the business and I started to feel a connection again. Not with my parents, but with my grandma. She loved this place and I think she would be happy I'm here taking care of it. I've made it into my own."

"Well, Jess is right, it's gorgeous."

"Thanks." Charlie grinned.

Emilie needed Charlie to stop giving her those little smiles. The woman clearly had no clue what they were doing to Emilie's heart and panties.

"Looking forward to spending time in Canada?" Jess asked.

"Yeah, I've only been a couple of times and they were flying visits. Whereabouts will we be staying exactly?"

"My house is a few hours north of Quebec City. I hope you like forests," Emilie laughed. Her house was on one of Canada's many many lakes. The cabin was surrounded by trees and there wasn't a soul in sight, not for at least five kilometres.

"Forests are good, no issue here. Have you decided what I'll be doing?" Charlie asked, her eyes fixed on her food.

"I thought it would be good to document the more personal side of my life. Not for the fans, but for me. I have a million and one photos of myself on stage or at some award ceremony, but I have hardly any of my friends and family. Just doing normal stuff. I was also thinking about organising a few local gigs—"

"Since when?" Jess interrupted.

"Since now. Wouldn't it be nice to do some smaller, more intimate shows? I was thinking we could visit some of the local towns. After all, *those* are the people that started my career. Not all of them can afford to travel to my concerts, or afford the ticket prices. I think it's time I showed my appreciation."

"Jack is going to shit a brick, Em. No way he's going to put up with that."

"It's not Jack's choice," Charlie spoke. Emilie and Jess stopped their bickering and stared at her. "Sorry, didn't mean to overstep," she added.

"You didn't overstep. You're right, it's not his choice."

"Hey, I'm with you, Em, but you know he's going to fight it."

"Why?" Charlie asked.

"He wants me to start writing another album. Even though I've told him repeatedly that I need a break."

"Well, he works for you, right?" Charlie commented.

"Yeah, but you would think it's the other way round sometimes." Jess replied.

"I think you gotta do you, Em. If you want to do smaller gigs to give back to the community, then do it." Charlie shrugged.

"I'll talk to Jack. Now enough shop talk. That's what the flight is for. Let's get back to this wonderful dinner. You sure know how to cook a Shepherd's Pie, Charlie."

"I know my way around a kitchen, that's for sure. Does it live up to your impossible Shepherd's Pie standards?" Charlie grinned. Emilie couldn't help the fact she liked a *good* Shepherd's Pie.

"I'll give you nine out of ten," Emilie laughed.

"Why did I lose a point?" Charlie mock sulked.

"You didn't serve it with crusty buttered bread."

"Bollocks, I had it ready, look it's on the counter," Charlie protested, fetching the bread. "I get the point now, right?"

"Alright, you can have it. Ten out of ten for Ms Baxter," Emilie laughed.

# Chapter 9

Had Charlie's bed always been this uncomfortable? The answer had to be yes, because it must have been the millionth time she'd turned over. At this rate, she was starting to resemble a spit roast pig: Back. Side. Front. Other side. Nothing she did allowed her to settle. Okay, maybe it wasn't so much the bed but the woman sleeping in her spare room.

Ever since Emilie had cornered her on that country road, Charlie spent every second questioning whether she was doing the right thing. Sam certainly thought so. When Charlie had gone back to the car to tell the girls what Emilie had asked her, all three of them gave her a resounding "Do it."

Sam had been the one to convince her. "Charlie, this is a great opportunity. Not only will it give you time to get to know her again, but it will be great for your portfolio. Shit, after a few months tailing Emilie Martin, you're going to have your pick of jobs."

If she were being honest, she needed little encouragement. As resistant as she seemed on the outside, her insides were screaming at her to go along with it. So she'd agreed. Why she had invited Emilie and Jess to her place was a mystery. Her mouth just blurted the offer out. She couldn't take it back once it was out there, though. That would have been rude.

Waiting for Emilie to arrive at her house had been anxiety-inducing. It would be the first time that Emilie saw Charlie's life as a fully formed adult. Would she be impressed? Silly to get hung up on those kinds of thoughts, but it was only natural. Charlie didn't feel the need to impress many people, but Emilie was definitely an exception. She led such an accomplished life. How could Charlie *not* be a little insecure?

Their dinner together had been nice. There was no awkwardness, no stiff silences. The conversation had flowed easily. Jess was cool, although Charlie noticed the appraising looks thrown her way now and then. Charlie did her best to ignore it, she didn't want Jess *or* Emilie to think she was open to flirtation. This needed to be a business-only kind of arrangement.

Yes, she wanted to get to know Emilie again. They were, after all, more than just lovers back in the day. They'd been best friends first and foremost, and it would be nice to form that kind of relationship again. But as far as romance between them was concerned, that just seemed like a recipe for disaster.

The gala had allowed them both to let go of some of the hurt, that was certain. Forgiving two decades' worth of pain had needed to happen for both their sakes. Opening back up to Emilie again was something different entirely. The anguish Charlie suffered as a teen had been terrible. What would that feel like now as an adult? She wasn't sure it was something she could come back from. No, they just had to try for friendship. That was safer for everyone.

With her brain still buzzing with thoughts and feelings, Charlie resigned herself to a sleepless night. Not one to stare at the ceiling, she peeled herself from her bed and shuffled to the kitchen. Thankfully, there were no squeaking floorboards to contend with. The last thing she wanted was for either Emilie or Jess to hear her.

102

Popping the light on above the oven, Charlie set about warming some milk. Alcohol wasn't an intelligent choice, she would *definitely* do something stupid if she indulged in a glass of something. Instead Charlie would be a good adult, she'd have a soothing glass of honey and milk, listen to some soft jazz on her wireless headphones and then maybe do some yoga. Yes, centering herself was good! Thinking of Emilie wrapped up, possibly naked, in her spare room was bad. *Bad Charlie.*

There was only one place Charlie could relax when she felt like this, and that was in the armchair by one of the large arched windows. From her trusty chair, Charlie was offered a wonderful view of the manor's exquisite rose garden. It was here that Charlie felt closest to her grandmother.

Letting her head rest against the back of the chair, she closed her eyes. The soft melody of her favourite jazz playlist lulled her into a state of calm. The milk coated her throat and made her feel warm and safe. For a moment, her warring mind was peaceful.

The sensation of a warm hand touching Charlie's forearm nearly gave her a coronary. "Jesus, fuck," she squealed.

"Shit, sorry, I didn't mean to scare you," a very shocked looking Jess said. "I saw the light on when I went to the bathroom and wanted to check everything was okay." Her eyes were just as wide as Charlie's. A few beats passed before they fell into laughter. Still clutching her chest Charlie, pressed pause on her playlist and patted down her lap making sure she hadn't catapulted warm milk all over herself.

"No worries, I was in a world of my own," she chuckled.

"I take it you couldn't sleep?" Jess asked, leaning against the armchair.

"Nope, my mind wouldn't shut up. I thought a nice mug of warm milk and some music might help me relax."

"I get it. I'm the same on tour. My sleep pattern goes right out the window. Especially when we're hopping into different time zones. Messes with everything."

This was probably the most Charlie had spoken to Jess alone since school. Honestly, Charlie hadn't given Emilie's bandmates a second thought. Her focus had always been on the star.

"Hey, do you mind if I sit with you for a second?"

Charlie registered the sudden nervous energy radiating off of Jess. "Yeah, sure, you want some milk? My grandma used to swear by it."

"Thanks, that would be great." Together, they went to the kitchen. Charlie silently went about heating more milk and grabbing a mug from the cupboard. Jess sat herself down at the breakfast bar. The atmosphere had changed slightly. Jess seemed more nervous than ever. Charlie put the steaming milk on the bar and took the seat next to Jess.

"I wanted to apologise," Jess began, looking at the mug. "What happened all those years ago wasn't right, and I feel like shit."

"I don't see why you should feel like shit?" Charlie said plainly. The problem had been entirely between her and Emilie, as far as she was concerned.

"No, I should have stood up for you. I know we didn't exactly hang out or whatever, but you were a really important part of Emilie's life. I should have made more of an effort to be your friend. How the others treated you was bullshit. When Em accused you of going to the press, I should have done more. I told Em I thought she was wrong, but she wouldn't listen. I had no idea she was going to humiliate you like that. If I had, I would have warned you or tried harder to get Em to see sense."

Well, this was a turn up for the books. Honestly, Charlie had come to terms with the fact that most of the girls at the

104

academy never gave two shits about her. The only reason she was tolerated by ninety percent of the student body was because of Emilie. Jess had never been a dick to her, but she'd certainly never tried to bring her into the fold, either. The apology was welcome. If she'd had just a shred of support back then, she may have handled everything differently, but that hadn't happened so no point in wondering "what if".

"Thanks, I suppose. I don't really know what to say to be honest, Jess."

"You don't have to say anything, Charlie. To be honest, I needed to get that off my chest. I've carried the guilt around for a long time. I didn't realise it until the gala came up. Emilie was a nervous wreck for months, understandably. I was too if I'm telling the truth. I never wanted to be that girl in school, you know."

"What, a raging bitch?" Charlie laughed.

"Yeah," Jess grinned. "I think I was so focused on making sure I got through the academy unscathed that I didn't stop to think that my inactions were just as damaging as my actions."

"Wow, that's some deep shit, Jess," Charlie chuckled. She didn't want Jess to think she was making light of her apology. It was all just so far out of left field. Blimey, she'd only managed a small conversation with Emilie about what happened between them. Charlie certainly wasn't prepared for an in-depth discussion with Jess.

"Hey, I'm a deep person, thanks," Jess winked. "Seriously though, I am sorry."

"I appreciate it. Really." There was a question on the tip of her tongue, and Jess must have sensed it.

"Ask what you want," Jess pushed.

"Do you know who it was that went to the press?"

"No, but I knew it couldn't have been you. The pair of you together were sickly sweet and loved up. You were far too in love with Em to have betrayed her like that."

"So why the fuck didn't she believe me? If you could see all that, surely she did, too?" Charlie couldn't help her ire, no matter how hard she tried to forgive and forget the injustice wedged itself in her chest.

"I think she was just so shocked to have had all those private conversations aired in public she lost her damn mind."

"Yeah, but some arsehole suggested it was me."

"I agree. Emilie never told me who it was though."

The righteous anger that had been coursing through Charlie mere seconds ago evaporated, leaving her fatigued. A bigger conversation had to happen with Emilie. Maybe they were now in a position that wasn't entirely fueled by decades of hurt, they could wade through the shit and finally find out who had ripped their lives apart.

"Well, this has been enlightening. Thanks for saying sorry. I think I needed to hear it. I hope we can build a friendship on top of it?"

"I'd really like that, Charlie." Before Charlie could protest, Jess flung her arms around Charlie's neck, pulling her into a tight embrace. It was awkward, but Charlie allowed it for a few seconds. She then carefully pulled away and said good night. Sleep might not come, but she wasn't going to spend any more time out in the open. No, she needed the sanctuary of her room.

\* \* \*

The buzzing of her phone roused Charlie. Around five a.m. she'd finally fallen into a dream-filled sleep. Her head felt groggy, like she'd been drinking, but in fact, it was the contents

106

of the dream. Maybe nightmare would have been a more appropriate way to describe it. The last day of term was the sole premise of it. Christ, it had been a long time since she'd relived it in her sleep. Not wanting to give it any more focus, Charlie grabbed for her mobile.

"Hey," she grumbled down the line. What she would give for eight more hours of sleep.

"You sound like shit, mate," Sam laughed down the phone.

"I got bugger all sleep, that's why," Charlie argued.

"You didn't sleep with her again, did you? Christ, Charlie, I thought you weren't going to go down that road again?"

"No, I didn't sleep with her. I just couldn't sleep. This is all kinds of fucked up Sam. Jesus, last week I hadn't seen Emilie Martin for twenty years. Now she's in my bloody house sleeping and I'm about to fly off to Canada with her. It's a mind fuck."

"Yeah, you're not wrong."

"And I ended up having a midnight heart-to-heart with Jess."

"Really? How did that come about?"

"I was in the living room—"

"Listening to jazz and drinking warm honey milk—"

"And suddenly Jess was there. Anyway, I make her a drink and then she's spilling out an apology for everything back in school. Telling me how she should have stood up for me. That she'd tried to tell Emilie that it wasn't me who went to the press, yada, yada."

"Wow, how do you feel about all that?"

"Well, I appreciate it. I could have used someone back then. It hurts to know that Emilie didn't believe Jess either. She was so focused on blaming me."

107

"You need to hash it out with her, Char. I know you had that chat in the toilets at Pickerton, but I don't think it's enough, do you?"

"Deffo not, buddy. The thing is, Sammy, I need to be professional. When all's said and done, she's hiring S.C. Photography. I can't make it all about me and her."

"Obviously, but you can separate the two, Charlie."

"Yeah."

"Do you think Jess is after something?"

"What?"

"Don't play daft, Charlie. That woman wants to bang you ten ways to Sunday. Just be careful, alright."

"I'm not interested in Jess. I think we can be friends." Did Charlie believe what she was saying? Jess had made it clear that she wanted Charlie for more than friendship at the gala and the way she'd looked at her through their dinner together yesterday. Surely Jess' apology wasn't to get in Charlie's good graces so she could make a move?

"So, when do you fly out?" Charlie appreciated the conversation change.

"Tonight at eight."

"Packed?"

"Yeah, you know I travel light. How's Anna?"

"Still horny." Sam laughed. "I'm thinking of buying Red Bull in bulk."

"Toy play, that's what you need. If you haven't got the energy to bang all the time, buy some gadgets that will get her there just as well as you can."

"I'm not being replaced by silicone, thank you very much. No way."

"You're the one bitching about being tired."

"I'm allowed to bitch. It's your job to listen."

108

"Alright, alright, keep your knickers on. Anyway, I'm going to grab some breakfast and do some exercise."

"It still shocks the shit out of me to know you're exercising on purpose."

Charlie rolled her eyes. Yes, she hadn't always liked exercise. In fact, she detested it. It was only after having an hour lecture from Sam that she'd agreed to do yoga. Turned out she was pretty good at it and enjoyed the benefits. She would *never* admit that to Sam. "Yeah, yeah. Right, mate, I'll call you when we land. Give Anna and my niece/nephew a kiss from me."

"Will do, Char. Love you."

"Love you, too."

Chatting with Sam always made Charlie feel better. At least her head felt clearer. Throwing on her yoga shorts and tank, Charlie headed to the living room. For a split second, she forgot there were other people in the house. Seeing Emilie sitting on the sofa nearly gave her a second coronary. "Jesus," she hissed.

"Morning, sleep well?" Emilie asked, smiling.

"Nope, but never mind. I was… well, I was going to do some yoga," Charlie said, pointing to her TV like an idiot.

"Well, don't let me stop you," Emilie grinned. Good God. How the hell was she supposed to concentrate with Emilie watching her? No, scratch that with Emilie *and* Jess watching her. Jess walked in and plonked herself on the sofa next to Emilie.

"Do you want to do it with me?" Charlie threw the question at both women, who simultaneously shook their heads, declining her offer. Wonderful.

Throughout the entire forty minute class, Charlie felt two pairs of eyes on her. She could have sworn that Emilie had gasped when she'd moved into downward dog.

Finally, the session ended. Charlie was a sweaty mess, but not all the heat she felt was from exercise. Knowing Emilie was

109

watching her was a massive turn-on. "I'm just going to shower," she mumbled. Both Emilie and Jess nodded silently, their cheeks a little pink.

How in the hell was she going to survive this? What was she thinking? Pulling herself from her wandering mind, Charlie slipped under the shower. Without overthinking, she pleasured herself until release. If she was going to have to spend time with Emilie, she was going to make damn sure she wasn't horny when doing it.

The shower was soothing, but only for her sore muscles. Grabbing the towel from the back of the door, Charlie was surprised to see Jess standing in the now open doorway.

"Oh, shit, sorry," Jess mumbled, but made no attempt to leave. Charlie stood, towel in hand, stark naked.

"No worries," Charlie replied. She wasn't shy about her body. There was no need to overreact at another human seeing her sans clothing, but she wished Jess would sod off. "Um, Jess, could you—" Charlie pointed to the door indicating Jess should leave.

"Right, of course."

"Jess, what are you doing?" Oh good, Emilie had joined them. Charlie watched her eyes dart from Jess to her naked body and back again several times.

"Jess was just leaving."

"Total mistake on my part," Jess mumbled as she reversed out of the bathroom. Emilie stood for a moment longer before departing, too. Letting the towel slip to the floor, Charlie massaged her temples. The conversation with Sam swam in her mind. There was no way Jess had "accidentally" entered her bathroom. It was an ensuite for fuck's sake. Sam was right, Jess wasn't just being friendly. Charlie felt like an idiot for believing everything Jess had said last night was because of genuine remorse. It was looking more likely that she was just trying to get into Charlie's knickers.

Why did it feel like she was still in high school? She should have left them all behind when she had the chance. No luck now though, she was committed to work for Emilie. Distance, that's what she needed. Taking a step back was the sensible option. She'd make sure, her and Emilie would discuss the past and then she would move on. Leave it at that.

# Chapter 10

Today had been a day, and it was only eleven in the morning. Emilie had gone from elation to pure anger in the space of a few hours. Everything about yesterday evening had been perfect, okay not totally perfect, but as close as it could get. Charlie seemed to loosen up as the evening progressed. The conversation had been fun and all three of them were relaxed. As far as Emilie was concerned, her and Charlie's new relationship was off to a brilliant start. Should she call it a relationship? Maybe not. They were getting to know each other again, nothing more. Yet.

So imagine Emilie's shock and confusion when she entered the kitchen last night to grab some water, only to be met with Charlie and Jess in an embrace. Not wanting to get caught looking, Emilie had retreated to the guest bedroom, feeling sick to her stomach. What had she missed? Since when was Charlie interested in Jess? What was Jess playing at? She was supposed to be Emilie's best friend. Safe to say Emilie got hardly any rest after that. Suddenly, the bed had seemed too big. She felt as if she were drowning in her loneliness.

As dawn broke, Emilie had already taken a shower, eaten breakfast, and settled on the sofa, pleased that neither Charlie nor Jess had woken up. No matter what she did, she couldn't get the image of Jess draped over Charlie out of her mind. Was this revenge? Was Charlie going to punish her for the past by getting with her best friend? No, surely not. The Charlie she knew would never play those games.

This wasn't the Charlie that she knew though, was it? No, she couldn't bring herself to believe it. There had to be an explanation, and Emilie promised to ask Charlie before coming to the wrong conclusion. She'd done that before and ruined something wonderful.

What she needed was a distraction. Planning a few small gigs would provide that. Emilie had been telling the truth when she told Charlie and Jess that she wanted to give back to her local community. Those people had nurtured her and supported her when she needed it the most. Doing something for them was the least she could do.

Pulling out her phone, Emilie used the map app to locate her cabin. There were only a handful of local towns, all of which she had performed in when she'd started out. Five in total. Jess was right in saying that Jack was going to lose his shit. He did *not* like it when Emilie went off script and so far she'd done it twice. First by inviting Charlie to stay with her and second by planning these gigs.

It didn't matter. Jack could throw a tantrum all he wanted. This was something Emilie wanted to do and, by god, she'd earned the right to choose her own concerts. Shaking her head, Emilie got down to business jotting notes on her phone. The sound of bare feet on the wooden floor pulled her attention. Emilie wanted to groan out loud when Charlie walked towards her in sexy yoga shorts, a tight tank and her hair whipped up in a messy bun. It wasn't fair really. The universe shouldn't be allowed to make someone as stunning as Charlie. Those tattoos! Fuck, Emilie would never tire of looking at them. What a shame she couldn't see the other works of art she knew lay beneath those clothes.

The conversation between them was lost on her. They conversed, sure, but if anyone was to ask what they'd said, she wouldn't have been able to say. All she knew was that she wanted to watch Charlie do yoga. She wanted nothing more in this world.

The fantasy was dulled somewhat when Jess sat next to her, intending on doing the exact same thing. Forty blissful and orgasm-inducing minutes later, Emilie was about to combust. Did Charlie know what she was doing to her? She'd tried her hardest to keep her lust hidden, but when Charlie shifted into downward dog, Emilie knew she'd let out a gasp. Charlie's ass was phenomenal! Sharp images of Emilie grasping that backside swam into view. Oh yes, the night of the gala had been eye opening. Emilie would pay good money to get her hands on that ass again, especially if it meant Charlie was grinding on her again.

"Em?"

Was someone talking to her? "Hm?"

"Charlie's gone for a shower, I'm going to put the kettle on, you want a tea?"

Right, yes, she couldn't just sit fantasising all day. Had Charlie spoken to her? Damn, she needed to get a grip. "Tea, yeah, thanks." Emilie watched Jess leave. She'd been so distracted watching Charlie that she'd forgotten that she was very pissed at Jess. They needed to talk.

Out of the corner of her eye, she spotted Jess round the corner and disappear down the hall. Call it intuition or a gut feeling. Either way, Emilie knew she should follow Jess and see what she was up to. There was no sign of her in the room she'd slept in last night or the one Emilie had been in. Was she in Charlie's? Cautiously, Emilie entered Charlie's room. Everything in her body wanted to stop and peruse, but the sight

114

of Jess inside Charlie's ensuite where Charlie was standing naked stopped that thought in its tracks.

Emilie remembered calling Jess's name, and she remembered Jess making a lame excuse before leaving. She also remembered staring for too long at Charlie before removing herself from the situation. A red mist ascended over her mind. If she confronted Jess now, she'd likely rip her head off. Before she did or said anything, she would come to regret she needed to calm down.

Emilie prided herself on being a reasonable person. It was rare for her to lose it, and she wasn't about to do it now. Storming through the apartment, Emilie stomped to the front door. It was too early for anyone to be at work downstairs, but she found the main doors unlocked. *Carol must be here somewhere.*

The sun was bright, but the air was frigid when she stepped out of the manor. Shit, she hadn't put on a coat. Well, she couldn't go and get one now, not without running into someone and that would be extremely counterproductive to her wellbeing, or theirs. If Charlie and Jess were fucking, Emilie was going to have to address it now. There was no way she was going to be a third wheel. No way she could spend time with Charlie, knowing there was no chance for them. Not in her own home.

The front of Bowman Manor was pretty, but nothing compared to the back garden. The term garden didn't do it justice, though. The area was perfectly landscaped. Ornate hedges trimmed into complex sculptures. A water fountain that bubbled away in the middle, surrounded by a gavel pathway that was so discreet it didn't look as if it was there. Everything had been expertly planned to look and feel like a magical secret garden. The pièce de résistance were the rose bushes. Apart from Charlie's arms, Emilie had never seen roses so vibrant or diverse.

There seemed to be every colour under the sun surrounding the back of the manor. *Does Charlie tend to them?*

"They're not my handiwork." Charlie's smooth voice startled Emilie. She'd been so lost in the garden's wonder she hadn't heard Charlie approach. Not even the crunch of gravel had alerted her.

"Are these your grandma's roses?" Emilie knew all about Estelle's famous roses. Charlie had recounted many a fond memory to Emilie of her time spent in the garden with her grandmother. Although, if memory served, it was in a care home garden, not the manors.

"Yup. They were a little neglected until I took over ownership of the property. Unfortunately, I didn't really inherit my grandmother's green thumb. I mostly spent my time feeling the petals and sniffing them," Charlie laughed. "I have a gardener now who is as enthusiastic about roses as she was. He does a fab job. I hope wherever grandma is, she knows her roses are in safe hands." A lump formed in Emilie's throat. Sometimes when Charlie spoke, she was so deep and emotional it took a minute to digest what she said.

"They look gorgeous. Just like your tattoos."

"Oh, yeah, Max is a genuine artist. He captured what I wanted perfectly."

The conversation lulled awkwardly. *Why have you followed me, Charlie?*

"Are you packed?" It was the worst attempt at small talk ever. Emilie cringed inwardly. Charlie wasn't stupid. She could always read Emilie well. Surely she'd picked up on Emilie's mood, especially after practically sprinting out of the manor the way she did.

"I don't know why Jess was in my bathroom. I didn't invite her." At least Charlie was straight to the point. Never one to beat around the bush. Emilie felt herself heat at her

116

inappropriate thoughts. Charlie definitely knew how to beat around her bush! *Jesus, Em, grow up.*

"I have to say it was a surprise, especially after witnessing you both last night."

"What do you mean? Witnessing what?" Charlie scrunched her eyebrows together.

"I went to grab some water and walked in on you two, in an embrace." God, how she wished she could erase that image from her brain.

"We weren't embracing, Em. She hugged me after she apologised for the way she acted in school. That was it. End of!"

"What did Jess have to apologise for?" Why was Jess inserting herself into their past? Emilie was the only one that needed to make amends.

"She said she should have been there for me. Apparently, she tried to convince you I hadn't sold you out." Emilie's anger boiled. Jess had said nothing of the sort.

"That's what she said, huh?" Emilie wasn't going to expose Jess' lie. That could wait until they were alone together.

"Is that not what happened?" Charlie was studying Emilie closely.

"Maybe I just remember things differently. It doesn't matter now.

"Really?" Charlie cocked her eyebrow. Why was every sexy woman on the planet able to wield their eyebrows like that?

"Really. Do you want to take a walk around your enormous garden with me?" Jess could wait, everything could wait. Finally, Emilie had a chance to spend some alone time with Charlie and she wasn't going to waste it.

"I'd love to, but shouldn't you go grab a coat? It's Baltic out here."

Emilie rolled her eyes dramatically. "You are such a lightweight, Charlie Baxter. You do know that winters in Quebec

117

are a little more harsh than here, right? I'm talking lower than minus ten in December. Even colder in January."

"Oh, I'm sorry I don't have the constitution of a fucking polar bear, Em. Still, it doesn't mean you should tempt fate by walking around in the cold without a coat. That's just inviting trouble. I know you, Emilie Martin. You turn into a massive pain in the arse when you get sick."

"Hey," Emilie protested.

"Oh please, as if you can argue!" Charlie scoffed, tilting her head to the side, waiting for, Emilie to respond. Emilie wasn't going to. Charlie had her, she was in fact, *the* worst person when sick.

"Fine, I'll admit I can be difficult."

"Go grab your coat and we'll take a walk."

Emilie grinned as she passed Charlie to head back inside.

* * *

As the manor grew smaller in the rearview mirror, Emilie sighed. She was going to miss that place. It wasn't as if she had stayed there long, but even a short time had given her a clear insight into Charlie's life and she liked what she saw. Charlie had grown to be a kind, funny, and interesting woman. Putting Charlie's ridiculously good looks to one side, her character was just as stunning.

The walk in the garden had been wonderful. They hadn't hashed out any more of their past. That was still to come. Instead, they'd asked silly questions about each other, listened to stories and laughed at shared memories. There was hope for them, Emilie could taste it.

The car ordered to take Emilie, Jess and Charlie to the private airport whizzed through traffic easily. Normally Emilie would take the travel time to go through emails, check in with

Jack, do all the stuff she hated. Not this time though, instead she kept up light conversation with Charlie. Jess had been unusually quiet, which spoke volumes in Emilie's mind.

"Jesus, is that yours?" Charlie blurted when the car pulled into a hangar that housed Emilie's private jet.

"Yup, that's mine. Don't get me wrong, I have no issue travelling on commercial jets, but sometimes I need the privacy the jet affords me."

"Sod commercial, Em," Charlie laughed, scrambling out of the car. "She's a beauty." Without waiting, Charlie skipped to the plane's steps and rushed inside, causing Emilie to laugh. Charlie was never one to dampen her enthusiasm. Well, not around Emilie anyway. In school, Charlie would reserve this kind of excitement for Emilie's company only. It seemed that grown up Charlie was a lot more free with herself now.

"Em, you've got a bedroom," Charlie shouted from somewhere inside. Emilie laughed harder, even Jess cracked a smile.

Emilie left her driver to collect their luggage. Charlie was nowhere in sight when she finally stepped on board. As usual, she was greeted by Inga, the flight attendant. Inga had been with Emilie for six years and she was fantastic. That woman could anticipate Emilie's needs before she knew what she needed herself.

"Evening, Emilie, did you have a pleasant break?" Emilie insisted everyone call her by her first name.

"Oh, yes, Inga, thank you. We had a blast."

"Excellent. I've set you up on the sofa. There is a bottle of Champagne open. I poured three glasses and set out snacks. You have a little time before takeoff, so relax." Emilie smiled warmly at Inga and squeezed her upper arm in appreciation. Jess had already flopped herself on the sofa, picking up a bowl of nuts from the table.

119

"Charlie?" Emilie called. There was a scuffle of movement before Charlie poked her head around the toilet door.

"Your toilet is massive. Not the actual loo, but the space. I bet you've had some fun in here," Charlie said, waggling her eyebrows. Emilie went scarlet. No, she had never done anything of the sort in the plane's toilet, but now she was thinking about it.

"Stop inspecting the lavatory and come have some Champagne." Charlie didn't need much arm twisting. As the attendants worked, Emilie, Jess, and Charlie settled down with their drinks.

"Cheers everyone, here's to a fun and productive break," Emilie held her glass up in cheers.

"Em, that was a terrible speech," Charlie clucked. "Here's to new adventures and getting into trouble," she winked. Rolling her eyes playfully, Emilie swallowed her drink.

"I'm going to stick my headphones on if that's cool. I don't like takeoffs," Charlie said a few minutes after Inga informed them they would start taxying to the runway.

"Go for it," Emilie replied. This was the opportunity she needed to talk to Jess. Once she was sure that Charlie couldn't hear anything but her playlist, Emilie pulled on Jess's arm sleeve, directing her to follow.

Emilie sat in one of the large comfy chairs behind Charlie. Jess followed and sat next to her, looking uneasy.

"What's up?" Jess asked. It irked Emilie. She hated it when people tried to act as if they had no idea what was going on.

"Want to tell me what's going on? First you're flirting with Charlie at the ball, then I find you all over her in the kitchen last night, then you're in her bathroom whilst she's naked. I mean really, Jess, you have to ask what's up?"

Jess shifted uncomfortably. "Okay, I'm sorry for flirting. I just couldn't help myself. I mean shit, Em, have you seen her? She's not the girl I remember."

"Of course I've seen her, Jess," Emilie spat. "But this isn't just some girl from school, this is Charlie. You know how I feel about her, how I've always felt and you're what? Hoping to get in her pants?"

"No, of course not. Look, I shouldn't have flirted. As for the 'finding me all over her', it wasn't like that at all, I swear. You're not the only one who feels bad for how things played out back then, Emilie. Alright, the main issue was between you two, but I should have stood up for her more. She was nice enough and didn't deserve the way you and the others treated her."

Emilie wanted to strangle Jess. How dare she act so high and mighty? Jess had never shown the slightest interest in Charlie, even when Emilie and Charlie were a couple. So all because Charlie had grown into a hot as hell woman, Jess now felt she could get on her high horse.

"Where was this attitude back then? You never said a word. And I do not appreciate you telling Charlie that you tried to talk me round. That's horseshit, and you know it."

"No, it's not. I told you I thought it wasn't Charlie. You were just too blinded by rage to listen." They were both breathing heavily. This was possibly the first time in their friendship that they were close to blowing up at each other.

"And the bathroom this morning?"

"It was a genuine mistake. I went in to ask Charlie for a towel so I could use the other shower. I really had no idea she'd be standing naked. I swear, Em. I'm not trying to be underhanded, and I am sorry for acting the way I have. Charlie is a friend, that's it. I would never do that to you."

Emilie studied Jess' face. Over the years, she'd got pretty good at sussing out lies and deceit. Unfortunately, it came with the job. Jess had been nothing but true to their friendship. Could she still trust that now?

# Chapter 11

Travelling by private jet was something Charlie could definitely get used to. Seriously, it was awesome. The leather seats were like marshmallows. The carpet was so thick it was bouncy and the toilet... probably not something Charlie should be so excited about to tell the truth, but it was an opulent bog!

Flying was never something Charlie overly enjoyed. She didn't hate it, but there was always that sliver of fear hanging in the background of her mind. Knowing she was so far from the ground was unnerving. Surely that was natural, though. It's not like humans were born to fly, no wings and all that. Charlie's mind was going off on a tangent.

Back to reality, which was funny because her current reality was so beyond her norm. Jazz belted out through her earphones. The plane had successfully taken off and she could feel her queasy tummy settle. It was weird. She never felt like that on the landing.

Inga, the very friendly attendant, stopped by to tell them that the seatbelt sign had been shut off. Snapping open the buckle, Charlie peered round to the seats behind her. Jess and Emilie were looking a little tense. It didn't take a genius to figure out why.

The events of last night and this morning still played on Charlie's mind. Jess had crossed a line coming into her

123

bathroom. There wasn't a real excuse for her to have been there. Jess had apologised and given a frankly lame excuse about towels but, not wanting to rock the boat, Charlie had accepted it and moved on. By the look on Emilie's face, she wasn't being so forgiving.

"The takeoff wasn't so bad," Charlie said, hoping to break whatever was going on between Emilie and Jess.

"Grant is an excellent pilot. Always smooth sailing," Emilie replied a little too sweetly. Charlie recognised that as her *I'm pissed but can't show it* voice.

"So, what should we do for the next seven hours?"

"Whatever you want. There's plenty of booze. A TV with all the streaming services. If you want to sleep, you can use my bedroom."

"I might nap later. How about we go through some of my work? Would be good to dial in on what you want from me... job-wise, I mean." That hadn't come out how she wanted it to at all.

"Sure, let's move to the sofa." Emilie unbuckled herself and scooted past Jess, who smiled tightly at Charlie.

"Jess, you want to join us?" Charlie asked. The last thing she wanted was any more hostility. Jess and Emilie had been friends forever, and Charlie hated she was coming between them.

"Nah, I'm going to get some sleep. Thanks though."

Taking that as her cue to leave, Charlie grabbed her iPad and sat next to Emilie. She had to address the elephant in the room. The thing was fucking huge. "You guys okay?" Charlie mumbled.

"We will be, now let's take a look at your stunning work."

They spent the best part of an hour going through Charlie's portfolio. The work was good, Charlie knew that. Especially the projects that she'd done with a few bands. None of them had Emilie's status, but she'd still done a fab job. Charlie loved the atmosphere of shooting photos at gigs. The atmosphere and energy given out by the crowd was intoxicating.

Over her career, Charlie had lost count of the amount of pictures she'd captured that reflected how the crowd affected a band or individual artist. Flipping to her favourite piece, Charlie pointed to the singer's face. "Look at that. You can feel that she's in the zone. God, that night was epic. The venue wasn't huge, but it was packed. Trip, the singer, had the crowd eating out of the palm of her hand. She was so captivating. I snagged this picture as the crowd chanted her name. Look at her face. She's basking in their adoration."

"It's why we do it," Emilie said, looking closely at the picture. "There is nothing in this world like the energy of an audience. You must remember, Char, we had a few concerts that were wild."

"Wild? Ha, I don't think I'd say wild. We were teens. We didn't know what being wild was! Oh, we *thought* we were the dogs' bollocks but we most definitely weren't," she laughed. "I've been to gigs that were wild. This gig was wild," Charlie replied, pointing back to the picture.

"I still think we did okay back then. We had a little fan base. You have to admit, it was addictive. That feeling we got just before going on stage."

"Yeah, I'll give you that. I didn't miss it though. When I stopped playing, I didn't miss the shows."

"That's sad to hear, Charlie."

"Not really. My love of music was always different to yours, Em. You thrived on the concerts. It was your dream to be a star. I just wanted to bash some piano keys."

"Well you bashed them beautifully," Emilie laughed. "I hope you'll play for me when we get home. I have a wonderful piano just begging to be used." Charlie took a moment. Her first

125

instinct was to rebuff the offer. That had been her modus operandi for so long it came as second nature now. But that's not what she wanted anymore. Sitting and playing the piano was a gift, one that she desperately wanted to reclaim. Honestly, she felt foolish that she'd given up something she loved so much because her adolescent brain had linked it permanently to Emilie.

"I might have a little go," she grinned. "I can't wait to see your music room."

"How do you know I have one?" Emilie smirked.

"How do I know the sun will rise in the morning or the tide will rise and fall? It's inevitable, Emilie. You without a music room would be like Mr Eccleton without his bushy hair." Emilie barked out loud at the comparison.

* * *

Seven hours can pass pretty quickly when having fun, and that's exactly what happened. Before Charlie knew it, the Captain was announcing they would be landing shortly. Charlie and Emilie had spent hours chatting. It was just like in the garden back at Bowman Manor. They were learning about each other, getting to know each other as adults that had led such different lives. They flirted mildly, but it never went beyond that.

"Shitting hell, it's freezing!" Charlie exclaimed as she deplaned the jet. The icy wind slapped her around the face as soon as she'd stepped out of the comfort of the cabin and onto the metal stairs. Maybe she should have worn more layers. Wrapping her coat tightly around her body, she leapt down the steps and jumped straight into the back of the waiting car. "You are here for Emilie, right?" she asked the driver. Hopefully, she hadn't just hijacked someone's ride.

"Yes, ma'am," the driver replied.

126

"Nope, never call me that again, mate. Charlie will do, ta." The driver grinned and nodded. Charlie willed her body to heat up.

"Doing okay, Charlie?" Jess laughed as she climbed in, taking the seat opposite.

"Oh yeah, fab. I am seriously worried about the clothes I bought. I'm going to freeze to death."

"I told you to bring your warmest clothes," Emilie called from the boot of the car.

"I did, but you're seriously underestimating my wardrobe, woman. I have like four outfits. Black jeans, band shirts and like three jumpers. I packed my entire wardrobe."

"Why the hell didn't you say anything? We could have stopped off and bought you some appropriate attire. You look like an icicle." Emilie groaned, climbing into the car. "Mark, put the heating up to full. We need to thaw this one out."

"I hope your house is warm." Charlie's teeth chattered as she spoke. Where had all her body heat gone?

"Come here," Emilie said, yanking Charlie into her side.

"If I die of hyperthermia, I am going to be pissed," Charlie barked, causing Emilie and Jess to laugh.

"You are so dramatic. We'll get you warm again. Tomorrow I'll send out for some clothes. How do you feel about thermal underwear?" Emilie giggled.

"I feel fantastic about it. Can I have a set with the flap thing on the arse, like the ones in the movies?" Charlie was sincere in her request.

"If you want a butt flap, Char, I'll get you a butt flap," Emilie grinned. Jess shook her head, laughing.

Halfway through the car journey, Charlie could feel her face again. Even though she was warmer, she didn't move away from Emilie's body. "Ah, thank god, I can feel my limbs again," she sighed.

"I cannot believe you thought a few jumpers would be enough. I get you like the whole rock chic thing, but really Charlie, the weather here isn't to be laughed at."

"Are you scolding me right now, Em?" Charlie laughed. "I didn't do it on purpose. The clothes you see really are all I own. I've been wearing the same things for twenty-five years. It's not about style but comfort."

"Comfort? How comfortable were you half an hour ago?" Emilie shot back. Charlie was a little confused by her attitude.

"Whoa, alright, take it down a notch. Sorry it didn't occur to me to prepare for the fucking arctic circle. Why are you getting so bent out of shape?"

"Because I don't want anything to happen to you. The cold is no joke." Emilie shot. Charlie lay her hand on Emilie's thigh, stroking small circles, which used to calm Emilie down. Charlie hoped it still worked.

"Sorry, I promise next time I will wear layer upon layer of thermal clothing. Please don't be mad at me." Charlie saw Emilie's body relax.

"I'm not mad, Charlie. I just want you to be safe."

"And I am. Look, you warmed me right up." They looked at each other for a beat too long. No matter how much Charlie tried to keep that invisible barrier between them erect, Emilie had a way of toppling it with just a look.

"Two minutes out, Emilie," Mark, the driver, announced. Charlie was grateful for the interruption. Peering out the window, Charlie did a double take when they rounded the corner and were presented with Emilie's cabin.

"Holy shitballs, batman, that's your cabin?" Charlie shouted. Was there nothing in Emilie's world that wasn't massive and luxurious?

"Home sweet home," Emilie sang.

Shoving her beanie over her head, Charlie grumbled as she left the warmth of the car. There was no way she would ever get used to this kind of cold. At least her trusty Doc Martens protected her feet from the freshly settled snow. If she were in a better—warmer—mood, Charlie might have stopped to take in the Christmas card worthy scene that she was currently standing in. But no, there was no time for dilly dallying. Not when her nipples were freezing off her chest.

Rushing into the cabin, Charlie nearly dropped to her knees and thanked every goddess out there that the space was so well heated. With her body happily warmed, Charlie looked around. It was safe to say her jaw nearly hit the floor. The cabin was gorgeous. Just like Charlie's place, the cabin had a delicate balance of old and new. I was an old traditional hunting lodge, but perfectly paired with modern twists. Thankfully, there were no dead animal heads hanging on the wall, so at least she would sleep at night. Who the hell wanted beady eyes staring at them all day and night? No ma'am, not this chick.

"So…?" Emilie stood by the closed door. Jess was already hiking her bag up the cabin stairs.

"Wow, I mean wow, Em. This is beautiful." Similar to the cottage in Pickerton, the cabin was open plan. The large kitchen fed into the living room that was warmed by a huge open fire.

"Come on, I'll show you to your room. It's been a long day. I think we should get some sleep and start the tour tomorrow."

Charlie followed Emilie up the stairs and into a bedroom she presumed was her new lodging for the foreseeable future. Yeah, she definitely needed some shut eye because tomorrow the adventure began.

\* \* \*

*What the fuck is that? Is it raining indoors?* Why was Charlie's face wet? Her mind whirred as she cracked open her eyelid. Something slimy smacked her square in the face. "Jesus," she moaned, swiping at her face. Suddenly a warm tongue plastered her entire face. Dragging her hands down her cheeks to wipe away the offending goo, Charlie opened her eyes fully, only to be confronted with a large and very wet black nose. "I take it you're Spud," she muttered to the dog that was staring at her with wonder. Another long swipe of a tongue caused Charlie to giggle. Dogs were the best.

"Get off, you brute," she laughed. Instead of obeying, Spud lay prone on Charlie's body, shoving her face in Charlie's.

"Spud, come on girl, where are you?" Emilie called from down the hall.

"I think your mum's looking for you," Charlie said. Spud wagged her tail enthusiastically but didn't move.

"Eeeem," Charlie shouted. Spud didn't look like she was going to move anytime soon. Side note, though, the dog was super warm. Charlie was definitely stealing her at night. *Furry water bottle sorted.*

"Charlie?" A light tapping resonated through the door before it creaked open.

"Em, I think your dog has taken a liking to me," Charlie laughed.

"Oh my god, Spud, bad girl, get down this instant." Spud looked back at Emilie and ignored her.

"Spud, now!" Emilie growled. Charlie burst out laughing as the dog continued to ignore Emilie, focusing solely on Charlie. Her cute eyes shone with excitement. She was clearly over the moon at the prospect of having a new friend.

"Charlie, I am so sorry. She never disobeys me." Emilie strode over and picked Spud up, setting her down next to the bed. Emilie froze, looking down at Charlie. Oh right, she'd fallen

130

asleep naked and her girls were showing. A smirk etched itself on Charlie's face. Emilie was making no bones about the fact she was looking at Charlie's nipple bars. *Yeah, she likes those, if I remember well.*

"How's the view?" Charlie asked.

Emilie's eyes snapped to hers. Instead of embarrassment, Charlie saw a tinge of defiance. "Well, if you're going to parade them, I'm going to look."

Charlie chuckled. She'd do exactly the same. "What time is it?" Charlie was completely disoriented. She certainly wasn't used to being woken by dog kisses.

"Almost nine-thirty. You can sleep longer if you want. Jetlag is a bitch."

"No way, I've got exploring to do, although I will need some clothes. My faithful band tees aren't going to cut it this time."

"Already sorted. I've got a bunch of clothes waiting for you. Grab a shower and I'll leave them on the bed. Breakfast will be ready in ten and then we can start the day."

"Why couldn't you have been this accommodating back in the day?" Charlie laughed. "The amount of times you shoved me out of bed to grab you breakfast from the cafeteria was ridiculous."

"Hey, I made it up to you tenfold." Emilie smiled. Yeah, she had. Every time Charlie came back with a bagel, Emilie always thanked her with oral. Ah, to be sixteen and horny.

"Are you expecting me to thank you for my breakfast in the same way, Emilie?" *Whoa stop, what are you doing? Warning, warning, danger. Stop thinking with your crotch!*

"I hadn't thought of that," Emilie winked. "Not this time, though. Too much to do. Come on Spud, let's go. Ten minutes, Charlie. Don't wash your hair, we haven't got time." Charlie stuck her tongue out. A big downside of very long hair was the time it took to wash and dry.

Eleven minutes later, Charlie strolled into the kitchen. The pile of pancakes set her mouth watering. Spud sat by Emilie's feet, watching her every move. Was she hoping for a bit of food to magically fall to the floor? Yes. Was Spud getting what she wanted? No. Smiling at the expectant pooch, Charlie hopped on to one of the many stools. "Do you like to entertain people at breakfast, Em? This is a lot of stools!"

"Is it? There are only eight."

"Sorry, my bad. Eight kitchen stools is a totally reasonable number to have."

"I've just made you pancakes, and you're in here busting my ass about the number of stools in my kitchen?"

"Just saying," Charlie mumbled through a mouthful of pancake. "Oh, yeah, now these are delicious." Fresh fluffy pancakes, the only thing that would make it better would be —

"Maple bacon, I cooked plenty, so tuck in."

"You're perfect," Charlie whispered. Either Emilie hadn't heard or she ignored Charlie's slip up.

"Ok, once you're done, we'll head out for a walk with Spud. I can't wait for you to see… everything!" Emilie beamed.

"Me either. Is Jess joining us?" Charlie had almost forgotten Jess had stayed over last night. It was way too easy to get lost in the fantasy of her and Emilie.

"No, Jess headed out already. Her house isn't too far. I'm sure she'll stop by soon. Honestly, it does us good to have some time away. We already live in each other's pockets for months on end. When I'm home, I like my privacy and space."

"Hey, say the word Em, and I'll make myself scarce. I can start planning shots and stuff. Now I have an idea of what you're looking for. I don't want to get in the way."

"Charlie, stop. I invited you here. I want to be around you. Yes, I know you're going to be working, but I want us to connect again. We can't get back the time that's passed, but we can start again. I want you with me."

Emilie's frank statement left Charlie spinning. Nothing that she'd said was a surprise, but now she was here, in Emilie's life. It was real. After twenty years, she would reconnect with Emilie. What that meant, she wasn't sure.

# Chapter 12

Emilie rejoiced at the sound of sticks breaking underfoot. The smell of pine in the air rid her body of months and months of stress. Finally, she was home. Finally, she could completely relax.

Walking through the forest was so calming. Spud ran around, unable to contain her joy. *Squirrels beware*, Emilie thought. It was laughable because if Spud ever caught one, Emilie was certain she'd lick it to death rather than harm it. The pooch was just a barrel of love.

The sun shone through the trees; the air was chilly and there was a decent amount of snow on the ground, but it didn't matter, Emilie loved all of it. Charlie, on the other hand? So far, Emilie had laughed more in the last 48 hours than she had in the past six months. Charlie was just too much. Turning round to make sure Charlie was keeping up, Emilie had to bite her lip to stop herself from laughing again. Poor frozen Charlie.

Dragging up the rear of their threesome, Charlie waddled along in the thickest coat ever made. Her trousers were insulated, and she wore a scarf so long it wrapped around her a dozen times. Add the thick beanie perched on her head and all Emilie could see was a pair of vivid green eyes.

"Alright?" Emilie called. Charlie replied, but the words were completely lost in the fabric cocooning her mouth. "Didn't quite catch that," Emilie giggled. Taking her gloved hands out of her pockets, Charlie set about pulling at the scarf.

"I said I'm fine," Charlie grumbled.

"Charlie, we can go back inside if you're miserable."

"I'm not miserable. I'm actually quite warm now. I'm sure I resemble the Pillsbury Doughboy, but I'll own it. I wish I was one of those women who could make winter wear sexy."

"What are you talking about?"

"You know. Cute bobble hat, nice little knitted scarf over a peacoat."

"You look fine," Emilie said, trying not to crack up at Charlie's face.

"You are a shitty liar, Emilie Martin. You, on the other hand, are one of those women. Look at you." Emilie looked herself up and down. Yeah, she had the thick peacoat, knitted scarf and bobble hat. Her hair hung down her back.

"That's only because I'm accustomed to the cold. As soon as your body acclimatises, you'll be rocking this outfit in black, I'm sure of it."

Spud zoomed out of the trees with a stick in her mouth. She ran around Emilie and Charlie several times before running off again.

"Does she want us to throw the stick?" Charlie asked.

"Oh no, she just likes to do that now and then. It's her thing. If she ever drops the stick in front of you, it's a warning there is a bear close by."

"I beg your pardon. Did you say bear?" Charlie hissed. Her eyes scanned the trees feverishly. Oh dear, Emilie shouldn't have dropped that little nugget of information so casually.

"Don't panic. It's a rare occurrence. The bears are further north, but they do wander. They're black bears, not grizzlies. If we see one, we just back up slowly. No drama, okay."

"I cannot believe you didn't tell me about bears —"

"Well honestly you should be more worried about moose." *Oh, for the love of beans Emilie, shut up!*

"Moose. Why should I be worried about moose?"

"Erm, they can just be a little aggressive, is all."

"A little aggr... Emilie, what the hell? Can we go back please? I'm too young to die by moose!"

Not wanting Charlie to freak out any more than she already was, Emilie turned them around to head home. Shame really, she would have loved another hour in her special place. Looking at Charlie though, she could still be with her special person, so that would do.

Charlie had practically jogged back to the house, which Spud had thoroughly enjoyed. She thought Charlie was magical, and Emilie couldn't disagree. They entered the back door and Emilie watched Charlie shed her many, *many* layers. Underneath all those layers was Charlie's signature band tee. Under her thick trousers were a pair of black ripped jeans. Emilie sighed. She would never tire of Charlie looking so... well, Charlie.

*Buzzzz Buzzzz Buzzzz*

Yanking her phone out of her pocket, Emilie groaned out loud. The message she'd just received from Jess warning her that Jack was on the warpath popped her magical little Charlie-filled bubble. Great, she was going to have to talk down an irate Jack. She wasn't even supposed to be working, well, not on anything official.

"I think we're about to get a visitor and he's going to be pissed. You'll have to excuse me for a little while."

"Is it Jack?" Charlie asked, her posture tensing as she spoke.

"Yeah, seems he's found out I hired you. He really doesn't like it when I go 'rogue',"

"Rogue? Seriously?"

"Well, yeah. I mean, he is my manager. I should take things through him."

"He doesn't run your life, Em. Anyway, you didn't just hire me."

"What do you mean?"

"Well, you asked me here so we could get to know each other again. That's a personal matter, Emilie, fuck all to do with him."

Emilie batted her toe on the floor. Charlie was right. Jesus, how long had Jack been running her entire life?

"Hey, I can stick around if you want. I bet he won't be so much of a dick if I'm here. You don't have to face him alone." Emilie wanted to scoop Charlie up into a hug. Even Jess never enjoyed sticking around when Jack went off on one of his rants.

The offer was so tempting, but she needed to sort it out with him alone. It was time she started taking back some control. "Thanks, but I'll handle it. Why don't you take a tour of the house?" Before Charlie could answer, the doorbell sounded repeatedly.

"Alright, I'll be upstairs, but I'm a shout away. Don't put up with his bullshit, Em. Let no one tell you what you can and can't do."

Emilie was transported back to their school days, when Charlie would say things like that to her daily. Being a teenager at the time meant that most of the adults in her life liked to tell her what to do, what to say, and how to think. A lot of the time it served *their* interests instead of Emilie's. Charlie was the only one that told it to her straight. Encouraged Emilie to forge her own path, trust in her own instincts.

With Charlie safely upstairs, Emilie opened the door to Jack. He didn't wait for an invitation. He barged right past her and went to the living room, where he began to pace.

"What's this I hear about you hiring your high school fuck?"

What the hell? That was way over the line. "Would you care to rephrase that, Jack?"

"Oh, come on, Emilie. I know you were hung up on seeing her again but bringing her back with you, really, after what she did? Surely you can spot an opportunist when you see one."

"I invited her here as a guest, Jack. This is personal. It's nothing to do with you, so why, may I ask, are you in my home raging about it?"

"You hired her as your personal photographer, for fuck sakes. You have one of those already."

"Yes, but I wanted Charlie for *strictly* personal photos. No events or award ceremonies. I want to make some memories over the next few months, away from the public, Jack. I asked Charlie if she'd do that. So I'll repeat my question. Why are you raging about this?"

"And the gigs you plan to do? Were you going to tell me about them?" Emilie didn't miss that he was dodging her question.

"How did you find out about that? And yes, I was going to tell you. I wanted you to help me. Isn't that what you're supposed to do, not just give me shit anytime I deviate from *your* plan?"

"I thought you wanted a break. That's why you keep saying no to a new album."

"I *do* want a break. I want a break from the studios and the touring. I want to get back to simpler times. Me singing for fun. I want to show all those people that supported me in the beginning how much I appreciate it. I just wanted to go to a local pub and sing for them. It's not a big deal, Jack, so why are you making it into one?"

138

"I just wish you'd run it by me Emilie, it's my job."

"No, your job is to do what I ask of you. Again, something you keep on forgetting. I can make my own decisions, Jack, you are not my keeper. I want to work with you, but it's clear that any time I have an original thought, you're ready to burn it down."

"I want what's best for you, Emilie. You are a star and I want that to continue."

"For who? Me or you?"

"Hey —"

"No, I have told you for a long time that I needed to slow down for a bit, but you just keep pushing. You tell me it's for my own good, but I highly doubt it. If you were doing things for my welfare, you would be listening to me and trusting that I know myself well enough to make that call."

Jack stopped pacing, his head dropping to his chest as he let out a giant breath. "You're right, Em. You are, I'm sorry. I'll do what I can to help. Tell me what you need." *Well, this is a quick change of attitude.*

"Can you discreetly enquire at the local pubs in the surrounding towns? Ask if they would like a private concert. I don't want any press Jack, no advertising, this is strictly personal, okay?"

"Okay, sure. I'll get on it. Do you want to charge anything?"

"Nope, I just want people to have a good time."

"I'll call when I have some dates and venues. Sorry, Em." With a quick pat on the shoulder, Jack left as quickly as he arrived. The blow up left Emilie exhausted. That was her general feeling nowadays, exhausted.

Taking a few calming breaths, Emilie headed upstairs to find Charlie. She wondered how much she'd heard of the row. After checking most of the rooms, Emilie smiled to herself.

Charlie must have found the music room. Stepping quietly, she peered round the open door to find Charlie sat at the white grand piano in the middle of the room. "Hey," Emilie said quietly, not wanting to break the silence. Charlie looked so calm and happy.

"Hey, everything sorted?"

"Yeah, finally. I think I got through to him." Emilie entered the room and took a seat on the piano bench next to Charlie.

"This is a magnificent piano, Em."

"I thought you'd like it," Emilie smiled. "Play something for me?" Emilie knew she was probably pushing it, but she couldn't help it. Charlie was a sight to behold when she tapped those keys. There was nothing more transfixing than watching Charlie lose herself so completely to the music.

"Okay," Charlie said softly. Emilie knew to be quiet. Charlie had a process, well, she used to. It was like she was summoning the music and wrapping herself up in it until it consumed her. Charlie was a formidable composer. Most of her creations brought Emilie to tears. *Does she remember them?*

Slowly, Charlie rested her fingers over the keys. Emilie held her breath in anticipation. And then it happened. The magic that was Charlotte Munroe. Emilie knew she should say it was the magic of Charlie Baxter, but right in that moment, she saw the genius sixteen-year-old that would blow her mind with her music. Charlie was lost, and Emilie watched as she swayed, the emotion of each note playing out over her beautiful face.

Closing her own eyes, Emilie let the melody engulf her. She allowed herself to go on the journey that Charlie was taking. She felt the crushing sadness and the elation as the story unfolded. Tears pricked at her eyes as Charlie played. When the last note rang out, Emilie could have collapsed. Charlie was a master of wringing out every last feeling, stripping Emilie's emotions bare for the world to see.

Silence descended. Emilie needed a few moments to collect herself. It was always the same way, after Charlie played, Emilie needed time to sooth her exposed nerves.

Opening her eyes, she looked at Charlie, who stared at the piano keys. "My god, Charlie, you're still the best."

Charlie turned to her with a shy smile. "It feels great to play again." As usual, guilt gripped Emilie's chest like a vise. Because of her actions, she'd robbed the world of Charlotte Munroe.

"I'm so sorry, Charlie," she sobbed.

"Hey, hey, whoa, what's happening right now?" Charlie asked, scooping Emilie into her arms. The guilt got heavier. Why did Charlie have to be so good?

"It crushes me that you gave up your passion because of me. I know we've talked, but I can't help feeling guilty."

"Maybe it's time we talked again. One argument in a school toilet isn't really us talking, Em. I think we can do it now, though. Neither of us are as angry as we were, right?"

Emilie nodded. They knew this day would come. They couldn't brush it under the carpet. "You go first," Emilie whimpered. Her emotions were way too fried to talk.

"Wow, okay." Charlie huffed. "First, I don't want you to carry that guilt about me quitting the piano. That was on me. I was young and ruled by my emotions. I should never have given it up because you hurt me. I just ended up punishing myself." Charlie turned her body so she was facing Emilie. "What hurt me the most and still does, if I'm honest, is you not trusting me. I could understand your anger, shit, Em, what the papers wrote about you was terrible. Of course, you were hurt and I could understand you taking it out on me. I was your person.

141

"I thought though, that when the shock wore off, you'd see how ridiculous it was to blame me for it. I couldn't believe that you truly thought I would do that to you, not after everything we went through together. I waited for you to calm down. I waited for you to see the truth, but you didn't, and then you screamed at me in front of everyone. I could have forgiven that if you'd just believed me in the end, if you'd come back to me and talked, but you didn't. You left and shattered everything we built."

Charlie rubbed her head and looked down at her lap. Emilie knew that everything she'd said was right. Emilie had done all those things, and she felt awful. There was nothing in this world she regretted more than walking away from Charlie.

"I can't give you a reason, Char. I was just so upset. I felt like my safe haven had been violated. Being at Pickerton with you was my safety, my home and when those details got printed, I lost the plot. The days went by in a blur. I honestly couldn't tell you what happened, only that I had friends telling me it had to have been you. They all knew that you were the only one privy to my life before Pickerton. I know a few of them resented you for it. I was lost in this black hole. Everyone around the world knew intimate details about me. The more my friends told me you were to blame, the darker I felt."

Emilie wiped her face. Tears streamed down each cheek. "I had so many people talking *at* me. I just lost it when you tried to talk to me and that's when I screamed at you. I have regretted nothing more in my life than that. It took me weeks to clear myself up and by that time, I'd ruined us. There was no way I could face you after that. I didn't deserve your forgiveness, so I left you alone."

"I didn't want leaving alone, Em. I just wanted you."

"I was a coward, Charlie, it's as simple as that."

142

"Do you believe me, that it wasn't me who called the papers?"

"Oh, Charlie," Emilie sobbed, "I knew you weren't lying. I fucked up and blamed you, but I knew in my heart you would never have done it. I'm so sorry, so, so sorry."

"Shh, shhh, come on Em, it's okay."

"How can you be so nice?" Emilie cried.

"Because we were kids, and we made mistakes. I should have reached out. I would have if it had happened when we were older. I just didn't have the emotional maturity back then. We lived in a vacuum, Emilie. Everything was so intense. If we'd been a regular couple, it wouldn't have blown up like that. We just weren't capable of fighting all the outside influences. Yes, I wish we could have communicated and worked it out, but maybe we weren't meant to back then."

"What do you mean?"

"I mean, how the hell were we meant to survive as a couple? We had fanciful dreams, but neither of us actually had a clue how we would have made them into a reality. Maybe by breaking up back then, we were given the opportunity to grow, find our own paths. We've come back together after twenty years and the attraction and passion is still there, but we've also gained experience and, dare I say, a little wisdom. If we were good before, imagine what we could be now."

"Do you want there to be a now?" Emilie's heart rate was through the roof. Could she be given the one thing she desired most in the world? Not fame, not fortune, but the love of Charlie Baxter. Was she lucky enough to be offered a second chance?

"Eventually," Charlie said. Emilie felt Charlie cup her chin, lifting her head so they were face to face. No hiding. "It's going to take time, Emilie. We have to build trust and we need to keep learning about each other. If we do that, I think we will get to where we both want to be."

143

# Chapter 13

When Emilie had fallen silent after Charlie's heartfelt speech, she was worried that maybe Emilie wasn't as invested in them working things out as Charlie had first thought. Then Emilie kissed her so passionately that *all* thoughts went out of the window. They sat for a good hour kissing, connecting. Just being surrounded by Emilie was enough.

They promised nothing; they made no plans. Charlie recognised that she'd done a 180° turnaround on her decision to keep things strictly professional, but that was okay. The great thing about being human was the ability to change one's mind. She wasn't going to be stubborn just for the sake of pride. Whatever was happening between her and Emilie was worth exploring.

Maybe it was a sign of their new commitment to each other that they didn't fall into bed. It would have been so easy to have taken Emilie in the music room. Show her how much Charlie had missed her, but they'd refrained.

A week had passed since that evening in the music room. Something had shifted between Charlie and Emilie, something profound. Talking openly and honestly had bridged a two decade old gap. The relationship was a work in progress, but it was certainly heading in the right direction. Charlie felt comfortable with herself. She reflected on the situation daily, checking in with her thoughts and feelings.

Whenever a question arose, Charlie felt no stress voicing it, and Emilie seemed to have no problem answering it honestly. That's what had been missing all those years ago. How could two teenagers be expected to deal with such deep emotions?

Their situation at the time had been incomprehensible, and neither of them had good enough role models in their lives to help them wade through all the bullshit. Yes, Charlie was as convinced as ever that coming back into each other's lives now was how it was supposed to be for them. Okay, so she could have done without the complete wreckage that had occurred back then, but, hey, time had passed and she had healed, even more so now.

As well as spending their days talking and getting to know each other, Charlie also wandered around the property — never too far though, because, bears! — taking in her new normal. So far, she'd done no official work. The most important thing had been to fix things with Emilie. Now that was well and truly on the way to being completed, Charlie focused on work.

Emilie said she wanted Charlie as her personal photographer and, looking at the sparse walls and empty spaces around the cabin, she could understand why. There were plenty of pictures of Emilie with other celebrities, at award shows, magazine covers. There were zero pictures of Emilie with friends and family. Everything in the house celebrated the artist Emilie Martin, but nothing reflected her as a woman, just a regular person with likes and dislikes. Charlie had pictures everywhere in her house. Sure, she had framed photographs she was proud of, but mainly, she had silly pictures of her and Sam. There was a brilliant picture of the whole friendship group out celebrating

Kim and Hélène's engagement. Why didn't Emilie have those kinds of memories displayed?

"Em, you have like no pictures of your friends or family around here." It was a statement, one she hoped wouldn't upset Emilie.

"I know. Why do you think I hired you?" Emilie laughed.

"But why don't you have those pictures?"

"Because I'm always working, Char. Everything I do usually ends up as a promotional stunt. I once had a birthday party where I only invited my closest friends. Well, that got busted up when Jack invited all these celebs. The night turned into just another promo party. That's why I have no private memories. I'm never given the chance to experience them." Charlie's heart raged and broke at the same time. Nothing had changed from when Emilie was a teen. She was still surrounded by arseholes who saw her as a money pit. It was a miracle the woman hadn't burned out years ago.

"Well, that shit stops now! Get here, we're having a selfie." Charlie watched Emilie's face transform. Her smile was as bright as the sun reflecting off of fresh snow. "And don't give me that bloody Emilie Martin pose shite. I want fun Em, to come out and play."

Twenty minutes passed, and the poses got sillier and sillier. Poor Spud got roped in and together the three of them had nearly an album's worth of daft photos to laugh at. "Oh my lord, these are too good, Char!" Emilie giggled.

"I especially like the one with Spud sticking her tongue up your nose," Charlie laughed.

"Ew, don't remind me," Emilie chuckled.

"Okay, so now we've made a good start on your private photos. What's next? What do you want me to capture?"

Emilie sat pondering for a second, which Charlie didn't mind because it meant she could sit and watch Emilie. Her hair

146

was in its signature messy bun. Charlie loved that Emilie looked so chilled in sweatpants and a band tee, especially since it was one of Charlie's.

"Everything I suppose. I know that doesn't really narrow it down," she smirked. "I want to be reminded of all the things that bring me happiness and peace. Like the forest. Spud, obviously. You, my friends. Not too bothered about the family part," she joked. Charlie knew that Emilie's family was a mess. "Although I would like photos of my uncle."

"So these friends, who are we talking about?"

"Gosh, I suppose Jess and Lydia." Charlie visibly cringed when Lydia's name came up. "I don't get what the problem is between you pair," Emilie commented.

"There was never a problem from me, Em, it was all Lydia. She hated me from the very first day she met me and I have no idea why. I wasn't strong enough back then to stand up for myself, but now, well, now she can suck a bag of balls."

"Gross, Char."

"You asked," she laughed. "I was going to suggest you have a little party. Just your friends. Have a night to just relax with them, gossip, do whatever you want to do. I know I couldn't go without my friends for very long."

"You and Sam are really close eh?"

"Yeah, she's like my sister. I was still quite shy by the time I started uni. I put on a brave face, though. Anyway, I met Sam, and she became my roommate. We just hit it off. Sam was like this lesbian superhero in my mind. She could get any woman she wanted because she was confident, but not cocky. She was just happy with herself and it shone through.

"I think I was able to draw from her strength and I finally found my own confidence. It was liberating. Plus, her mum Sandy, who is this awesome artist, treated me like I was her own

147

kid. Together, they gave me the family I had been starved of. I would do anything for them."

"That's beautiful to hear. I love that story and I can tell that you definitely gained confidence. Jesus, Charlie, when you entered the ball, I think everyone's jaw hit the deck! That was a power move if I ever saw one," Emilie laughed.

"Yeah, it was. I was about to meet you again after a fuck ton of time had passed. I was a nervous bag of bones. It was Kim who told me I needed a shit hot entrance," Charlie chuckled.

"I can totally see Kim saying that. She's fierce. I'm not usually intimidated by people, but, hell, that woman made me nervous."

"God, don't be nervous, honestly. All my friends are awesome. I would love for you to get to know them and I swear as soon as Kim knows she doesn't have to play the protective friend, you are going to see how much she adores you." Kim would definitely become Emilie's number one fan.

"Why don't we invite them here for a few days, then? I'll ask Jess and Lydia and you ask your lot. We could have a repeat of the after party."

"Are you serious?"

"Of course. I said I wanted to get to know you, Charlie. And now I know, to do that, I need to get to know your friends. What do you think? Will they come?"

"I'll call them now and ask." Charlie wasted no time pulling up Sam's number. It would be early evening time in Paris so no reason Sam wouldn't pick up unless Anna was getting frisky.

"Sammy," Charlie shouted with excitement.

"Charlie," Sam returned with just as much enthusiasm. "What's cooking, mate? You having fun?"

"Yeah, it's awesome here. I wanted to forward an invitation to you and Anna from Emilie."

"What kind of invitation?" Charlie could hear Anna in the background questioning Sam.

"Hang on, Anna wants to know what's going on. I'm putting you on speaker."

"Hey Anna, how's the bump?"

"All good. I've stopped feeling nauseous, so that's a win."

"What's this invitation?" Sam asked.

"You're so impatient. Fine, Emilie, wants to know if you fancy coming over here for a few days?"

"Are you being serious?" Anna squeaked, causing Charlie and Emilie to laugh.

"I am very serious, Anna, I would love to get to know you better," Emilie chimed.

"Am I on speaker, Charlie? *Merde*, you could have warned me. So sorry, Emilie."

Charlie cackled. Her friends were ridiculous. "Don't get your knickers in a bunch. You're not coming to meet the famous Emilie Martin, you're coming to meet my dear friend Em, okay?"

"When?" Sam asked. Anna had fallen silent, probably too nervous to speak.

"How about next weekend?" Emilie asked. Charlie nodded. That worked for her.

"Call Kim and extend the offer to her, too. I haven't got the energy to wrangle her enthusiasm," Charlie grinned. Kim was going to lose her shit. "Just message and we'll get everything set up."

"Can't wait," Sam gushed.

"Love you," Charlie called, speaking to both Sam and Anna, who parroted back the sentiment.

"Are you sure you want to do this, Em, they can get a bit wild?"

"Well, now I'm even more intrigued and excited. I can't wait."

* * *

With the plans for their little party arranged, Charlie was buzzing with excitement. Not only was she going to get to spend time with Emilie and her closest friends, but they were also preparing to do the first concert in the local town.

Charlie didn't have much time for Jack, but she had to concede he was decent at his job. He'd done everything that Emilie had asked of him, arranging five intimate concerts in the towns surrounding Emilie's cabin. There had been no press and as far as Charlie knew, it was only the owners of the bars that knew what was happening.

"Okay, so the girls will be here in ten minutes. Kim just messaged me. It took me a few minutes to get past all the fangirl bollocks before I actually got the information I asked for," Charlie laughed. Kim was definitely not keeping her cool about any of it. Thank god for Hélène and her "Kim calming" ways.

"Jess and Lydia will be over in about an hour," Emilie called from her bedroom.

"All the food is ready and the booze. Are you sure you're up for this?" Charlie asked. It was sure their little soiree was going to turn messy.

"Oh, yes, I think you're more nervous than me. I just ask that no one post pictures online," Emilie said. Charlie had already had that talk with her friends, but she wasn't concerned.

The doorbell shrieking jolted Charlie from her seat. Ripping open the door, she launched herself at her friends, who were just as excited to see her.

"Fuck me, doll. This is gigantic," Kim blurted as soon as they'd stopped hugging.

"C'est très belle," Hélène added.

"Come in, come in. The rest is just as spectacular." Just then, Emilie descended the steps. All eyes were on her. Charlie could understand her friends being starstruck. Even in boyfriend-cut jeans and a plain sweater, Emilie was stunning.

"Oh, I'm so pleased you're all here. Welcome." Emilie stepped forward and hugged each of them. Charlie laughed out loud when Hélène had to physically remove her fiancé from Emilie's body.

"Will you calm down?" Hélène laughed. Kim didn't seem in the least bit sorry.

"Hey, it's not everyday you get to hug Emilie Martin. I'm getting in as much hug time as possible." Hélène rolled her eyes playfully. Charlie turned to Sam and Anna. Anna really was glowing. "Mama, you look radiant!"

"I feel huge," Anna mumbled, and Sam took her wife in her arms, kissing her head.

"You're gorgeous, honey." They were going to be such wonderful parents.

With the greetings over with, the six women headed to the kitchen to pour drinks and start their evening. Kim was already snapping silly photos. Sam almost lost her mind when Spud waltzed in with a little party hat on and a rainbow bow tie. Safe to say, Spud had plenty of human time filled with cuddles and ear scratches.

The atmosphere became a little tense when Jess and Lydia walked in. Charlie wasn't thrilled that Lydia had agreed to come. Apparently, she'd been planning to stop by, anyway. Jess had already invited Lydia over to stay with her for a few days.

It was fine. Charlie could avoid Lydia for a couple of days. Tomorrow was the gig, and there was no way Charlie was going to let Lydia put a damper on it.

151

The night was full of laughter. Charlie regaled Emilie with stories of her and Sam's time in university, which lead nicely to the story of Anna and Sam. Kim told Emilie how she and Hélène met and fell in love on holiday.

Charlie discreetly took photos of the group. The pictures got incrementally worse as the night wore on. Charlie wasn't great at focusing with half a liter of rum coursing through her bloodstream. Soon the music got turned up and everyone was dancing on the makeshift dance floor in the middle of the living room.

The same flame of desire that had sparked at the ball came roaring back with a vengeance when Charlie watched Emilie dance. This time, though, she wasn't going to give in to lust. They were building something special and that took time. Charlie had to resist for a little longer. That was easier said than done, though.

* * *

"How is everyone feeling this fine morning?" Emilie shouted, which was especially mean. Six groans emanated throughout the kitchen as the group sat nursing coffees and hangovers. Why the hell wasn't Emilie hanging out of her arse like the rest of them? Anna also sat smugly, watching the girls suffer.

"Why aren't you dying with us?" Charlie moaned.

"Because I switched to water, like a responsible person," Emilie laughed. "I'll get breakfast on. You lot drink coffee. We have a big night tonight."

"Don't you worry, we'll be right as rain in no time. Hélène, babe, whip up your magic hangover food. That will do the trick."Kim said, patting Hélène on the bum. Hélène dragged herself off the kitchen stool and began raiding Emilie's fridge. Charlie watched as Emilie stepped back, smiling. Yeah,

Emilie was just as pleased as Charlie that her friends felt comfortable.

Half an hour later, the group had picked up a little. Hélène's hangover sandwich really was magic. Already Charlie could feel herself perk up.

"What's the skinny for tonight, then?" Sam asked.

"So the gig tonight is in the next town over. It's in a lovely little pub. It's not a massive venue, but it's a local hotspot, so I think we'll have a blast. The people are so nice. I think it's going to be a fantastic night all round."

"Is Jess up there with you, Em?" Lydia asked. Charlie grimaced. Lydia's sweet voice rubbed her the wrong way.

"Nope, it's not a band thing, it's just me with my guitar."

"Oh, wow, it's going to be so good," Kim crooned.

"Let's have a chill day. We can have a wander in the woods and then we'll get ready for tonight. Sound good?"

"Don't wander too far though because there are bears!" Charlie blurted. Emilie laughed and patted her shoulder.

"Yeah, like Charlie the worry wart said. There are bears in the area, but don't panic."

"Still a wimp then, Charlotte?" Lydia laughed. Charlie knew she was baiting.

"It's Charlie, and when it comes to massive fucking bears, you bet your fat ass I'm scared. Right, I'm going to shower and chill." Charlie hopped off the seat and left before Lydia could reply. It felt good to get the last word in for a change.

The day went just as planned. Everyone seemed to relax and enjoy the cabin. Charlie was even able to relax a little on their walk. Tonight though, chilled Charlie had to stay at the cabin and professional Charlie would take over. Even though Emilie had been strict about no social media and videos,

153

Charlie was still going to document the evening with her camera.

Emilie had told the group that the dress code was casual and everyone looked comfortable as they entered the little bar. Charlie felt immediately welcomed. There wasn't a sudden rush of adoring fans. The locals embraced Emilie like she was a long-lost daughter. They all knew her by her first name, and Emilie seemed relaxed around them. The pub had done a great job of keeping the gig a secret because everyone was surprised to see her. They were even more surprised when she stepped up to the little stage.

"Evening, everyone," Emilie said, her voice like velvet. "I thought it might be nice if I sang for you lovely people tonight." The small crown whistled and shouted their approval. "Can I ask that no one films it? I would really like to keep this between us."

"Damn right," a patron near the bar shouted. Charlie liked these people. They were here for Emilie, not for her fame.

# Chapter 14

Pete's Pub was one of Emilie's favourite places in Canada. The space wasn't massive. It had a long wooden bar and several tables. The décor was very much hunting lodge/old English pub. The lights were always low, but it wasn't a dive.

Pete had known Emilie since she was a young girl and she'd spent many an afternoon drawing at one of the little wooden tables that littered the room. Pete and Emilie's uncle were lifelong friends and would often meet up. This was the perfect spot to kick off her local town tour.

What more could she ask for? Nothing. This was the first time in a very, *very* long time that Emilie could say she was perfectly content. The rush of a twenty-thousand strong crowd was awesome. She always loved it, but there was nothing that could compare to singing the songs she loved on a little stage with just her old guitar. There must only be around fifty people in Pete's, but that was more than enough. The atmosphere was fantastic. Everyone was in high spirits, and Emilie could relax. Really relax, which was rare. Add the fact that Charlie and her friends were with her made the night perfect.

Speaking of Charlie. Emilie had nearly swallowed her tongue when Charlie had descended the stairs in the cabin earlier. Skin tight leather trousers, body hugging black sweater and faux fur-lined black boots. Her hair was loose down her back and shining like the night sky in the moonlight. In all black, Charlie's eyes shone like emeralds. Emilie had seriously considered nipping back upstairs and changing her underwear because that was the effect of Charlie Baxter. Utterly devastating.

There were several people in the bar that clearly agreed with Emilie's observations of Charlie because they were not being subtle with their leering. The men didn't bother her. It was the very cute bartender that gave her pause. The woman must have been around twenty-five. Did Charlie like younger women? Her hair was butter blonde, and she had perky boobs. Emilie couldn't help but glance down to her own chest. They were good boobs, maybe not as perky as the young bartender, but not bad.

After she'd announced the set list to the waiting patrons, Emilie settled on the stool that had been set on stage by Pete. Taking out her old guitar, she tried to put Charlie and the pretty bartender to the back of her mind. It was time to do what she did best.

Emilie was having the time of her life. The small crowd sung along, danced and cheered throughout the night. During one of her breaks, Charlie climbed up on stage with a pint of Emilie's favourite beer.

"You brought me Moose Head," Emilie beamed. Her throat was dry and she could already feel the soothing effects of the amber liquid in her mouth before she'd taken the glass.

"Thought you could do with a drink. You're fucking killing it, Em. Seriously breathtaking, as always." Emilie felt herself blush. Thank god the lighting was low.

Suddenly, a wolf whistle pierced the crowd. Emilie looked at Charlie, who grinned. It occurred to her that Charlie was bent over in front of Emilie, revealing her very nice derriere to the crowd, and someone had clearly appreciated the sight. Standing up straight, Charlie turned to the crowd and did a little bow, causing several shouts and whistles. Emilie caught sight of the bartender fanning herself with a beer mat.

"I'll leave you to it," Charlie said, climbing down off the stage. Emilie let herself watch Charlie for a second. The ethereal goddess of photography picked up her camera and slung the strap around her neck. She was all business. Not wanting the rest of the pub to notice her ogling of Charlie, Emilie cleared her throat and strummed her guitar. *The show must go on, Em.*

There were several shouts for an encore when Emilie finished her set. Obliging, she sang one more song and then headed for her friends. Could she call them her friends yet? Jess and Lydia, sure, but what about the others? Hopefully, because Emilie liked them all a lot.

Kim rushed up to Emilie and koala-hugged the shit out of her. This wasn't the first time since she'd met the blonde bombshell. The move seemed to be her signature hug. Probably because she only reached the shoulders of most of her friends.

"That... Oh. My. God Emilie, that..."

"Take a breath, babe," Hélène said calmly into Kim's ear. Emilie couldn't hide her grin. Kim was just this ball of love and fun.

"You really liked it?" Emilie asked, casting her gaze to the rest of the group. Even after decades on the stage, she still felt nervous about people's reactions to her music.

"Stunning. You have made my life!" Kim bellowed.

"Surely marrying Hélène will make your life," Emilie laughed.

"No, it's definitely this," Hélène grinned.

"You were fabulous," Lydia whispered, way too close to Emilie's ear. Why did she have to make things uncomfortable?

"I'll get you another drink," Charlie muttered. Emilie caught the eye roll at Lydia. Charlie stalked off to the bar and immediately began talking to the sexy bartender. Great.

157

It took fifteen minutes for Charlie to extricate herself from the bartender. Well, maybe Charlie didn't mind the blonde chatting her up. That would explain why she stayed at the bar for so long.

Eventually, Charlie came back to the table with a tray of drinks. "I think that wonderful performance deserves a toast," Charlie called. Everyone raised their glasses. "To the formidable Emilie Martin. You are the queen of music and sexy to boot, cheers."

A chorus of cheers cried out and everyone drank. Feeling a little hot under the collar, Emilie excused herself to go and meet some of the crowd. She knew most of them from her childhood, and it was nice to just chat to people like a regular human. No one asked her about future albums or tours. Actually, the most common question she got asked was how Spud was doing. That goof was loved by everyone.

Pete cleared a few tables away and hooked up his sound system. With a mix of country and pop playing, it didn't take long for the crowd to dance. Emilie nearly peed her pants when "Cotton Eyed Joe" came blaring through the speakers and Charlie grabbed Sam so fast it was comical. Clearly, the pair had memories attached to the song. Sure enough, Sam and Charlie were belting out the words, dancing like a pair of idiots laughing. Emilie caught Anna's eye, who laughed and shook her head. This was a side to Charlie that Emilie had never witnessed.

Pickerton had hosted several discos back in their school days, but Charlie *never* let herself relax and have fun. Emilie knew why. All the kids were arseholes to her. No one wanted to make themselves the target of ridicule. Thank god Charlie had found her confidence. Clearly, she didn't care what anyone thought now.

Looking back into the crowd, Emilie laughed harder when Pete scooped Charlie up into a dance. Charlie flung her head back, laughing. It was a sight to behold.

"Want to dance?" Lydia said. Emilie nearly jumped out of her skin.

"Jesus, Lydia, you scared the shit out of me."

"Sorry, Em, I didn't mean to. Still, wanna dance? It's been a while?" Emilie studied her friend. Normally Emilie would decline. Ever since Lydia's blow up, Emilie had avoided situations like this. Now though? *It should be okay, Lydia has a partner apparently.*

"Sure why not."

They'd only just got into position to join in the fun when the song changed to a slow ballad. What were the odds? Emilie looked at Lydia, who shrugged. Taking the lead, Lydia began to slow dance, pulling Emilie into a gentle sway. The dance felt anything but innocent.

Conscious that other people could see them, Emilie leaned back as far as she could. Movement to her left snagged her attention. Charlie making her way through the crowd, away from the dance floor. She arrived at the table, picked up her drink and downed it in one. Emilie was just about to break away from Lydia when Charlie picked up a napkin that had been under her glass. Emilie watched Charlie read it, turn her head to scan the room and then pocket the napkin.

*Right, so Charlie isn't that bothered because she's just kept the bartender's number.*

Emilie hadn't seen what was on the napkin, but it didn't take Sherlock Holmes to figure it out. Knowing that Charlie had happily accepted another woman's phone number was sobering. The elation of the night was seeping out of her, only to be replaced with a sick feeling clawing at her stomach.

159

They were supposed to be building something together, right? Emilie hadn't misunderstood Charlie, surely? *Maybe she took the number so the bartender didn't feel rejected?* That's definitely something Charlie would do. She would never want to upset anyone. Clinging on to that hope, Emilie gave Lydia a tight smile and headed to the table. She needed a drink, and she needed to talk to Charlie.

The talk never happened. As soon as Emilie joined Charlie at the table, so did Sam, Anna, Hélène, and Kim. The only person not there was Jess who was chatting up a woman by the stage.

"I think I'm about ready to call it a night," Anna said, yawning.

"That's fine by me, it's been a wonderful evening," Emilie said. Staying and drinking more wasn't an option. They were having a farewell dinner party tomorrow night and there was plenty for Emilie to do in the morning. Doing it with a hangover wasn't a wise choice.

With all the ladies in agreement, Emilie called for her car. A new batch of snow had settled whilst they were in Pete's. If the weather carried on like this, they were going to get snowed in.

Anna and Sam bid everyone goodnight as soon as they got back. Kim and Hélène settled in front of the fire with Emilie and Charlie. One small glass of port couldn't hurt. Thankfully, Lydia hadn't pressed to come back to the cabin with them. Instead, she'd hung back, waiting for Jess to finish salivating over the woman she liked.

"What a day!" Kim sighed contently. "This trip was a fabulous idea, thank you Emilie for inviting us."

"It has been my pleasure. Anyway, it's not over yet. Tomorrow we can build snowmen. No one sing, please," Emilie shot a look at Charlie, who snapped her mouth shut looking guilty. She had certainly been about to sing a rendition of "Do you Want To Build A Snowman." "After that we have our dinner party which I'm really excited about."

"I think we should ask Anna and Sam if they want to reserve a hotel in Quebec City for a few nights," Hélène said to Kim. "Anna isn't going to be able to travel much longer. Would be a shame to miss out on the opportunity."

"That's a fab idea," Kim replied, kissing Hélène.

"Do you want to go with your friends?" Emilie whispered to Charlie. They had the shows scheduled, but Emilie didn't want Charlie missing out on time with her friends.

"No, I'm here with you, Em."

"Right, we're off to bed, ladies. Don't do anything I wouldn't do," Kim winked.

"FYI, that doesn't leave a lot," Hélène laughed. Kim playfully slapped her arse.

"Your friends are great, Charlie. I know I've already said it, but they are."

"Yeah, they're good eggs."

"Want another drink?" Emilie asked. She wasn't ready for the night to be over.

"I think I'm going to go up if that's cool. I want to get all the photos loaded onto my laptop before I sleep."

Emilie nodded her head and smiled. "Sure, see you in the morning."

"Em?" Charlie said, standing up. "You really were magnificent tonight. You blew me away." Charlie leaned down and kissed Emilie on her cheek. When she knew that Charlie had gone upstairs, Emilie finally let out a big breath. Her hand caressed her cheek where Charlie had kissed her.

Lord, she was in trouble. They were supposed to be going slow, building trust and forging a new relationship, but all

161

Emilie wanted to do was have Charlie rip her clothes off and fuck her into next week.

* * *

"Have you actually given your snowman boobs?" Emilie asked, staring at Charlie's creation. The group had been playing in the snow for the past hour. Sam had suggested they make the snowman building into a competition. The winner got bragging rights and a trophy. God knows where they were going to source a trophy.

"Well, yeah, there isn't a rule saying my snowman can't have breasts."

Emilie looked Charlie up and down. "You're serious, aren't you?"

"Fuck yeah, I'm serious. I'm going to win this competition with originality." Charlie stood with her hands on her hips, assessing her snowman. Emilie silently chuckled. Amazingly, Charlie had acclimatised to the cold. Sure, she still wore three times the amount of clothes as anyone else, but at least she wasn't turning blue anymore.

"Nice baps," Kim called over.

"Thanks," Charlie replied.

"Baps?" Emilie questioned.

"Yeah, baps, funbags, melons, you know, tits."

"Jesus," Emilie mumbled.

"You know my friend's husband calls them Tattybojangles," Charlie grinned.

"How are Max and Ben?" Sam asked.

"Really good. They said the video of my work is really boosting their appointments."

"Is Max someone you've done photography for?" Emilie asked. She hated that there was still so much she didn't know about Charlie.

"I mentioned Max before. He did all my tats." Emilie's mind wandered back to the garden at Bowman Manor. Charlie had mentioned Max then. "His husband did a video of the finished product. I have taken plenty of photos of Max's work, though. He really is a master."

"I'll say, your tats are phenomenal," Emilie stated. "I always thought I might get one, but I chickened out."

"Max will sort you out. Next time we're in London, I'll get you an appointment."

That sentence almost floored Emilie. Charlie was thinking about their future. She had to be. Charlie could see them together in London. *Alright Em, calm down, don't jump to conclusions. Nice and slow.*

"That would be great." Emilie smiled sweetly and turned back to her own snowman. She needed a few minutes to calm her nerves.

"You have three minutes remaining," Sam bellowed. Emilie looked at her snowman. She'd gone the more traditional route. With one minor adjustment to the snowman's scarf, Emilie stepped back and announced she was done.

The tinkle of Sam's alarm signalled the competition was over. Emilie slipped into the house to collect a tray of hot chocolate whilst Anna judged the snowmen. There had been an outcry when Anna volunteered to be judge. Those women took their competitions seriously. Anna hadn't the energy to build, so it made sense. She also promised that she wouldn't be biased. Emilie found the whole thing highly entertaining, especially when Sam winked at Anna, blowing kisses. Anna shook her head and Charlie made the motion of "I'm watching you" to Anna and Sam.

163

To Emilie, the winner was clear. "I declare Kim the winner," Anna announced to the boos of everyone else. It was all good natured fun. Kim had created a *Devil Wears Prada* masterpiece. It looked more like an ice sculpture than a snowman.

"She's called Sylvia," Kim proudly called.

"Why Sylvia?" Emilie asked.

"Why not?" Kim laughed.

"How the hell did you get her in heels?" Charlie asked disbelievingly.

"If I can do anything in heels, so can Sylvia."

"Come on, everyone, grab a hot chocolate and warm up. Let's toast to Kim and Sylvia."

"Hear, hear," Charlie shouted. The moment was shattered when a very excited Spud came belting out of the forest with a stick. Even though every woman shouted "STOP" at the top of their lungs, Spud ploughed through their snowmen before stopping in front of Emilie and dropping the stick. *Uh Oh!*

"Alright, everyone inside, quickly now." Emily shouted, trying to usher the group inside.

"Move your arses," Charlie bellowed. Emilie looked at Charlie, who kept turning her head toward the forest. Yeah, she'd definitely remembered what Spud dropping a stick meant.

"What's happening?" Anna asked.

"Big fuck off bear, that's what's happening," Charlie practically screamed. Well, that got everyone moving alright.

With the group and Spud safely inside, they stood by the windows, peering into the trees.

"There," Hélène gasped, pointing to her right. Just waddling through the trees was a momma black bear and two cubs.

"Oh, wow," Kim gulped.

"They are so cute," Anna added.

164

"Yeah, until they rip your face off," Charlie mumbled, causing Emilie to laugh. They stood and watched the creatures amble by. When they had disappeared back into the forest, the group settled down in the living room. Emilie left them to talk about the bear sighting whilst she prepared for the dinner party.

Everything was in place. The table was set, candles were lit, and the food was ready. Emilie had never thrown a dinner party that was just for her friends. Jess and Lydia had turned up half an hour before and were dragged into the living room so Kim could retell the bear sighting story.

"I just want to say thank you," Emilie said, standing up with a flute of Champagne. "It's been wonderful having you all here. I've loved every minute and please know you are all welcome back any time."

"Cheers," the collective group sang.

"You look stunning, Em," Charlie whispered in her ear. They hadn't got dressed up, but Emilie had put a little effort in. She wore fitted jeans and a nice jumper. Emilie looked into Charlie's eyes and was surprised to see lust staring back at her. Nothing had happened to warrant Charlie's sudden desire, not that Emilie could remember.

"You look stunning too, Char," she replied. It was true. Charlie looked edible.

"Will you stay with me tonight?" Charlie asked.

Where the hell was this coming from?

# Chapter 15

The past twenty-four hours leading up to Charlie asking Emilie to stay with her for the night had been illuminating. It all started at the pub last night. Watching Emilie perform was always thrilling, but seeing her so relaxed, truly enjoying herself, was beyond gratifying. Emilie's soul came alive when she took to the stage. It was something that had always drawn Charlie to her, right from their very first meeting at Pickerton.

Everyone in the pub had been so wonderful and genuine. Charlie had laughed when she got wolf whistled on stage. She'd only gone to give Emilie a pint of beer. Next time, she wouldn't parade her arse to the rest of the patrons. Next time? Yeah, she wanted there to be a next time. It was strange, but being here with Emilie gave her a sense of belonging. Cheesy right? But for Charlie, that sense of safety and belonging had always been absent.

Growing up rich was great, Charlie got she was very privileged. What people might not understand is that even though she had money, that was all she had and really it wasn't even hers. Her parents funded her life because they weren't willing to give her anything else. The term "Absent Parent" didn't come close to covering how neglectful they were. Estelle had been Charlie's caregiver — in that she spent time with her at the nursing home — for as long as she could, but as soon as

Estelle was too old, Charlie had been alone. No friends, no family.

Pickerton had been a temporary reprieve. For once, Charlie didn't have to be completely alone. Emilie had become her family. No matter what shit was happening in her life, Charlie could rely on Emilie. When they'd parted ways, Charlie had lost so much more than a girlfriend.

Last night in the pub, it hit Charlie hard in the chest. Those familiar feelings of Emilie being her safety and her home flooded back, catching Charlie unaware. The feeling had been so potent she'd had to take herself away for a few minutes to catch her breath.

They were going slowly, and it was nice. However, taking it slow with someone so magnetising felt almost impossible. It was a daily struggle to keep her feelings at bay. Trying to be a reasonable, level-headed adult was bullshit.

As the night progressed, the crowd got louder. Charlie loved dancing with everyone, especially Sam. "Cotton Eyed Joe" was their jam. Flinging each other around the miniscule dance floor had been hilarious, even more so when Pete joined in. Then it became less fun when Charlie spotted Lydia and Emilie dancing. White hot anger had erupted in her chest as she witnessed Lydia hold Emilie in her arms.

Acting like a jealous idiot was not Charlie's thing. She hated that kind of shit. It didn't take a genius to get that Lydia wanted Charlie to react. For Charlie, watching Lydia behave this way was nothing new. For as long as she could remember, Lydia had always hated her and made it painfully clear that she didn't think Charlie was good enough for Emilie. Watching the two of them dance had raised a question that made Charlie nauseous. Had Emilie and Lydia ever been more than friends?

Not wanting to give Lydia what she so clearly wanted, Charlie had slipped off the dance floor and back to the table to

167

grab her drink. Slamming the rest of her beer didn't quite have the same effect as ripping Lydia off Emilie by her hair, but at least she wouldn't get arrested. The napkin placed under her drink was a surprise. Maybe the cute bartender had written her number on it. Oh, how wrong Charlie had been.

*Stay away from Emilie. I'm warning you. Don't test me, bitch.*

Charlie didn't recognise the handwriting. Casting her gaze around the room, no one caught her eye. Who the fuck had left it? Slipping the napkin in her pocket, she grabbed for Sam's drink that was still half full. Should she take the threat seriously? Probably not. Honestly, there was only one person Charlie thought it could be and if that was the case, she could handle it.

The next day had been so much fun until Spud scared the living shit out of her by dropping that bloody stick. No way was Charlie going to forget Emilie's warning about bears. When the group scrambled inside to watch through the window, Charlie almost melted when Emilie stood nestled into her.

Charlie was taller than Emilie, so she could see over her head. Emilie had backed herself up into Charlie's body. It felt so natural and so right. The depth of feeling that ran through her body was indescribable. It was only getting harder to resist what Charlie really wanted, and that was Emilie, in every way she could have her.

As Emilie had worked to get the dinner party ready, Charlie had taken the time to observe from a distance. Her body wanted to seek Emilie out, go to the kitchen and help, just to be close but she didn't. However, that was the great thing about the cabin. The open plan meant that no matter where or what Emilie was doing, Charlie could always see her without invading her space. Charlie conceded she might come across as a creepy stalker but tough shit. The alternative was to drag Emilie

168

upstairs and fuck her senseless, regardless of who was downstairs. That would have been rude. Awesome, but rude.

Emilie had grown into an incredible woman. Years of stardom hadn't changed her. Charlie still saw the kind, warm girl she fell in love with all those years ago. Maybe it was because they were in such close quarters that everything felt more intense than if they were casually dating. Was that the reason her feelings were so strong, so fast?

Jess, turning up with Lydia in tow, threatened Charlie's Zen more than she would've liked. Flashbacks of Lydia dancing with Emilie were unwelcome and impossible to stop. The napkin also came to mind. If Lydia wasn't behind it, Charlie would have a giant dick tattooed on her forehead.

Sam, Anna, Kim and Hélène had all told Charlie that they loved Emilie. Considering her friends were the most important people in Charlie's life meant their approval was everything. And now she was here, sitting next to Emilie at the beautifully dressed dining table, whispering into Emilie's ear that she wanted to spend the night with her.

It could have been the glass of wine that finally crumbled Charlie's defences. She didn't know. What Charlie *did* know was that she needed Emilie in her bed, on her body. Charlie wanted–no–needed, to feel that closeness, the security that only Emilie Martin could give her.

"You... you want me to spend the night?" Emilie whispered back. Her eyes darting around the table, making sure no one else was listening.

"Yes, Emilie, I want you with me tonight!"

"Oh... just so there's no misunderstanding. When you say 'spend the night' you mean –"

"You, me, naked, doing very naughty things to each other." Charlie wanted to laugh as Emilie's eyes widened and her face blushed.

169

"Char, you can't say things like that to me in front of everyone." Charlie was about to respond when they were interrupted.

"What are you two whispering about?" Lydia asked, her eyes narrowed into slits. God, Charlie hated that bitch.

"I was just telling Emilie that I have a great idea for a piece of art that would fit wonderfully above the fireplace." Charlie should get a fucking prize for pulling that bullshit out of her arse. *Way to go on the improv Char.*

"Oh, really?" Lydia drawled, arching her eyebrow. "And what art would that be?"

"A vagina painting by Sam's mum." It was the first thing that came to mind. Sandy had gifted a painting to Charlie a few years ago for her birthday and it was one of Charlie's favourites. Come to think of it, even though she'd lied about mentioning it to Emilie, a Sandy Chambers piece really would look great in the living room.

"A vagina painting," Lydia mocked.

"Yeah, a vagina painting," Charlie repeated.

"Oh god, do we have to bring that up again?" Sam moaned. "It was bad enough the first time round."

"So your mum is an artist?" Jess asked Sam.

"Oh yeah. She did a collection a few years ago that was basically a load of multicoloured vaginas."

"Wow," Jess laughed.

"Yeah, wow, is one word. Mum isn't shy about sharing her art with me, unfortunately."

"And she gave you one of those paintings, Charlie?" Emilie asked, looking amused.

"Damn right she did. That woman is a genius. It hangs pride of place above my desk in the office."

"About that, Char. Couldn't you put it somewhere else? I really don't enjoy looking at it when I visit."

170

"For the last time, Sammy, it isn't your vagina. What's the problem? It's a beautiful bit of art that I will *not* be moving. You need to build a bridge and get over it. Anyway, Anna likes it, too."

All eyes shifted to Anna, who was silently chuckling. "Sorry, *mon amour*, I'm with Charlie on this one."

"See, ha! Out voted. I'm going to call Sandy tomorrow and ask her to paint one for Em. Would you like that?" Charlie ignored Sam's grimace and focused on Emilie, who was a delightful shade of red.

"I'd love that, thank you."

"Right, that's your Christmas present sorted, then." Charlie smiled, delighting in the smoke that was coming out of Lydia's ears.

"So does your mum only paint erotica?" Jess asked. Charlie burst out laughing when Sam let her head drop to the table. Charlie would never tire of Sam's embarrassment.

The conversation flowed and everyone relaxed, including Lydia, who seemed to have gotten bored with shooting hateful looks at Charlie. Charlie couldn't have cared less because as the night wore on, Emilie shifted closer, eventually resting her hand on Charlie's thigh under the table. Lightning bolts were shooting to very intimate parts of Charlie's anatomy, and she was getting jumpy.

By eleven o'clock, Charlie was getting testy. She wanted everyone gone so she could get her hands on Emilie. Anna was the first to retire, followed minutes later by Sam, Hélène, and Kim.

"Can we crash tonight, Em?" Jess asked. The snow had continued to fall and Charlie could fully understand not wanting to drive on the roads. Unfortunately, that meant Lydia would stay, too.

"Of course. Are you two okay sharing? The other rooms are full."

"No worries, see you in the morning." Jess must have sensed Lydia's hesitation to leave, because she grabbed the woman's hand and practically dragged her up the stairs.

"Thank fuck for that," Charlie wailed comically. "I thought they'd never bugger off."

"Oh, and why would you want that, Charlie?" Emilie grinned, her eyes twinkling in the firelight. After the food had been consumed, the group had retired to the living room. Now it was just Charlie and Emilie on the couch next to the open fire.

"Well, Emilie, I thought we could play some cards. Oh, or we could read! How about dominos?" Charlie smiled when Emilie rolled her eyes and shifted closer. Charlie's heartbeat thudded in her chest. She wouldn't be surprised if Emilie could hear it.

"I think we can come up with something better than that, don't you?" Emilie purred.

Even though everyone had gone to bed, Charlie was well aware that they weren't alone. They could be disturbed at any minute. The sensible option would be to take Emilie to bed. Her brain wasn't operating sensibly though, it was operating on need. Right now, Charlie *needed* Emilie naked in front of the roaring fire.

"Come here," Charlie whispered. Emilie slid across the last bit of space on the sofa. Although carnal need still bubbled under Charlie's skin, she didn't want to rush this. Yes, they could ravage each other like they had the night of the gala, but tonight needed to be more. They needed to re-connect, wholly, body and mind.

Charlie cupped Emilie's face and took a moment to just drink her in. Gently, Charlie pulled Emilie toward her. The mellow scent of Emilie's perfume engulfed Charlie's senses.

Emilie softly rubbed her nose against Charlie's. The delicate touch was so sensual, Charlie heaved in a deep breath. Closing her eyes, she sighed with joy when she felt Emilie's lips brush her own. They were so soft, so plump and warm. They moved in synchronicity, their tongues exploring knowingly in each other's mouths. How could they still know each other so well? Twenty years may have passed, but nothing had changed. Their kisses held more confidence than those of teenagers. Even so, their hands and mouths danced together to their own beat, just like they always had.

Without breaking their kiss, Charlie pulled Emilie up to standing. With their bodies flush, Charlie allowed her hands to wander. Her fingertips skimmed Emilie's breasts, lingering only for a second. The feel of soft skin made Charlie groan out loud as her hands reached under Emilie's sweater. The possessive squeeze on Charlie's arse signalled Emilie's impatience and desire. Emilie had always liked Charlie's bum.

"Take off your clothes," Emilie said against Charlie's lips.

"Take off yours," Charlie replied. Emilie broke their kiss, stepped back, and began discarding her clothes. The firelight licked Emilie's body as she revealed herself slowly. Charlie's eyes raked up and down Emilie feverously. *Jesus, she's sublime.*

"Now you," Emilie purred when she was down to her underwear. Very nice blue lace underwear. Charlie unbuttoned her trousers, sliding them to the floor. Emilie's eyes bugged when she noticed Charlie had gone commando. Feeling more than satisfied with the reaction she'd just elicited, Charlie whipped her top off and discarded her bra.

"Good god, Charlie," Emilie panted. Charlie stepped forward, running her hands over Emilie's chest.

"Can we get rid of this?" she asked, snapping Emilie's bra strap. Emilie reached round and unclipped the bra, letting it fall to the floor. Charlie hooked her thumbs under the waistband of

173

Emilie's knickers. Looking into Emilie's eyes, she silently asked for consent. Emilie nodded.

As soon as the lace fabric hit the floor, Emilie crashed into Charlie. Hands grabbed and caressed, tongues battled and licked. The world around them faded as they took what they needed.

"Down here," Charlie gasped. Shifting away slightly, she tugged Emilie down so they were lying on the rug in front of the fire.

"Please touch me, Charlie. I've missed you so much."

Charlie lay Emilie down. She positioned herself between Emilie's legs. The fire crackled and flared as Charlie looked down at Emilie. She could spend a lifetime expressing how much Emilie meant to her, how much she'd missed her body, her spirit. Now wasn't the time for words, though.

"I'm going to lick every inch of you," she growled. Charlie craved the taste of Emilie's skin. Dipping her head, she gently sucked on Emilie's pulse point. Emilie instantly reacted. Her hips jolted and rolled. Slowly, Charlie kissed her way down. Emilie's nipples were hard peaks, desperate for attention. Charlie licked them once but carried on her journey. She bit, licked, and sucked Emilie's stomach, her hips and thighs. When she was satisfied, she flipped Emilie over to her stomach. Emilie was putty in Charlie's hands. The soft gasps and murmurs emanating from Emilie were further proof that she was lost in Charlie's touch.

"Oh, Charlie, please, for the love of god fuck me," Emilie huffed frustrated. Charlie smiled widely against Emilie's arse.

"Patience, Em," Charlie chuckled. Taking Emilie's wrists, Charlie pinned them above Emilie's head, her body lying flush against Emilie's back.

"I love the feel of your boobs," Emilie muttered, her face turned to the side. "I also love the feel of your pussy on my ass,"

174

she added. Charlie gave a slow, sensual roll. They both moaned loudly.

"If you love that, wait until I really get started on you," Charlie said, sucking on Emilie's earlobe. "Keep your hands up there, okay?" Emilie nodded. Charlie kissed her neck. Releasing Emilie's wrist, she snaked her hand down Emilie's ribs. Using her knee, she gently ushered Emilie's legs apart. She was careful to make sure her weight was on her elbow and knees. "Are you alright?"

"I'm perfect, I love to feel you on me," Emilie sighed. Charlie lifted her hips slightly, encouraging Emilie to do the same. Sliding her hand under Emilie's body, she gently cupped Emilie's mound.

"Take what you need," she whispered in Emilie's ear. Understanding what Charlie wanted, Emilie began to roll her hips, Charlie's hand giving her the friction she needed. With Emilie's arse rolling steadily against Charlie's clit, she had to bite her lip to tamp down her own arousal. *God, I'm going to explode.*

Emilie's hands gripped the rug, her knuckles whitened as she picked up the tempo. Charlie was losing the battle to keep her orgasm at bay. Knowing that she was almost at the tipping point, she reached up and laced her free hand with Emilie's and gripped hard as Emilie's body convulsed, sending waves of pleasure through her already stimulated pussy.

"Oh fuck, oh fuck, Charlie," Emilie moaned, burying her head into the floor. Charlie let herself go, her screams muffled by Emilie's neck. Their bodies stilled. Charlie shifted and lay beside a very satisfied looking Emilie.

"Are you ready to go again?" Charlie asked. Emilie laughed into the rug, shaking her head.

"Ready when you are," she panted. Charlie leaned in and kissed her deeply, rolling her onto her back.

Suddenly, Emilie pushed her away. "I'm no pillow princess, you know," she smirked. Sitting up, Emilie pushed Charlie down and straddled her waist. "Do you remember the one thing I always wanted us to try, but we never did?" Emilie asked with a raised eyebrow.

"How could I forget," Charlie replied, hauling Emilie up her chest by her arse. "Turn around," she demanded. Emilie turned her body and looked down between her legs. Charlie's chin was just visible. Opening her legs wider, she lowered herself to Charlie's waiting tongue. Charlie couldn't help but grab Emilie's arse cheeks. Having Emilie on her face was a dream! Having Emily eat her out at the same time was just perfect.

# Chapter 16

Emilie was in sexual heaven. Her pussy ground down on Charlie's face. Where the hell had Charlie learned to do what she was doing? *Oh fuck*. No time to get lost in thought. Emilie had her tongue buried deep in Charlie's folds. The taste and scent of Charlie was overwhelming. She was delicious.

"Keep going, Em, shit I'm close," Charlie mumbled from beneath her.

Her own orgasm was a second away from ripping her to shreds. Being eaten out was fantastic. Eating Charlie out at the same time was magnificent. Emilie was kind of glad they'd never done this when they were younger. She was sure that it wouldn't have been as good. Not with them both being so inexperienced. Now, though, holy shit, they were electric. The flames roaring in the fireplace were nothing compared to the fire that stoked between their bodies.

"Yes, yes, oh shit," Charlie cried. Emilie doubled down. She nuzzled her face in further, sinking her tongue into Charlie's entrance as Charlie came. As soon as she felt Charlie's body relax, she pulled her face away. Charlie didn't waste a second, though. She plunged her tongue into Emily hard. Emilie rocked back and forth, loving that her pussy slammed into Charlie's face. Gripping the rug again, Emilie held on for dear life as

Charlie brought her to climax. There was no dampening her scream, which rocketed around the cabin.

"My god, that was…"

"Yeah, it was," Charlie finished. Emilie had crashed onto Charlie when she'd come. Her head lay on Charlie's thigh, her legs spread-eagle on Charlie's chest.

"Of all the views in Canada, I think this is my favourite," Charlie said before swiping her tongue up Emilie's slit again, causing her to jump.

"Give me a sec and I'll move. I'm like jelly at the minute." In fact, Emilie could have easily fallen asleep right then and there.

"Don't move on my account, honey," Charlie chirped. "I can keep doing this," she said, swiping her tongue again.

"Oh, fuck," Emilie gasped. As spent as she was, her clit was already responding and getting ready for round three.

* * *

"I need coffee," a distant voice grumbled.

"You need three," another voice added.

"I'll make it. You go and wake Charlie. She'll oversleep otherwise," a third voice said. *Where the hell am I?* There should be no voices in Emilie's bedroom. *Oh no!*

"Uh, don't think we have to worry about finding Charlie," the first voice sang. Emilie kept her eyes tightly shut. Oh shit, they hadn't made it upstairs, which meant they were still very naked in front of the fireplace. Emilie could feel Charlie's body curved around her own. At least it wasn't her ass on show.

"What's going on?" a fourth voice called.

"Um, you probably don't want to know," the first voice said.

178

"Oh, for the love of…" Jess said. Emilie was awake enough now to know whose voice was talking. "Jesus, I'm going to go ward off Lydia. She'll throw a fucking fit if she walks in to this."

"So who's going to wake them, then?" Hélène asked.

"Not me," Sam blurted. "Charlie is a miserable arse in the morning."

"You're all ridiculous," Kim snapped lightly. "I'll do it. Can you grab a blanket or something?" There were a few shuffling and muttering noises.

"Charlie, you need to wake up." Emilie felt Charlie stir. There was no way in hell she was going to move first. "Charlie," Kim bellowed, causing Charlie to jump.

"Fuck me, why are you shouting?" Charlie grumbled, her head still buried in Emilie's neck. This was ridiculous. Emilie was straining to keep her nervous laughter from spilling out.

"I'm shouting because you need to get up. You're naked on the living room floor," Kim laughed.

"Am I? Oh, shit, yeah. Hang on, pass me that blanket. The warmth of Charlie's torso evaporated the moment she moved from Emilie. Still keeping her eyes closed, Emilie waited a few moments longer. A blanket was placed over her body.

"Jesus, Charlie, can you cover up?" Sam grumbled.

"Sam, you've seen me naked plenty. We're all women, calm down." Emilie couldn't hold on any longer. Rolling over, she opened her eyes and looked up to see Charlie standing proud and tall in all her naked glory. Kim was laughing, as were Hélène and Anna. Sam was bright red, shaking her head.

Shifting to her elbows, Emilie hoisted the blanket around her body. "Morning," she said shyly. This had never happened to her, and she had no way of knowing how to deal with it.

"Hey, babe," Charlie said, smiling. Emilie laughed at Charlie's utter disregard of her friends' embarrassment. Standing up, Emilie moved so she was standing behind Charlie. The ethereal goddess might not be bothered about showing off her body, but Emilie wasn't so carefree.

"Um, sorry about this," she said, motioning to Charlie and herself. "We fell asleep," she added.

"Well, it certainly looked like you had fun," Kim winked. "Right, we'll get breakfast going whilst you two get dressed. Be ready in twenty." With that, she ushered everyone over to the kitchen island.

Charlie turned around and beamed at Emilie. "Wanna take a shower?" she asked, wiggling her eyebrows. Emilie chuckled, stood on her toes and kissed Charlie soundly. Yes, she absolutely wanted to take a shower.

With everyone fed and happy — bar Lydia, who had obviously heard about Charlie and Emilie being found in the nude — Emilie began tidying up the house. It was amazing how much crap could accumulate in just a couple of days.

Charlie was sitting on the sofa with Héléne, Anna, and Kim. Emilie noticed Sam walk in with a very odd look on her face. Sam made a beeline for Charlie. Emilie couldn't hear what was going on, but it must have been important. Emilie moved to the other side of the kitchen island when Charlie and Sam stepped away from the others. They were acting very odd. What did Sam just pass to Charlie?

Emilie placed the cleaning sponge down and walked over to where the women were huddled. Something wasn't right.

"Hey, what's going on?" she asked. Charlie looked from the scrap of paper in her hand to Emilie and then Sam.

"It's nothing, it's fine," Charlie answered.

Sam didn't seem to agree with her friend's assessment of the situation. "It is not fucking fine, Charlie," Sam growled.

"Charlie?" Emilie wasn't stupid. She could see from Charlie's face everything was far from okay.

"Fuck," Charlie huffed. "Sam found this in her luggage." Charlie handed over the piece of paper she'd been gripping.

*If you know what's good for your wife and baby, you will get Charlie to leave Emilie now. I will hurt you.*

"What the hell is this?" Emilie demanded. "Who left it?"

"No idea," Sam said. "I only just noticed it. I've no idea how long it's been in the bag."

"Why aren't you more surprised?" Emilie asked Charlie, who in her opinion was being far too calm about it.

"I got something similar the other day," Charlie mumbled.

"What? Why the hell didn't you say anything?" Emilie bellowed. The one thing she took seriously was her safety and the safety of her people. Emilie never took these things lightly. She couldn't, not in her line of work. Seven years ago, she'd had to get the authorities involved with a besotted fan. It was one of the scariest things she'd ever gone through, and she certainly didn't want a repeat performance.

"Em, it's nothing, just bullshit," Charlie said, trying to soothe her, which wasn't working in the least.

"No, Charlie, you can't say that. You need to trust me. When it comes to threats against me, I have to take them seriously."

"They aren't against you, Em," Charlie shot.

"No, but they may as well be, Charlie. I can't risk you getting hurt."

"No one is going to hurt me, Emilie."

181

"You don't know that, Charlie." Their voices had risen to shouting level. Kim, Hélène, and Anna rushed over to see what the crisis was. Emilie shoved the note into Kim's hand. Her blood was boiling.

"Shit," Kim hissed, passing the note to Hélène.

"I'd never let anything happen to you or Anna, you know that, Right?" Charlie was gripping Sam's shoulders.

"I know, mate, but I think it's time for us to leave. I want us home, safe."

Without another word, Sam left the room, taking the stairs two at a time. Anna had a hold of the note. Her face visibly paled. "Charlie, come home with us," she pleaded. "Just until Emilie can investigate this," she said, waving the paper around.

"Not a chance. I'm staying right here," Charlie shot defiantly.

"Char—" Emilie began.

"No, Emilie, I'm not leaving." Charlie stormed out of the room.

"Dammit," Emilie whispered. What the hell should she do?

"She's stubborn, she won't budge now," Anna said to Emilie. "Just take care of her, okay?"

Suddenly Emilie found herself alone. With the group upstairs collecting their luggage, Emilie slid onto one of the kitchen stools, her hands in her hair. *Okay, you know what to do. Call Buddy, report the notes, and keep a close eye out.*

Buddy Marsh was the detective who had dealt with Emilie's overzealous fan. She kept in contact with him. He was a fantastic guy and an excellent detective.

"Hey, Buddy," Emilie sang down the phone line when it connected.

"Emilie, how you doing? It's been a while."

182

"Yeah, sorry I haven't called more."

"You're a busy woman, no worries. What can I do for you?" Emilie spent the next few minutes explaining the situation. "Okay, keep the notes. I'll swing by and collect them as evidence. You know the drill. If you see anything or notice anything out of the ordinary, anything at all, you call 911. I'll get the incident recorded, so there is an open file."

"Thanks, Buddy," Emilie sighed. Just having Buddy note the incident made Emilie feel better.

"You need to tell your friend the same thing, okay? Do you have any idea who it is?" He asked.

"None."

"What about your friend?"

"I'll ask her and let you know. We're just about to take her friends to the airport, so we'll have time later to talk. I'll let you know, okay."

"Sure thing. Try not to worry too much. We'll figure it out. Speak soon."

"Bye." Okay, that's all that she could do for now. As soon as their friends were safely on board the jet, she and Charlie would talk.

* * *

The car journey to the private airstrip was tense and almost silent. The threat against Sam, Anna, and their baby had shocked everyone. Emilie tried several times to catch Charlie's eye. She wanted desperately to know what she was thinking. If her face reflected what was in her mind, then Emilie could see she was seething.

"We're here," Emilie said quietly as the car pulled up. Everyone exited the car and went about collecting their belongings.

183

"Are you sure you don't want to come home?" Sam asked Charlie.

"I'm good, Sammy, please don't worry. I'm sure it's nothing serious." Sam clearly wanted to argue, but Anna squeezed her shoulder, pulling her away.

"Thank you for a wonderful time," Anna said to Emilie, wrapping her up in a hug. One by one, they wished Emilie and Charlie farewell, giving them each a tight hug. Charlie still hadn't said a word. Together they stood by the car and watched the plane taxi to the runway and then takeoff.

The car journey back to the cabin was just as silent. Emilie felt like screaming. By the time they arrived back, Emilie was ready for several glasses of wine.

"Want one?" she asked Charlie, who was perched on the sofa, staring outside.

"Yeah, thanks." *Well, at least she answered.*

Emilie poured two very generous glasses of red wine and sat herself close to Charlie.

"Can we talk?" she asked tentatively. This was the first time she'd ever seen Charlie looking so furious. Charlie by nature was a calm, gentle person with a flair for the dramatic, but she was never angry. "I called a detective I know and reported the notes. He wanted to know if I had any idea of who it could be. I said I didn't, but he wanted me to ask if you had a clue?"

"I think it's pretty fucking obvious who it is," Charlie spat, taking Emilie by surprise. The venom in Charlie's voice was abundant.

"Who?" Emilie asked, her voice high-pitched. Did Charlie really know who had sent the threatening notes?

"Oh, come on, Em."

"What do you mean 'come on Em'? Why would I know who it is?"

"There is only one person we know who has hated me so passionately and for a very long time that just so happened to spend the night here." Emilie scrunched up her eyebrows. Surely Charlie wasn't suggesting Lydia. Sure, Lydia was intense, but she wasn't someone who would threaten a pregnant woman for god's sake.

"Do you mean Lydia?" Emilie asked, shock evident in her tone.

"Of course I mean fucking Lydia. That bitch has had it out for me since our first day at Pickerton. She's never hidden the fact that she didn't think I was in your league. She's never hidden the insults and digs. You can't seriously be surprised."

"Of course I'm surprised. She's one of my oldest friends, Charlie. I think I would know if she had a screw loose, don't you?"

"Would you? Really? That fucker has been nothing but antagonistic to me since the ball. Now suddenly I'm receiving threatening notes. Both of which happened to coincide with Lydia's visits. She was at the bar and here last night."

"Lydia was dancing when you got that note. I remember now because I thought it was the bartender giving you her number. Lydia was with me and last night she never went upstairs alone, plus she arrived after everyone. When did she get the time?"

Charlie was looking at Emilie with fire in her eyes and not the kind that had been present last night. "You don't believe me?" she said flatly.

"It's not that, Charlie, but come on, that's a heavy accusation to throw at someone without proof."

Charlie shook her head and laughed. "Yeah, you should know, being the expert at that kind of thing." Charlie's words pierced Emilie's chest. "I can't believe you're doing it again. Twenty years later and I still can't get you to believe me, can I,

185

Em?" Charlie wasn't shouting, her voice wasn't even above normal level. Her voice was resigned, as was her body language. Words wouldn't come. Emilie opened her mouth to talk, but nothing materialised. Charlie stood up and placed her wine on the coffee table. "I think it's best I go after all. I don't want anything to happen to Sam and Anna." No, no, no, this couldn't be happening. *For fuck's sakes, Emilie, say something.*

"Charlie."

"No, Em, it's fine. I get it. You know Lydia better than me. Of course you would believe her. You have decades of friendship between you. Who am I? I'm just someone you fucked for a little while twenty years ago." Emilie watched as a tear slid down Charlie's cheek.

"Charlie, please, I'm sorry," Emilie shot. She could not let history repeat itself. Charlie's parting words burned through her brain as she watched Charlie leave. *"Who am I? I'm just someone you fucked for a little while twenty years ago."* Sprinting up the stairs, Emilie burst into Charlie's room. Charlie was stuffing her clothes into her duffel bag.

"You're not leaving. I won't let you." Hell would freeze over before she let Charlie Baxter walk out of her life again.

"Em, please, let's not do this."

"No, we're doing it. Talk to me, explain what I'm missing. If you really think Lydia is behind the threats, tell me. I'm sorry I didn't listen. I'm sorry you think I don't believe you. It just came as a shock is all. Talk to me, Char, please." When she saw Charlie's shoulders relax a little, Emilie knew she'd won a reprieve.

Charlie dropped her duffel on the floor and sat on the edge of the bed. "Em, I had plenty of people in school dislike me for whatever reason, but no one like Lydia. Before we became an item, she never paid me much attention, but as soon as you showed an interest in me, I became a target. You knew

186

about the snarky comments, but what you didn't see were the thinly veiled threats, the 'accidental' trip ups. You name it, that fucker did it. It was a well known fact that Lydia had always held a torch for you. You can't tell me you didn't know."

"Yeah, I knew. I told her it would never happen though, that we would only ever be friends."

"And how did that work out? If she didn't try it on with you, I'll be a monkey's uncle," Charlie stated.

"Okay, yeah, she did a couple of times."

"It went beyond a crush for her, Em. There were times I'd catch her watching you, watching us. Not in the context of a group. I'm talking about Lydia following us and watching.

"Why didn't you ever say?"

"I didn't want to overthink it and honestly, Em, you were so desperate to have friends, I didn't want to take that away. I know how hard it was with your family and trusting people. I didn't want to sow seeds of doubt. Plus, me and you were going to go away together after Pickerton, so I had no reason to worry. Lydia wouldn't have been a part of our lives."

"You really think she's held this hatred for you for so long?"

"Fuck, yes. It's like no time has passed. There is no one else that hates me the way she does. It's possible it's a crazed fan, but the location of the notes tells me it's someone close and the only person in my mind it could be is Lydia."

"I'm not saying you're wrong, okay? I just need to sit with the idea for a while." Emilie knew she was riding a thin line. One false move and Charlie would bolt.

# Chapter 17

Charlie stood by her bedroom window looking out onto a field of white. Even the trees were covered. Last night had been a rollercoaster, one that Charlie had not enjoyed. A familiar feeling had snaked its way through her body ever since her talk with Emilie. It was a familiar feeling that she never thought she would have to deal with again. Emilie disbelieving her.

Now that things had calmed down a little, she could understand why Emilie needed a minute to process what Charlie was saying. Of course, it was a serious accusation she was levying against Lydia, but Charlie knew in her heart she was right. There was no other explanation. No other person on this planet wanted Charlie away from Emilie like Lydia did.

With that said, was it wrong for Charlie to want Emilie to believe her off the bat? No questions needed? Probably, but Charlie needed that from her. There was no way she could go through the humiliation and pain of Emilie choosing to believe someone over her. Not again.

Once Charlie had agreed to let Emilie sit with what she'd said, they'd parted ways. After their delicious night together, it was certainly not what Charlie had been expecting to happen. No, they should have been holed up in a bedroom doing all kinds of naughty things to each other. Instead, they had been in separate rooms all night and now Charlie was hiding out. She didn't want to go downstairs and see the uncertainty in Emilie's eyes.

Maybe she should have returned home with Sam and Anna? That way, everyone would be out of danger, and it would have given Charlie and Emilie a bit of space to figure out if they were on the same page. Charlie needed trust. There was no point in moving forward if that fundamental element was missing.

The bang of the front door drew Charlie into the hallway. Jess's voice echoed through the house. Charlie tensed. If Lydia was here, she wouldn't be able to hold herself back. No one threatened her family and walked away. Charlie would do anything for Sam and Anna, and that included jail time if needed. Who the fuck did Lydia think she was? Gripping the stair rail, Charlie willed herself to calm down. This wasn't just about her. There were other people involved.

With her breathing somewhat normal, Charlie descended the stairs. A quick scan of the room told her that Lydia was not there. "Hey, Jess."

"Hey, Charlie, you okay? You don't look like you've slept at all," she winked. Jess obviously thought that Charlie's tired eyes were the result of hours of debauchery with Emilie. If only.

"Yeah, bad night. You look like you're dressed to do some woodchopping," Charlie said, hoping Jess would go along with the change of subject. To Charlie's relief, she did.

"I'm heading into the woods, but not for wood chopping. I'd thought I'd take a hike and camp out for a couple of nights. There's a really nice campsite about forty minutes away."

"Camping, it's like minus a thousand out there," Charlie spluttered.

"Jeez? Dramatic much. The temperature has actually risen slightly since you arrived. Anyway, there is *nothing* like camping in the woods to clear the mind. I do it now and then when I need to reset." Reset? That sounded exactly like what

189

Charlie needed. So far, Charlie hadn't spotted Emilie. Presumably she was hiding away in her room too.

"Can I tag along?" The words were out of her mouth before she could think her request through. This was the woman who nearly froze to death on a quick jaunt into the woods with Emilie and Spud. Why the fuck was she volunteering herself to camp out in the woods for a few nights?

"Seriously?" Jess's face mirrored Charlie's surprise.

"Yeah, fuck it. I could do with a change of scenery. We've been cooped up in the house for too long. Plus, it would be great to get some shots of the wildlife around here." The more Charlie tried to talk Jess into the idea, the more she realised how much she wanted to go. It was her firm belief that if she and Emilie didn't get some adequate space between them, then nothing would be resolved. If anything, the situation would probably get worse.

"Em won't come along. I'll tell you that for a fact," Jess said, looking around the house. She was probably wondering why Emilie hadn't come out to see her.

"That's fine. We're not joined at the hip," Charlie stated. At some point, she'd probably have to tell Jess the two of them were in a kind of fight.

"Well, alright then. I've got a bunch of extra gear. Have you got walking boots?"

"Yup, nice furry ones, so all good."

"Okay, you go get your stuff and tell Em what's happening. I'll go back to mine, load up, and meet you back here. Let's say an hour, cool?"

"Brilliant, thanks, Jess. See you soon."

Jess gave her a thumbs up and left. Now all Charlie had to do was explain to Emilie she was taking an impromptu camping trip for a few days.

Charlie took the stairs slowly. No matter what she said, Emilie would think she was running away, and she was. No, not running, just distancing. With a deep sigh, Charlie knocked on Emilie's door. A few seconds went by with no answer. God, was she being ignored? Bracing herself, Charlie pushed open Emilie's door. The room was empty.

Charlie shook her head. She should have known the only place Emilie would be was in her music room. Any time Emilie felt overwhelmed, or needed time to think, she would go to a music room. That had always been her go-to place in school. No reason to think that had changed now.

Following the corridor, Charlie stopped by the partially open door that led to Emilie's music room and, sure enough, there she was perched on the window seat, pen and paper in hand, looking out into the snowy landscape. Charlie's tummy tingled at the sight of Emilie lit up by the light reflecting off the snow.

Clearing her throat, she stepped into the room. "Hey." Emilie slowly turned her head and offered a small smile.

Just like Charlie, Emilie had dark circles under her eyes. "Hi."

"Um, so Jess stopped by. She's going camping."

"Oh good, she always feels better after a few nights in the open."

"Yeah, um, so I decided to go along. You know, experience the Canadian wilds for a day or two." Charlie was desperate to make it sound like the trip was about sightseeing rather than their obvious argument and subsequent tension.

"Oh." Emilie's eyes dropped to her notepad. Charlie's heart clenched. "Yeah, cool. I'm sure you will enjoy yourself. Just wrap up warm." Charlie appreciated Emilie wasn't making a big deal out of her decision to skip out for a few days.

Charlie nodded her head numbly. What else was there to say? "Right, I'll see you soon then."

"Will you be back before the next show?" Emilie's voice was saturated with insecurity and vulnerability. She really wasn't making it easy on Charlie.

"Em, of course. It's just two nights, maybe three." Emilie smiled, nodded, and turned back to the window.

The atmosphere between them was horrible. Charlie hated everything about it. Leaving was definitely the best option. Emilie could work through her feelings about the whole "Lydia being a psycho stalker," without feeling pressure from Charlie, and Charlie could work out if she could move past these feelings that had taken over.

Shoving her belongings into her duffel, Charlie paced around her room. She still had a good half an hour to wait for Jess. Only one thing for it, she needed her family.

"Sam, hey."

"You okay, Char, has something happened?" Charlie hated her friend was panicking.

"I'm absolutely fine, honestly nothing to panic about. I'm going camping. I thought I'd let you know. I'm not sure if I'll get reception in the woods."

"Camping? You? Why?" Sam asked incredulously.

"Hey, I can camp."

"I'm not saying you can't. I'm just surprised, is all. When was the last time you went anywhere that didn't have a king size bed and a double shower?" Alright, so Sam might have a point. The last time Charlie had done anything remotely like camping was in school. It's not her fault she preferred warm comfort over bug-infested cold hard floors!

"I think it's a good idea. I can do some sightseeing!"

"Is that the only reason, Char?" Sam knew Charlie wasn't telling her everything.

192

"No, not entirely."

"What happened?"

Charlie told Sam about her theory involving Lydia and the notes. She also told her that Emilie hadn't believed her and things had gotten heated.

"I think that's a good idea, mate. No harm in taking a bit of time for yourself."

"Do you think I'm overreacting?"

"I get why your first response would be to assume that Emilie doesn't believe you. Hell, it's only recently you've been able to process and move on from what happened between you both at school. I'd just say not to make any rash decisions. If someone threw accusations against my friend, I would certainly need some time to mull it over. You guys need to work together to sort this out."

"I just feel like I'm waiting for it all to fall apart again. It's like, when it's just the two of us, it's amazing. All the feelings are there. It's as if nothing has changed, but then other people get mixed in and I feel like we're not as strong as I thought. Have I rushed into this?"

"Take a breath, Char. Go camping and use the time to clear your head. Only you can decide what's right for you."

* * *

The drive to the campsite had been relatively silent. Jess knew something was off, but hadn't pushed. Charlie needed to be careful. After all, Jess was Emilie's friend, not hers.

"Wow, this place is amazing," Charlie gushed. She wasn't lying. The landscape they were travelling through was nothing short of magical. Snow capped the tall pine trees and covered the ground. Thankfully, the road had been gritted.

193

"This has got to be my favourite place in the world. Nothing beats it."

"When did you move here?" Charlie asked. Jess had been kind enough to let Charlie come along. The least she could do was get to know the woman a bit.

"After the first tour with Em. My family is pretty shit. I only got grief whenever I went home. I started staying with Em on our breaks and I fell utterly in love with the place. It really wasn't a hard decision."

"Sorry about your family. I know how that goes."

"Are you alright, Charlie? Look, tell me to sod off if I'm butting in, but I know there's something going on. Emilie always comes to see me off before I go camping."

Charlie chewed her lip. She wished she could pull her beanie over her head and hide away. "We had a bit of a fight last night."

"Can I ask what about?"

"I'm not sure you'll want to hear it."

"Try me, Charlie. I was serious when I said I wanted us to be friends."

"Yeah, but the fight was about one of your other friends."

"Lydia?" Jess sighed.

"Yeah."

"Okay, come on out with it."

"Did Emilie tell you about the notes I found?" It only occurred to Charlie in that moment that Jess may have no clue about the threats. She and Lydia had left before Sam discovered the paper in her bag.

"No? What notes?"

"I've had two notes threatening me. Well, actually one. The other threatened Sam, Anna, and the baby."

194

"What?" Jess gasped, taking her eyes off the road to look at Charlie.

"Yeah. I found the first one under my drink glass at the pub the other night. It told me to stay away from Emilie or I'd be sorry. I dismissed it. Then Sam found a second note in her bag, threatening her family if she didn't get me to stay away from Emilie."

"And you think…"

"I think it's Lydia. Emilie wasn't inclined to agree, and we fought."

"Fuck." Jess remained silent after that, her face deep in concentration and contemplation.

"Do you think I'm full of shit, too?"

"Emilie said you were full of shit?" Jess asked, surprised.

"Not in those exact words."

"Then she didn't say it, Char. Cut Em a break. You know how she is about people betraying her."

"Oh, yes, I'm intimately familiar." Charlie couldn't help the snark.

"Sorry, I didn't mean you. Emilie is going to be gutted if what you think is true. You know that. She won't make the same mistake as she did back then though — of that I'm certain. If you need to hear it, I'll say it. What she did to you is the single biggest mistake she ever made, and she's regretted it from the moment she left Pickerton. I should know, I've had to deal with this for two bastard decades. Let her have a moment to accept that one of her oldest friends could have done something like this to the one person she has always loved. Can you do that?"

Charlie felt like an arsehole of the highest calibre. Instead of acting rationally, she'd let her old insecurities and

195

anger take over, clouding her judgement and reaction. "Well, thanks Jess, I feel like a right dick now," she laughed.

"I'll always tell you how it is. That's what friendship with me is. Listen, you came here to get to know her again and put some past shit to rest, right?"

"Yeah."

"Then let it rest. Fuck, you're both approaching forty. Let the schoolyard shit go."

"Hey, we're mid-thirties like you."

"Stop kidding yourself. We're closer to forty now. Own it," Jess laughed.

"Alright, I hear you. You didn't answer my question, though. Do you think I'm full of it with the Lydia theory?"

Jess blew out a massive breath. "Shit, I don't want it to be true, but she's always been crazy when it comes to Emilie."

"Crazy enough to threaten me?"

"Maybe, I honestly don't know. I know that she wanted to leave pretty quickly the next day after the dinner party. Make of that what you will, I suppose."

Charlie scrubbed her face with her hands, blowing out a frustrated breath. "Right. I'm not going to think about it for a bit. We're here in this beautiful place and I want to enjoy it."

"Great, because we have just arrived."

Charlie cast her eyes out of the window. They pulled up to a small wooden hut. "Give me a second to let them know we're here and then we can go to the campsite." Jess hopped out of the truck and headed inside. Now that Charlie had relaxed a little, she comprehended the magnitude of what she had got herself into. What was she thinking? There was nothing but trees all around them, and where there were trees there had to be bears and other animals that would most likely want to snack on Charlie's body. *Oh shit, Char, you really did it this time!*

"Ah, I see the panic has set in," Jess laughed as she climbed back into the truck. "Out of ten, how much are you regretting this now?"

"Twelve, that's how much. Are there bears?"

"What is your obsession with bears? Yes, there are some around, but don't worry. We have bear containers for our food and we aren't camping in tents."

"We're not?" Charlie squealed in delight.

"No, you fool, it's like really fucking cold outside," Jess laughed harder. "We have a little cabin and when I say little, I mean tiny. We will have to share a bed. You okay with that?"

"Fine, just don't get handsy," Charlie winked.

"God, someone thinks highly of themselves," Jess tutted playfully.

"Well yeah, have you seen me?" Charlie wiggled her eyebrows. Jess shook her head, laughing.

"Anyway," Jess said, elongating the word. "We are safe from bears. So, you cool?"

"Totally, let's do this."

Jess manoeuvred the truck up a winding gravel path. There were several tiny cabins dotted around. After a minute of bumpy road, they finally stopped. The little wooden hut was cute. There was a picnic table and grill tucked around the side. The trees were dense, and the air smelled of pine and moss. Charlie took a second to breathe in the air, which was possibly the freshest air she'd ever experienced. In the distance, Charlie could see a clearing. "What's through there?"

"Let's dump all this and I'll show you."

A few minutes later, Charlie followed Jess through the trees to the opening. What lay before them was out of this world beautiful. "Oh, my god," Charlie gasped. The trees opened out onto an immense lake. There were snow-capped mountains in the distance. The water was so still and clear that

197

it reflected the scenery as clear as a mirror. Above them circled what looked be to eagles. Had she stepped into a fucking movie set? "Jess, this... wow."

"I know, right!"

Whipping her camera from her bag, Charlie set about snapping everything and anything. It had been a while since she'd felt this free with her photography. Usually she was on such a tight schedule she rarely had time to enjoy the process at all. That had been different since being in Canada. The photos taken of Emilie and the gang had been a lot of fun, but nothing serious. Here in the woods, Charlie felt the rush of inspiration rain down on her. Taking landscape and wildlife photos was well out of her usual wheelhouse, but, hell, she couldn't wait to give it a go. Everything else could wait for a few days.

# Chapter 18

The cabin was way too quiet for Emilie's liking. Charlie had disappeared with Jess to go camping. Camping! Of all the things Emilie thought would happen, that was the last thing she would have ever guessed. Charlie couldn't even take a stroll in the back garden without freaking herself out, for crying out loud!

The conversation—or disagreement—she'd had with Charlie was on a constant repeat in her head. Obviously, Emilie could understand why Charlie jumped to the conclusion that Lydia had left the notes. After the initial shock, it wasn't unreasonable to think that. Lydia had done nothing but show disdain for Charlie. The thing was, Emilie just couldn't see Lydia going that far.

Having not slept for most of the night, Emilie found herself in her music room. Being surrounded by her instruments and sheet music always comforted her. Even after Charlie left, she couldn't find the strength to leave. In times like this, she oddly became inspired. Maybe it was the raw, unfiltered emotion? Whatever it was, Emilie had written several new songs.

Emilie also found herself looking back to their time at Pickerton. Charlie had said a few things last night about Lydia that Emilie was unaware of. Yes, she knew Lydia had never really taken to Charlie, but Emilie had never been told about the threats Lydia had supposedly doled out. *Supposedly*. Why had she instantly attached that word? If Charlie said it happened, there should be no "supposedly" about it. Why couldn't Emilie ever just trust Charlie's word? Out of every single person she knew, Charlie had never lied or betrayed her. Was there something wrong with Emilie that she found it easier to trust untrustworthy people over her one constant source of comfort and security?

For once, Emilie had to give Charlie the benefit of the doubt. She owed her that much. Picking up her phone, Emilie dialled. "Buddy, hi, sorry to call again."

"That's what I'm here for, Emilie. Have you got an update?"

"Honestly, I'm not sure. I spoke to my friend and… well, she's pretty convinced Lydia Beecham is responsible."

"Okay, Lydia Beecham, isn't she a friend of yours?"

"Yes, I've known her since school, but so has Charlie, my friend, who received the threats. It's safe to say that Lydia has never liked Charlie."

"Enough to send threats?" Buddy asked.

"Possibly. I really don't know. I trust Charlie and if she's saying it's Lydia, I think it's only right you should know."

"You made the right choice. It could turn out to be nothing, but at least we will have followed the lead through. Give me a few days and I'll dig into Lydia."

"She was present each time a note was left."

"Okay, that could be something, or it could be a coincidence. Leave it with me alright. I suggest you don't have any contact with Lydia until I've got to the bottom of it. Same for Charlie."

Emilie laughed, "No chance of that happening."

"Speak in a few days, Em."

Good, Okay, she'd done something positive. Her belly didn't feel great about it, but that would pass, right? Sliding her phone across the window seat, Emilie stood up, taking her old guitar from its stand. The songs she'd written through the very lonely night were on repeat in her head, providing a strangely comforting background noise which helped dull her raging thoughts. Closing her eyes, she played. The melody was slow and painful. One song she'd written was about losing herself to insecurities.

On stage, Emilie Martin was *the* most confident woman on the planet. Nothing fazed her when she was standing in front of a crowd. Off stage was a different matter entirely. No doubt it all stemmed from her family. The world had *some* idea of the strife that had occurred between Emilie and her parents, but only her uncle, Jack, and Charlie knew the full account. For years, her parents had been stealing her money. Legally, they were supposed to have put all her earnings into a trust. Instead, they'd splashed out on houses, cars, Botox and hookers.

Thankfully, her uncle had swooped in and saved her. He'd talked Emilie out of pressing charges because of how it would have looked. Nothing could impact Emilie's image, not if she wanted to succeed. If faced with the same decision again, Emilie wouldn't have listened. She would have filed charges. It had taken even more money for Emilie to separate herself from her parents. The entire experience had been traumatic, and it warped her relationships with other people.

Charlie was the only person who Emilie had been able to fully relax with after everything happened. Their friendship had started slowly, with Charlie being super shy. Emilie had been the one to push for a friendship.

Jess came a close second, but Emilie still kept her at arm's length even now. Lydia, well, Emilie had shared nothing very personal with her. It was all surface stuff, it always had been.

201

Even though Emilie was closing in on forty, the experience with her parents had left her insecure around others. That's why she kept the same people around her, never really expanding her circle. If Lydia had sent those notes, then Emilie had once again trusted the wrong person. If that was the case, did she need to re-evaluate all her friends? Jesus, she felt like a paranoid bag of nerves.

The time passed quickly as Emilie played. By the end of the day, she'd written five new songs. No doubt Jack would cream his pants and insist she make a new album. Tucking her notes and sheet music into her diary, she slid it back into its hiding place. Emilie didn't even fully trust Jack now. Who was to say he wouldn't go snooping and find her recent work? There was nothing right about how she was feeling.

* * *

Three long days had passed, and Emilie had heard nothing from Charlie or Jess. Maybe that was a good thing, though. Hopefully Charlie was enjoying herself. Emilie had been productive and had written a handful of new songs on top of the ones she had written after the argument.

Tonight was the second small concert. It was to be held two towns over in a tiny jazz club. Emilie had been there a handful of times. It was an intimate setting, perfect for a private gig. Time was ticking by and Emilie was getting nervous. Charlie had promised she would be back for tonight's show, but there was no sign of her. Emilie would have to leave in an hour. Jesus, she hoped nothing bad had happened.

Visions of Charlie running through the forest screaming as a bear chased her sprung to mind. It shouldn't have been funny, but it was. Poor Charlie. Hopefully, the camping experience hadn't been too traumatising. As her mind

202

wandered, a set of bright car lights lit up the windows. Jack's SUV pulled into the drive. Emilie had agreed that he could attend the show. He was her manager after all, but she'd reiterated that he wasn't to do any promotional work.

"Hey," he called, sliding out of his seat.

"Hey, how are you enjoying your break?"

"You were right, Em, I needed it. I've played some hockey with the guys. It's been ages."

"I'm really pleased to hear it."

"So where is everyone?" he asked, peering around her shoulder into the house.

"Charlie and Jess went camping. They should be back any minute." Emilie felt uneasy talking to Jack about Charlie.

"Oh, cool. They getting on well? Shit, is Jess banging your ex?" Jack looked far too pleased at the thought, causing Emilie to frown. Why has *he* got a problem with Charlie?

"Not that I know of. Why would you say that?"

"I heard Jess had a thing for her, that's all. Anyway, you two are in the past, right?" He was fishing for information that Emilie was *not* going to give him.

"Come in, it's cold," Emilie replied, sidestepping his questions. The sound of tyres crunching through the snow saved Emilie from any more of Jack's probing questions. To Emilie's utter relief, Jess' truck came to a stop. The door flung open and a very happy looking Charlie stepped out. Damn, what had happened to make her beam like that? Jack couldn't be right, could he? Charlie wouldn't sleep with Jess, not after everything.

"Charlie, hey," Emilie said with gusto. She was *not* going to let on there had been an issue between them.

"Hey, honey, I'm home," Charlie called, laughing at herself. Emilie laughed as Charlie swooped in, picked her up, and swirled her around. Wow, something good must have happened.

"Put me down, you idiot," Emilie laughed. Releasing Emilie, Charlie stepped back, grinning. Her grin faded a tad when she spotted Jack.

"Oh, hi Jack, sorry didn't see you there."

"No worries. Had a good time, you two?" Emilie wanted to boot him straight in his nuts. Not only was he smirking, he was waggling his eyebrows suggestively. God, men!

"We had a fantastic time, thanks. Why are you doing that with your eyebrows?" Emilie wanted to kiss Charlie and laugh. Trust her to point out Jack's not-so-subtle attempt at insinuating Charlie and Jess had been up to salacious things.

"Well..." he spluttered.

"So, Em, you had a good few days?" Charlie bypassed Jack entirely.

"Yup, but we'll have to catch up later. You need to get ready."

"Shit, yeah. Sorry about that. We got stuck behind a broken-down car," Charlie said, rolling her eyes. Jess stepped up and dropped Charlie's bags.

"Here you go, your majesty," she mock saluted. "Next time get your own bloody gear," she laughed.

Charlie levelled her signature grin that made Emilie instantly wet. "God, she gets grumpy when she needs food," Charlie winked at Emilie, leaning in and kissing her on the cheek. "I'll be ready in fifteen." With that, she bounded up the stairs and disappeared into her room.

"Wow, she seems to have enjoyed herself," Emilie laughed.

"She did. Once she got over her ridiculous fear of imminent death by bear, she settled. Honestly, I saw little of her. As soon as she got her camera out, she was off." Emilie's heart warmed at the thought of Charlie bounding round the forest in her element, taking photos.

"Right, well, I'm grabbing a drink," Jack muttered.

"I'm going to nip home and change. I'll see you at the club."

Emilie joined Jack in the kitchen. His drink turned into three as they waited for Charlie. The sound of feet jogging down the stairs pulled Emilie from any more awkward conversation. When had talking to Jack gotten so hard?

"Ready to rock and roll, or, in my case, take photos and drink," Charlie grinned.

Jack slammed back his drink and headed for the door. Emilie rolled her eyes at Charlie's raised eyebrows.

The club was packed by the time they arrived, which was a little surprising. The jazz club wasn't huge, and it wasn't in a big town. Cheers erupted when Emilie stepped on to the stage.

"Hello, everyone." The crowd bellowed back. "Are you okay if I sing a few numbers?" Emilie asked playfully. The crowd cheered, and Emilie took that as her cue to start. Throughout the show, Emilie kept her eye on Charlie, who was weaving around the crowd taking photos. Not just of Emilie, but of everything. The décor, the people, the beer. Emilie smiled. She couldn't wait to see what Charlie had captured.

Halfway through, Emilie announced a ten-minute break. Joining Jess at the little table they'd reserved, Emilie was more than surprised when Charlie gave her a quick kiss on the cheek and headed to the stage. What was happening?

"Evening all," Charlie started, gaining the interest of everyone in the room. And why wouldn't she? With tight-fitting black trousers and a figure-hugging, sleeveless, high-neck top, Charlie looked stunning. Her hair was flowing freely and her eyes glowed under the lights. Her tattoos were on full display, and she honestly looked like a piece of art. "I hope you don't mind me gate crashing. I just thought I'd tickle some ivories for you whilst you wait for the incredible Emilie Martin to return." Was Charlie really going to perform? The crowd was enamored. Just like Emilie. Charlie's husky voice was bewitching.

Taking a seat at the bench of the piano that had been wheeled out, Charlie got herself comfortable. *She must have organised this for them to know she needed a piano.*

Emilie couldn't take her eyes off of Charlie. "Okay, lovely people, here goes." Charlie danced her fingers across the keys. "Now I'm no Emilie Martin, but I have been told I can hold a tune, so let's see." Emilie couldn't believe that Charlie was going to sing. She never sang in front of people. Hell, she'd only let Emilie hear her a handful of times.

The opening bars to "You and Me" by Lifehouse echoed through the silent room. Tears pooled in Emilie's eyes as Charlie sang. Her voice was low and gravelly. She sounded so sexy it hurt. Charlie poured out the lyrics with everything she had, and Emilie was gone, lost in Charlie's voice. The minutes passed as Charlie played to the crowd. Emilie knew better though, Charlie was playing to her. She knew it when Charlie's eyes found her as she sang the last few words.

*And it's you and me, and all of the people, and I don't know why. I can't keep my eyes off of you.*

Emilie could feel people's eyes on her as Charlie sang to her. She didn't care though, because Charlie had just given her the single most precious gift. Emilie would carry that song with her forever. With a quick "Thank you" down the microphone, Charlie rose from the bench. The crowd seemed to break from Charlie's spell at last and began whistling and cheering. Emilie didn't know what to do. Her feet were glued to the floor.

Charlie hopped off the stage and headed straight for her. "Was that okay?" Charlie asked as she stopped a few centimetres from Emilie.

"Was that for me?" Emilie knew it was, but she needed to hear it from Charlie. After the upset of the past few days, she couldn't afford to be wrong.

"Of course it was, Em," Charlie murmured, her face even closer than it had been a few seconds ago. Emilie surged forward, capturing Charlie's lips. All the passion she held for this woman poured out of her through that kiss. Charlie's arms swept around her and it felt so good. She was safe in Charlie's arms. She was home.

Eventually, Jess cleared her throat. Emilie still had half a fucking show to do. How in god's name was she supposed to concentrate now? Pulling herself away, she took a moment to look into Charlie's eyes. What had changed in those three days?

"Em, get up there," Jack growled. Trust him to piss all over her happy moment. Forcing her body to move, she slipped past Charlie and headed for the stage. There was no way to stop the red tinge on her cheeks as the crowd wolf whistled and cheered.

Four songs later and she was finally done. Charlie greeted her with a pint and a grin. "Let's have this and then go home. We have some catching up to do," Charlie whispered in her ear. Emilie's entire body came alive at the promise of what was to come. Well, by Charlie's intimation, it would be Emilie coming, and soon.

Never in all her years had she downed a pint faster. "Let's go," she called to Charlie as soon as the last drop had passed her lips. Charlie chuckled. Jack looked pissed.

"I'm not ready to go yet," he shot looking between Emilie and Charlie.

"That's fine Jack, you can crash at mine. You've had too much to drink, anyway. I'll drop you off in the morning to get your car," Jess said before Emilie could murder him. She shot

Jess a grateful look and practically dragged Charlie out of the club.

Charlie drove Emilie nuts the entire ride back. Her hand had got higher and higher up Emilie's thigh the longer they travelled. If it wasn't for the fact that her car wasn't soundproof she'd have ripped Charlie's trousers off and taken what she wanted. The car had barely stopped when Emilie yanked open the door, pulling a laughing Charlie along behind her.

Not even stopping to turn on the lights, Emilie continued in her quest to get Charlie upstairs and naked as quick as possible. Charlie seemingly was on the same page because Emilie suddenly found herself scooped up in Charlie's arms. "You weren't going fast enough," Charlie said, bounding up the stairs with her.

"Get naked, now," Emilie demanded as soon as Charlie threw her on the bed. This was not going to be a night of slow and steady. Oh, no. Charlie didn't need to be asked twice and Emilie was in no mood to wait around. Silently and efficiently, they undressed in record time. Emily leaned over to her bedside table and took out her harness. It had been a very long time since she'd had the pleasure of wearing it.

Emilie hiked up the straps while Charlie looked on. Her eyes shone devilishly as Emilie fitted the dildo. "Get over here," Emilie commanded. Charlie strode over in two long steps. Straddling her thighs, Charlie hovered over the toy. "Do you want lube?" Emilie asked.

"I don't need it," Charlie gasped as she lowered herself down. Emilie reached down and pressed the button on the base of the toy. Charlie's eyes almost disappeared to the back of her head when it started vibrating. "Oh, yes," Charlie panted.

"I can't take my eyes off of you either," Emilie whispered.

# Chapter 19

Raw pleasure coursed through Charlie as she lowered herself again onto the toy Emilie sported between her legs. With her hands cradling Emilie's neck and their foreheads touching, Charlie rolled her hips, relishing in the fullness the dildo provided.

"Oh, Em," she whispered. Not wanting to lose control too soon, Charlie continued her slow undulation.

"Wait," Em gasped. "Charlie stop." Did Charlie hear that right?

"Hmm?" Charlie wasn't in the headspace to understand anything. Her pleasure was spiking as she rode Emilie's lap.

"Charlie baby, wait." Charlie felt Emilie still her movement.

"What's wrong?" Had she missed something?

"Nothing, I want to do something." Charlie leaned back to look in Emilie's eyes. They were filled with lust and desire as much as her own.

"Em, you stopped me midway through fucking you because you want to do something?" Charlie was so surprised she laughed.

"Yes, now stand up." This was interesting. At least Emilie kept Charlie on her toes. Gently extracting herself from the toy, Charlie rose and stood in front of Emilie. "Stand at the end of the bed." She'd stopped them so Charlie could go from the side of the bed to the end of it? Seriously?

Curiosity piqued, Charlie followed Emilie's instructions. "Okay, now face the mirror." At the end of Emilie's gigantic bed was a long floor mirror. Charlie turned to look at herself. There she stood in all her willowy nakedness, waiting to see what Emilie had planned for her. Whatever it was, she was already turned on. The fact that she could see her own want glistening on her thighs proved that.

Looking at her own body didn't phase Charlie. Over the years, she'd learned to love herself. Kim had helped her massively. The blonde bombshell was all about self-empowerment and love. Body positivity was hard to accept sometimes, but Kim often spoke to her friends about it.

Now Charlie could look at her reflection and see how good she looked. Her breasts weren't huge but they were perky, a nice B cup. She loved her nipple bars. They added to her sensitivity. Charlie had them pierced for her own pleasure. Another thing Kim had discussed with her. Doing things for oneself. Charlie loved her nipples tugging and flicking during sex. She loved doing it to herself when she masturbated, so the nipple bars were a present to herself and future self-loving sessions.

Most people thought that Charlie's hair was her best feature. Maybe it was, but Charlie didn't see that. Yes, she loved her hair. Of course she knew it garnered attention, but, for Charlie, the best part of her body were her eyes. They dazzled.

In all her reverie, she hadn't noticed Emilie shifting on the bed. Charlie felt her presence behind her. Turning her head from the mirror, she looked over her shoulder at Emilie, who was now sitting on the edge of the bed watching her.

"You are stunning, Charlie. I wanted you to see what I see. How unbelievably sexy you are. To the point it's almost unbearable. I want you to watch as I take you, fuck you until you are a quivering mess."

Jesus, Mary, and Joseph, where the hell had this Emilie been hiding?

"How do you want me?" Charlie would attempt anything that Emilie wanted. Thankfully, she had always been adventurous in the bedroom and she was pretty sure there wasn't much that could shock her.

"I want you straddling my lap, but I want you facing the mirror." Charlie could do that, no problem. Backing herself up to the edge of the bed, Charlie took Emilie's hands and placed them on her hip.

"Keep me balanced," she said as she stretched one leg backwards and then the other to kneel on the bed above Emilie's lap. Emilie held her tight as she manoeuvred herself into position. When she felt comfortable, Charlie stared back at the mirror. It was possibly one of the most erotic scenes she'd ever partaken in.

The reflection showed Emilie gripping one hip whilst the other slipped down to position the toy back at Charlie's opening. Taking her cue, Charlie lowered herself once again. This time, though, she reached behind her to hold Emilie's neck. The vision before her was one of pure euphoria. Legs spread wide over Emilie's thighs, her hands thrown back, gripping Emilie and her hips beginning their slow movements.

It took only seconds for Charlie to see stars. Emilie's hand gripped her hip harder, the other hand lay palm down on the top of her back, anchoring her. Emilie thrust herself into Charlie. The combination of her rolling and Emilie's thrusting almost brought her to tears of sheer joy.

"God, Charlie, do you see yourself? Do you see how fucking beautiful you are riding me?"

"Em…" Charlie panted, her breaths coming harder. She felt Emilie's tongue trace her tattoos, felt her teeth nip at the art on her back. As the toy entered her deeper, she watched in fascination. She saw herself stretch, taking it in fully.

"I want to feel you all over me. I want you to come on my lap and then on my face. Do you want that, Charlie?" Charlie wanted nothing more. She never wanted this to end. Emilie Martin talking dirty to her was everything. Her body shook as she rode Emilie harder.

Emilie brought her hand round from Charlie's back and began twisting and pinching Charlie's nipple. That was it. That was all Charlie needed. The noise that escaped her throat was animalistic and powerful. Had she ever screamed in such rapture before? No, not like this. Emilie had extracted something from the very centre of her soul. She was playing Charlie like the strings of her guitar, so masterful and with exquisite results. Charlie's eyes clamped shut. As much as she wanted to watch herself transform into the very notes Emilie was conducting, she couldn't. The pressure in her body was too much, the lights dancing behind her eyes were blinding, and the music of her own orgasm deafened her to the world.

Charlie had never lost time before. Until now. She'd never been so encased in her own feelings that the minutes slipped by unnoticed. Until now. When she finally opened her eyes, she was lying on the bed, staring up into Emilie's eyes.

"You are a goddess, Charlie Baxter," Emilie whispered close to her lips. "I want to devour you, again and again." Charlie couldn't even summon the energy to respond. It was taking everything she had to corral her brain into resembling some feeling of normalcy. Sex had never left her this scrambled. By the time she'd entered some sort of situational awareness, Charlie felt Emilie making her way down her body.

212

"I love your tattoos so much, I can't get enough of them." Emilie licked and kissed Charlie's body art, worshipping every inch of inked skin. "Open up, baby," Emily whispered, her face nuzzling into Charlie's soft curls. Charlie was still addled, but instinctively her legs opened.

"Fuck," Charlie growled as Emilie swiped at her slit.

"You taste like honey," Emilie cooed, lapping at Charlie softly, consuming her. Charlie shoved her head back into the bed. Emilie was torturing her, and she fucking loved it. This side of Emilie was a welcomed surprise.

"Emilie," Charlie warned, her body feeling frenzied with need and anticipation.

"You come when I say you can come," Emilie said sternly, causing another zip of carnal lust to shoot through Charlie's pussy. Oh fuck, Emilie dominating Charlie was on another level. They were usually quite equal when it came to sex, neither one commanding nor submitting, but now, well now, Charlie was happy to submit. Emilie Martin could demand the world and Charlie would endeavour to give it to her.

Charlie's hips moved of their own accord. The pleasure radiating from her clit was immeasurable. Charlie willed herself to hold on, but it was becoming nigh on impossible with Emilie swirling and sucking Charlie's clit and lips.

"Come now," Emilie demanded and Charlie exploded, electricity shot from her clit to every inch of her body. Her limbs shook and vibrated. Emilie slowed her ministrations as Charlie came down from the stratosphere.

Only the sound of their joined panting pierced the stillness of the room. Charlie stared at the ceiling until she could feel her body again. Blindly, she reached for Emilie, tugging at her to join Charlie in an embrace. Charlie couldn't formulate the words needed to describe what she had just experienced, instead she hauled Emilie into her body and held her tightly.

213

Charlie blinked awake, the wet nose of Spud pressed into her cheek. Cracking open her eyelid, she looked deep into Spud's black eyes. The rhythmic *thump, thump, thump* of her tail against the floor brought a chuckle to Charlie's throat. Was there a more upbeat and happy dog in this world? Peering over her shoulder, Charlie checked Emilie was still sleeping. Their night had stretched on until the early hours. Charlie could feel her muscles complaining as she shifted. Gently, Charlie scooted out of bed. Emilie groaned softly and turned onto her stomach, her head buried in her pillow. The light from the unobstructed window cast a ray of sunshine over Emilie's bare back. She was a vision.

Creeping silently out of the room, Charlie rushed to get her camera. Spud could wait a few more minutes. Emilie hadn't moved a muscle, allowing Charlie to capture her in all her beauty. The setting was perfect.

Happy with her shots, Charlie set the camera down, leaned over, and peppered Emilie's back with soft kisses. Still, she didn't move. A smile spread across Charlie's face. This is what she wanted. All the other stuff didn't matter, not if it meant Charlie couldn't share her life with the woman that had captured and kept her heart for decades.

After letting Spud out, Charlie set about cooking breakfast. The simple task allowed her time to gather her thoughts. They needed to talk. Charlie had to tell Emilie how she was feeling. She needed to know how Emilie felt in return.

Putting the tray of scrambled eggs and pancakes on the edge of the bed, Charlie climbed back under the covers and pulled Emilie into her. Emilie sighed and gripped Charlie's hand.

"Morning, sunshine," Charlie said, kissing the side of Emilie's head.

"Mmm."

Charlie laughed, doubling her efforts to wake a very sleepy Emilie. Biting her earlobe seemed to have the desired effect. "Hey, I was sleeping," Emilie grumbled.

"But I made you breakfast," Charlie pouted. Emilie's grin told Charlie she'd won. Slowly, Emily opened her eyes.

"Ugh, fine. I suppose I'll get up then."

"I didn't say get up, just sit up so you can eat. We burned a shit ton of calories last night," Charlie smirked.

Emilie laughed and sat up. Charlie brought the tray of food over and placed it on Emilie's lap. Nerves had started to circle Charlie's tummy. The last thing she wanted was to burst their sex-induced bubble, but they needed to clear the air.

"Em, can we talk?" Emilie stopped chewing and cast her gaze to Charlie.

"Sure," she replied.

"I'm sorry I ran off into the woods after we had words. I acted impulsively. Remember when I said that we'd grown up and gained some wisdom since we were last together?" Emilie nodded. "Well, maybe not so much," Charlie laughed. "I let my seventeen-year-old self control me that day. Of course you were right to question me. I'd just accused one of your oldest friends of something very serious. If the situation was reversed, I would have absolutely done the same thing."

"I wasn't calling you a liar, Charlie —"

"I know. I jumped the gun. I still think Lydia is involved. I know I don't have proof, but I can feel it in my gut. There are too many coincidences. I won't, however, expect you to blindly believe me. This is a delicate situation. Em, at the end of the day, I just want us to be okay."

"Just okay?"

"No, you know I want more than that. Fuck, Em, there's no way we will ever just be friends. We both knew that going into this right? When you asked me to come here and work for you, I knew full well the invite had bugger all to do with working. We came into each other's lives again and we both wanted more."

"Well, you have been working," Emilie smiled. Charlie rolled her eyes.

"Yeah, okay, I took a few shots for you, but can you honestly tell me that's why you had me trek across the bloody ocean?"

"No, obviously not. Charlie Baxter, you haven't left my thoughts in all the time we've been apart. No matter what I did, I could never rid myself of your beautiful face."

"Did you want to rid yourself?"

"Yes, because it was so painful to have those memories of you and know I'd fucked everything up."

"But we're here now, Emilie. I don't want us to make the same mistake as before. We let other people interfere and it broke us. I won't let that happen again. When I was in those woods, yes shitting myself mostly at the thought of Yogi Bear coming along and eating me, I had time to stop and really look at myself. I was just as much to blame back then. I should have stuck by you, I should have realised that you were taking it out on me because you were terrified. I should have fought more."

"No, you shouldn't, Charlie, don't you see? You should never have to fight to have your loved ones believe and respect you. I let you down and I swear I will never do it again. Whatever happens with the threats, whether or not we find out it's Lydia, I'm here with you. We've waited too long. It's time we both got what we want, and that's being together, right?"

"I've wanted nothing more in my life." Charlie took Emilie's face in her hands and inhaled her. "It's you and me,

216

Em." They closed the gap, their lips parting as they sealed their promise with a kiss.

"Right, now we've got all that out of the way. Can I have some coffee? Some of us have been up for ages slogging away in the kitchen," Charlie huffed playfully. Emilie pinched her nipple before sliding back and shoving a fork full of eggs in her mouth.

Emilie's phone buzzed on the bedside table. Jess' name scrolled across the top.

"Hey," Em called down the line. She'd put the phone on loudspeaker so she could continue eating. Charlie nabbed a piece of pancake from her plate, earning her another nipple pinch.

"Em, I think you'd better turn on your TV or look at your social accounts," Jess said sternly.

Charlie reached for her own phone and brought up the local news. *Oh shit.* A video of last night's gig had gone viral. Charlie swallowed thickly. Emilie was going to hit the fucking roof. Knowing it was futile to keep the video from her, Charlie turned her phone. Emilie's face turned from confusion to rage instantly. Someone had filmed and leaked the concert.

Clicking on the remote, Charlie pulled up the news. To her own disbelief, Charlie watched as newscasters around the country reported on Emilie Martin's secret concerts. Footage showed journalists and fans alike descending on the local towns that surrounded Emilie's cabin. They both watched on as a woman who looked to be a fan was interviewed live on air.

"So tell me, why have you travelled all this way?" the reporter asked the giddy woman, who was flushed in the face.

"Oh my god, as soon as we heard Emilie was doing these little concerts we had to come. I'll pay anything to see her. I heard she's singing new songs, maybe for her new album," the woman squealed. Charlie muted the TV.

217

"Em?" she said gently. Emilie was staring at the TV with a blank look on her face.

"Em?" Jess's voice rang out. Charlie picked up the phone and took it off speaker.

"Jess, get over here and call Jack. Do these people know where she lives? If so, get some sort of fucking security here now." Charlie put the phone down and turned back to Emilie. "Em, honey, talk to me." Charlie was getting worried. Emilie hadn't uttered a word. Charlie moved the forgotten breakfast tray out of the way and positioned herself in front of Emilie. "Emilie," Charlie barked. The sudden noise pulled Emilie out of her head.

"What the hell, Charlie?"

"I know. Look, Jess is on her way over with Jack and security. Does the press know where you live?"

"The local press for sure. I've never hidden away. The national press has never had much interest in camping out here, especially in the winter."

"Well, I think that's about to change, babe. This video is just the beginning."

"No one in the jazz club would have done this, Char. I know these people. They were all local, none of them have an interest in attracting the press to me."

"Well, someone did. Whoever posted that video has made it look like an advert for a new album. If not an album, they've definitely used it to create buzz around you." Suddenly Emilie's features grew dark. A raging storm was building behind her eyes.

"He wouldn't have," she whispered. Charlie looked at her, confused.

"Who wouldn't have?"

"Jack," Emilie growled.

"You think he did this? Organised it?"

218

"Who else? Who else benefits from this?" Charlie almost felt sorry for Jack. If he had done this against the strict instructions of Emilie, he was in for a world of hurt. Charlie watched Emilie's shoulders sag.

"I just wanted to do one thing for me. I just wanted to control this one thing," she cried. "Now I'm going to have to deal with all this. The people of those towns are going to have to cope with intrusive reporters and fans."

"Hey, hey, it's okay. We'll deal with this, Em. You have me, okay, and Jess. No matter what, remember. It's you and me. I've got you."

# Chapter 20

Emilie didn't need to see Jack to know he was the one that had sent the footage to the press. There wasn't anyone else who would have done it. The people of the local towns had no motive. The last thing they would want were thousands of people turning up to badger them about Emilie's shows. The only person this situation served was Jack.

Hot raging fury burned her skin as she sat in her living room waiting for Jack to arrive. How could she have been so stupid? She'd seen the signs long ago! Every time he pushed her, did sly things behind her back, he was showing Emilie who he really was. Fuck, why hadn't she seen this coming?

For most people, having a show leaked to the press wouldn't be a big deal, but for Emilie, it was the epitome of her worst nightmare. Someone had lied and betrayed her yet again. Not just someone, Jack, her friend.

The front door opening with a crash startled her. Jess rushed in, looking pissed off and bedraggled. "Jesus, Em, it's bad out there. You've got half the country's bloody media trying to get to your front door."

"Shit," Emilie growled. Not only had Jack betrayed her trust, he'd also stripped her of her privacy. The cabin was her safe space, the place she could just be herself, not the great Emilie

Martin. Being home was sacred, and Jack had sullied it with his greed.

"Don't panic too much. Lola and the team are set up. No one will get past her, you know that." Jess laughed.

Lola Arnold was Emilie's head of security. Lola was simply terrifying. Being ex-military, she'd seen more battles than anyone ever should. Her persona screamed "I will hurt you" and her body was jacked. Emilie knew she was the right person for the job the second she'd laid eyes on the woman.

It was funny though, because Lola definitely looked like she could rip someone's head clean off. However, when Lola opened up and warmed to a person, she was delightful. Oh, she'd still fuck them up if necessary. No doubt about that, but she was a kind, gentle and lovely woman underneath it all.

Once Lola had been hired, she banded together her own team, informing Emilie that she would only work with people she knew and trusted. Emilie could definitely understand that mentality.

"Where's Jack?" Emilie asked, only just realising that Jess was alone.

"I rang him a dozen times, Em, he didn't pick up."

"I bet he didn't," Emilie seethed.

"It was him right, the one who set all this shit in motion?" Jess wasn't really asking, but Emilie nodded her confirmation, anyway. "Fucking idiot."

"I don't understand why though," Charlie interjected from the sofa next to Emilie. "I mean, surely he knows you're going to figure it out, right?"

"Of course, but my guess is that he's going to stay out of the way until he thinks Emilie is calm enough to talk her round to his way of thinking," Jess replied.

"How often does he do that?" Charlie asked, raising her eyebrows.

221

"Too fucking often," Jess said.

"Can you stop talking about me like I'm not here?" Emilie shot.

"Em, come on. This is his M.O. I'd say it's been the last year that he's *really* been pushing his luck, but you have to admit, he always talks you round."

Emilie hated Jess was right. She *had* let him get away with behaving that way. Probably because she thought that underneath it all, he was still her friend and wouldn't really hurt her. How wrong she was.

"And this time, what will you do?" Charlie asked Emilie. That was the question, wasn't it?

"Nothing until I've spoken to him." Snatching up her phone, she hit Jack's contact. It rang several times before going to voice mail.

"Jack, it's Emilie. You have exactly one hour to get to my house. If you are not here in that time, you're fired. I will instruct Rick to process your severance paperwork."

Jess and Charlie watched silently. Emilie calmly pushed the red End Call button and placed her phone down next to her leg on the sofa.

Fifty-two minutes later and Emilie's door opened again. Jack walked in with the air of a man about to be hung, drawn and quartered. Charlie sat close to Emilie. Jess having already left to follow up with Lola.

"Em, darling, I got here as soon as I heard."

"Well, that's bullshit," Charlie huffed.

"I don't believe this involves you, Ms Baxter. Would you mind leaving me with my client?" Jack shot.

Emilie looked at Charlie and nodded. She was more than capable of dealing with this. Plus, Charlie wouldn't go far, a fact that helped Emilie keep her courage. Once Charlie had left the room, Jack snapped his attention to Emilie. "Em, I can sort all of this out. We'll get to the bottom of it."

"Are you telling me this wasn't your doing, Jack?"

"Emilie, how could you think that?"

"You swear to me, Jack. On our friendship, you swear this wasn't you."

"Emilie —" he began.

"Before you answer, please know that I intend to throw a lot of money at this. I will hire whoever I need to in order to trace the source of that video. If you tell me this wasn't you and I find out you lied today. I will come for everything you have, do you understand? This is your chance to tell me the truth. I will listen to you, but only if you're honest with me." Emilie saw Jack's mind work. His cogs turning, trying to figure out the best way to deal with her.

"Okay, look, I sent the video. But only because the show last night was gold, Emilie. You were so relaxed and happy. I just wanted the fans to see that. They adore you. I know you keep telling me you don't want to start a new album, but I wish you would listen to me when I say the time is now. You are at your peak. You are more popular than ever. Every bit of attention we can get only drives up sales, sells tickets, ensures your legacy. I know you've been writing new songs. You are ready for a new album, Em. I know I push too much, but it's for your own good. Don't you see? I only ever do things to help you."

Emilie sat in silence, allowing her brain to process. Did he do it for her own good? Could she really believe that? No, not anymore, not after she'd asked him several times *not* to make her little town tour public knowledge. She'd explained her reasons for wanting to keep it private and he had willingly ignored her in favour of creating lucrative opportunities, ones that she didn't ask for.

Jess was right, this was his M.O. He would do whatever suited him and then worm his way back into Emilie's good graces. And why wouldn't he? Emilie allowed him to do it every damn time. But could she really fire him? Jack had been her manager for… well, forever. They'd travelled this road together and at times he had been a godsend to her. He was a damn good manager, but now? Not so much. If it weren't for the fact that Emilie and Jack were friends, she would have moved on from him a long time ago and Emilie guessed that Jack knew that, too.

Fuck, why couldn't she decide? Because she didn't trust herself, that's why. What would Charlie do? Yes, that's what Emilie needed. She needed to talk to Charlie. "Jack, can you issue a statement to the press? Reiterate that I am not producing a new album yet and that there will be no more concerts. This is your mess, so clean it up."

"On it," Jack chirped. Emilie knew he believed that she'd forgiven him as usual. Jack bounded out of the house with a skip in his step.

"Charlie?" Emilie shouted. Her body lacked the energy needed to scour the massive house looking for her. Seconds later, the rhythmic thumps of Charlie running down the stairs echoed around the silent house.

"Hey, how'd it go?" Charlie asked, parking herself next to Emilie, her arm snaking round her waist. Instantly making Emilie feel better.

"He did it. He gave me the same tired reasons. It was all for me, blah, blah, blah."

"Okay, so what did you say?"

"Nothing. I needed to talk to you."

"Me, why?"

"Because you are my calm, Char. My head is spinning with all this. Jess is right. I would normally let him talk me round. I think I'm scared to fire him. He's been with me forever.

224

If he goes, what then? I have to find someone else, someone I don't know."

"Maybe that's a good thing, Em," Charlie began. "You know the one reason I hated most of the girls in school?" Emilie shook her head. "Because they only ever saw you as the rising star. Jack is the same. I'm not refuting that he has probably been a skilled manager. Together, you have built an empire. But now you're not on the same page and instead of seeing you as his friend, as just Em, he is still seeing you as the star, the one that he can profit from. It's worse because he knows your history. He understands how hard it is for you to trust, and he plays on that."

"What would you do?" Emilie asked, her voice smaller.

"You know what I would do. If this was someone under my employ, he would have been kicked to the curb. I'm all for second chances, but I think you're way beyond that, Em."

"Why do I keep surrounding myself with people like this, Charlie," Emilie sobbed.

"You don't. Those people ingratiate themselves *into* your life. I believe Jack had all the right intentions to begin with, but now, well, now he's out for himself."

Charlie was right, of course she was. The path ahead was finally clear enough for Emilie to decide. The sound of Jack on the phone filtered through the house. He stepped through the door, looking satisfied.

"It's all sorted, Em, the press are clearing out. Now, what do you say to a drink?"

Standing from the sofa, Emilie squared her shoulders. Charlie, standing next to her, gave Emilie that extra support she needed. "Jack, you're fired." She hadn't meant to just blurt it out, but watching the man saunter over to her drinks cabinet like nothing had happened really pissed her off.

"What?" Jack looked as if he'd misheard what she'd said even though it wasn't possible.

"You're fired."

"You can't… Em, come on."

"No, you're not talking me round this time. I warned you, time and time again."

Jack's face flushed, his eyes darted from Emilie to Charlie. "This is you, isn't it?" he raged. Emilie flinched. She shot a look at Charlie, who hadn't batted an eyelid. If anything, she stood taller.

"This is me what?" Charlie asked calmly.

"You! You've come here and wheedled your way in. Turned her against me?" He bellowed.

"Are you hearing yourself, man? Get a grip. You screwed the pooch here, fella, not me."

"You wait until your uncle hears about this, Emilie."

"What has he got to do with it?" Emilie shot. It had been a long, *long* time since her uncle had played a part in her career.

"He knows I'm the best in the business. Call him, you need some sense talked in to you." Jack stood with his hands on his hips.

Alright, if that's what he needed, Emilie would give it to him. "Fine, I'll call him." The line rang three times before her uncle's voice sounded over the phone.

"Em, how are you, love? You enjoying the break? Although I see you're in the news already."

"Hi, Uncle Brandon, it's good to hear your voice." It really was. Emilie cringed at the time she'd allowed to slip by without contacting him. Maybe if she'd been better at that, she wouldn't be where she was right now.

"Brandon, hi," Jack shouted.

"Jack, my boy."

226

"Hi, Uncle Brandon," Charlie chirped, causing Emilie to snicker. "Sorry, I was feeling left out," she whispered to Emilie with a wink.

"Who's that?" Brandon laughed.

"Um, do you remember Charlotte Munroe?"

"Yeah, the name rings a bell… Pickerton, right? Oh, wow, you guys reconnected."

"Yeah, something like that, Brandon," Charlie chuckled. "I go by Charlie now, though. Just for the record, I did *not* sell your niece out to the press, just in case there was any lingering doubt."

"Jesus, I'd forgot all about that. Well, if Emilie is fine with you, then I have no grudge to hold. What's the call for, Em?"

"I've fired Jack," Emilie said matter-of-factly.

"Because Charlie here has been getting into her head," Jack bellowed, his chest puffing out.

"Oh, shut up," Charlie scoffed. "How about you let Emilie tell her uncle why she fired you?"

"Em? What's going on, kid?" Brandon asked, his tone no longer jovial.

Emilie wasted no time telling her uncle about all the times Jack had crossed the line. She saw several times when Jack had clearly wanted to interrupt, but Charlie had held up her hand and glared at him. Finally, Emilie finished speaking.

"Brandon, you must agree that as Emilie's manager, it's my job to push. I have to be the proverbial bull in a china shop to get things done. Look where we are, how successful Emilie is," Jack said.

"I agree with that, Jack," Brandon started. Emilie's breath hitched. Shit, *had* she made a mistake firing him? "But what you've done has gone far beyond that, boy." The use of "boy" rang through the air like a bullet. "After twenty years, Jack, I can't believe what I'm hearing."

227

"Brandon—" Jack stuttered.

"No. Emilie is right to fire you. I just don't understand what has taken her so long. You were an excellent manager, Jack, because you always had Emilie's best interest at heart. When did that change, hmm?"

"That hasn't changed, Brandon. Emilie, you're my chief priority."

"If that were the case, Jack, you would have done as she asked. Instead, you went behind her back. Worse, you leaked to the press. Why?" Brandon demanded.

Jack was almost purple. Emilie was a little worried that he was about to pass out. "Emilie *has* to create another album. I've already signed a deal. If she doesn't, I'm on the hook," he blurted. Emilie's eyes became saucers.

"What do you mean, you've signed a deal? Only I can sign, Jack, you've never had that power."

"I... I forged the documents, okay? You are contracted for at least one new album next year."

"You did what?" Charlie hissed, her hands curled into fists.

"The payout is immense Emilie, it was too good to pass up," Jack rushed.

"Get out," Emilie heard herself say. "Get out now."

Jack looked at Emilie, his eyes scanning her face. "You heard her," Charlie added. Emilie watched as her friend of twenty years slinked out of the house.

What in the world? This was unreal. Jack didn't do these kinds of things. Charlie must have anticipated the questions that were rolling around in her head.

"People change, Em, especially when money is involved," Charlie said, gently kissing her head.

"Em, love, I'm going to catch the next flight out. We have things to take care of. Charlie, look after her until I arrive."

228

"I've got her, Brandon, no worries." And Emilie *did* know Charlie had her. After Jack's revelation, Emilie should be freaking out. She should be panicking, but with Charlie's strong arms holding her as they were now, the anxiety and panic were kept at bay.

* * *

"Here you go, my famous hot chocolate," Charlie smiled, handing Emilie the biggest mug she'd ever seen. Was it hers? She couldn't recall seeing that monstrosity in her cupboard. "I bought the mug the other day, look it's got a moose on it." Emilie had to laugh at Charlie's excitement.

Not sure how she was going to tackle the behemoth mug piled high with whipped cream and chocolate drops, Emilie took her lead from Charlie, who unceremoniously shoved her face into the cream, lapping it up with her tongue. Damn, Emilie wanted to be that whipped cream.

"Stop staring. I'll do this to you later. Drink your hot chocolate before it gets cold." Grinning at the promise of naughty things to come later, Emilie ate as much cream as she could before sipping the drink. She spluttered as the powerful aroma of alcohol hit her nose milliseconds after she'd taken a big gulp.

"Boozy hot chocolate, proven to make everything feel okay," Charlie laughed.

"What booze is in it?"

"Spiced rum. Nice right?" Yeah, it was nice. It was damn strong, too. "You coping with all this?"

"Honestly, I'm not sure. I'm astounded by Jack's conduct. I hope Uncle Brandon can help me get out of the contract. He messaged me to say he was heading straight to the record label offices to straighten it all out."

229

"It's fraudulent. I can't see how they would enforce it. Don't fret, Brandon will get it worked out."

"Then there's the fact I need to find a new manager," Emilie added on.

"Brandon will help with that, too. I wish I could be more use, babe, but this is outside my purview. Now if you need a picture taken of your new manager, I'm your gal," she winked.

"Charlie, you're helping more than you know," Emilie said, her hand finding Charlie's.

"I'll do anything you need, Em, sincerely, just ask. Okay?" Emilie nodded and had to take a moment to stop herself from tearing up. "Maybe you should wait a little before hiring a new manager?"

"Why would I wait?"

"Because I think you need some time to figure out what your future holds, musically, I mean. From what you've said, you're feeling burned out."

"It's true. I love what I do, but I haven't rested properly in years."

"So take the time you need to rest and figure it out. You're Emilie Martin, there will *always* be people lining up to work for you. You don't have to rush this."

Emily sat with Charlie's words. Could she take a step back? Was this the time for her to focus on what she really wanted? Hell, she'd been saying it for so long, but never actually got the chance to do it. What could the future hold for Emilie Martin superstar?

# Chapter 21

Well, what a heap of dramatic bullshit the last few days had been. Charlie was about ready for a holiday. Emilie was holding up remarkably well, she thought. If Charlie had just had to dismiss one of her best friends like that, she'd be arse deep in a bottle of the strong stuff. Not Emilie though, she'd kept her poise. Charlie could see she was hurting, but she was doing her very best to put on a brave face.

Four days had passed since Jack's dismissal. The press had vacated the area pretty sharpish. At least Jack did one thing right. There was the odd fan still lingering about which Charlie expected. The sad part about it all was that she could see how lonely this life had been for Emilie. It hurt Charlie to think of all the times Emilie had dealt with this sort of thing alone.

Charlie had done her very best to give Emilie what she needed. That had ranged from cooking her dinner to lending her a shoulder to cry on. It had also involved lots of sex. Sad Emilie was a horny Emilie. Charlie kind of understood how Sam felt when Anna became a sex machine. Charlie was knackered. Whenever Emilie seemed to have a thought or emotion, she couldn't quite process, she jumped Charlie's bones. Evidently she had a *lot* of feelings and emotions she couldn't get to grips with.

"We're going to need more lube," Charlie muttered to herself as she lay in Emilie's bed. Emilie had fallen asleep half an hour ago after a very lively session that had pushed even Charlie's experiences. The morning was almost over, and Charlie had certainly worked up an appetite. Crawling out of bed, she headed to the kitchen to rustle up some food for them both. Emilie wouldn't wake, Charlie knew that much. As soon as Emilie was spent, she passed out.

Spud lay half on her bed and half off, upside down, with her tongue hanging out. Charlie laughed and scratched her belly. "I'll take you out soon, girl. I know we've been hauled up in here for too long. How about a nice stroll in the woods? As long as you're on bear duty. Deal?" Spud wriggled her back and thumped her tail. That was good enough for Charlie. A deal was struck.

Placing a steaming bowl of pesto pasta on the bedside table, Charlie set about trying to wake Emilie. It wasn't a delicate process. After the third soft poke, Charlie had to get a little rougher. "Waaaakee Uuuuuup," Charlie shouted, laughing when Emilie blinked rapidly.

"Wassup," she mumbled into the pillow.

"Babe, food. We need to eat, and then I'm taking Spud out for a walk."

"No need to shout," Emilie moaned, her eyebrows creasing.

Charlie let out a bark of laughter. "Em, it's nearly impossible to wake you up after sex. I've been at it for ten minutes."

Emilie grinned. "Well, honey, you do such a good job of wearing me out."

"Ditto, now, enough flirting. Get that down your chops. Do you want to come for a walk after?"

"I'm going to spend some time in the music room, if you don't mind."

"Go forth and make beautiful music, babe," Charlie said between forkfuls of pasta.

They ate in silence, but they always touched in one way or another. Charlie liked this routine they'd fallen into. Okay, not so much the constant acrobatic sex — honestly, she could do with a day off — but the rest of it was just what she always wanted. They had this comfortable ease about them. After their talk and the whole "Jack being a twat" debacle, they'd slipped into domestic bliss. Emilie often took herself to her music room to write. Charlie would grab her camera and snap pictures of Emilie in her element. Overall, she'd gotten a great selection of photos for Emilie to display around the house.

"Alright, I'm going to shower and take Lady Muck out. We'll only be about half an hour." Since Charlie's foray into the wilds of Canada with Jess, her nervousness had reduced dramatically. She wasn't stupid enough to discount the threat of death by bear entirely, but she wasn't jumping out of her skin as soon as she heard a noise.

The shower helped soothe her aching body a little. Donning her warmest clothes, she prepared herself for the brisk outdoor adventure she was about to take with her special girl. "Come on you, let's go chase some squirrels. Spud shot to her feet as soon as the *S* word had been spoken. Charlie giggled as Spud spun in circles, waiting for Charlie to open the door.

There was still plenty of snow on the ground. Emilie had paid to have certain trails salted. That way, Charlie could go out by herself and not get lost. It seemed a hundred years ago since Charlie was stomping around London, lost in the busy city surrounded by thousands of strangers. When she first came to Canada, she'd missed the hustle and bustle of the city, but now she couldn't think of anything she'd hate more. The silence here was wonderful. It wasn't creepy. There was always some sort of noise, like a bird or a squirrel. Maybe it was the silence that accompanied vast amounts of snow. Everything felt more peaceful in the snow.

Spud zoomed around Charlie, unable to contain her delight at being unleashed in her favourite playground. Charlie pulled out her phone. She had a little signal, but it wasn't great. It had been a few days since she'd spoken to Sam and she was eager to catch up. Charlie didn't enjoy talking to Sam about everything that had happened when Emilie was around. She felt as if she were gossiping, but that wasn't the case. Sam, Anna, Kim and Hélène were all genuinely worried about both of them.

"Hey, Sam, can you hear me?" she asked through her phone.

"Just about, you okay?" Sam replied. She sounded like she was in a tunnel.

"All good, mate. Just a quick check in. I'm walking Spud."

"No Em?"

"Nah, she's writing. Spud and myself were going a little stir crazy so we're just hiking one of the small trails."

"Look at you talking about 'hiking trails.' Where has my scared city dweller gone?" Sam laughed.

"She's still in here, just not as loud," Charlie grinned.

"Any updates?" Sam asked. Charlie knew that was code for *Have you had any crazy threats* which thankfully was a no. Charlie guessed that once the person *cough Lydia* realised the threats hadn't scared Charlie aways, they'd tucked tail and left.

"No, all quiet on the western front."

"Isn't Quebec on the east side?"

"Well, yeah, but I'm west of you!" Charlie tutted.

"Anyway, now the geography lesson is over. What's your plan? Have you got a clue when you'll be back?"

234

"Nope, I'll talk to Em about her plans. She's still taking time off. I thought maybe we could head back to her cottage in Pickerton. Gives me a chance to catch up on everything without us being thousands of miles apart."

"Have you thought about that long-term, mate? Surely, at some point, Em's going to get back out on tour or whatever."

Charlie had considered this. They hadn't spoken about it because Emilie was still dealing with everything else. In Charlie's mind, there was no reason they couldn't figure something out. Sure, Emilie could go on tour, but Charlie also travelled a fair bit for work, too. They would have to accommodate each other and compromise. They could do that, though. Hell, they'd planned to do that at seventeen, surely they were more than capable now in their thirties.

"We have time, Sammy. I know that whatever happens, I'm with her. We haven't had the 'big talk', I don't think we need it. She's my Emilie and I'm her Charlie —"

"She's my Emilie," a voice rang out. Charlie swung round to see who had spoken, but she was met with something hard crunching into the side of her head. Her eyes clouded. Another hit to her back brought her to her knees. The edge of her vision was turning black. Everything around her tilted on its axis. It was the second blow to her head that finally took her down. Desperately Charlie tried to move. She willed her legs to work. Why couldn't she get up?

The weight of another body crushed her to the snowy forest floor. "She is mine." The voice growled. Charlie wanted to move her head. She wanted to look into the eyes of that cold and vicious voice. She wanted to fight back, but it was impossible. Another blow hit her body. *Oh god, I'm going to die.* As the world faded, Charlie heard Spud in the distance. She felt the extra weight leave her broken body. And then everything went dark.

* * *

"Charlie, Charlie, can you hear me?" Who was that? The voice sounded so far away. "Charlie, it's okay, paramedics are coming. Oh, baby, what happened?"

The voice faded and Charlie heard nothing.

*What is that fucking noise? Can anyone else hear the incessant beeping?*

Charlie's head was pounding. Everything was still dark, but she could hear something. What was it? She couldn't tell. Where was she? The potent smell of cleaning product assaulted her nose. Why couldn't she see? *Are my eyes shut?*

*Beep Beep Beep Beep.*

*There it s again, the fucking beeping. Can someone shut it off? Hello?*

Something wasn't right. Charlie could sense something bad had happened, but what? Fuck, why couldn't she remember?

Everything went quiet again, everything faded into nothing.

"Charlie, baby, can you open your eyes now, please? Baby, please," the voice pleaded. Charlie heard the desperation. *I know that voice. Emilie, my Emilie. I'm alright Em, I'm here.* "Why isn't she waking up? It's been two days, she should be awake," Emilie's voices sobbed.

"She'll wake up," a second voice replied confidently. *Sam, that's Sam's voice. What is she doing here? I am awake, guys. Aren't I?*

"Oh god, I can't lose her, Sam, not now, not after just getting her back."

"Charlie is strong. She's a fighter, you know that. The doctor sai…" *What? The doctors said… what? Why can't I hear? Why am I so tired?*

236

*Beep, beep, beep.*

*I am going to murder someone if they don't turn that fucking beeping off!!*

"Charlie, did you speak? Baby, can you open your eyes?"

"Mmm." *That was a sentence, right? Come on, Charlie, for Christ's sake!*

"Sam, Sam, I think she's waking up." Charlie heard the sound of a chair scuffing the floor. *Open your goddamn eyes, Charlie.* Summoning all her energy, Charlie cracked open one eye. The light from above her instantly made her slam it shut again.

"Em, turn the light off. It's too much. Come on, Char, open those panty dropping eyes you've got." Charlie felt herself laugh. Her body moved slightly and fuck did it hurt?

"Did she just laugh?" Emilie whispered.

"I knew we would have to resort to stroking her ego to get her to wake up. Jeez Charlie, dramatic much." Charlie opened her eye again. The light was off, but it was still daytime because the sun shone through the window. Two fuzzy figures stood on either side of her.

"There she is," Emilie sobbed. Charlie felt Emilie's lips touch her cheek. She desperately wanted to take Emilie's face in her hands, but she couldn't lift her arms. *Oh god, am I paralysed?*

"I'll go grab the nurse," Sam said, running out the door. Finally, Charlie could focus on the beautiful face leaning over her.

"Is… is…"

"Shhh, don't talk just yet, love. Wait for the nurse to come, okay?" Charlie was growing frustrated that her body wouldn't do as she wanted.

A noise drew her attention to the door Sam had just left through. A short redhead bounced towards her with a huge smile. "Ah, Ms Baxter, good to have you back. You had us worried for a second."

Why had they been worried about her? Charlie's confusion must have been written on her face. "Do you know where you are, Charlie?" the nurse asked. Charlie let her eyes roam. *A hospital maybe? Is that where I am?*

"Can you speak, Charlie?"

"The… hospital?" she rasped out. Bloody hell her throat was sore.

"Good job," the perky nurse said. "You're in hospital in Quebec City. Do you know what month it is?"

"December," she said, her voice feeling stronger now.

"That's right, perfect. Well done. I'm going to ask the doctor to come in, okay?"

"What happened?" No matter how hard she searched her mind, there was only a blank space. Something had happened, she knew that, but she just couldn't get it to materialise in her memories.

"You were found in the woods, Charlie." Em whispered, her voice weak and small.

"Bear, was I attacked by a bear?" Charlie's eyes whipped to Sam, who started chuckling.

"I told you she'd say that as soon as you mentioned the woods." Sam winked at Charlie, and it made her feel better. Emilie was looking at her with fear pouring out of her eyes.

"Em," Charlie rasped. Christ, what did a girl have to do to get some water around here?

"Drink this sweetie, it'll help." *Oh, thanks nurse lady.* "Better?"

Charlie nodded, but her attention was solely on Emilie. "Emilie, were you hurt?"

238

"Oh, baby, I wasn't with you," she cried, tears falling rapidly down her face.

"Mate, you were attacked in the woods. Do you remember? We were on the phone and then suddenly there was a bunch of noise and I heard you—"

Whatever Sam was about to say, she stopped abruptly, her hand shot to her mouth as she gasped and started crying. Shit, everyone was crying.

"Sam, what happened?"

"You were attacked," Emilie answered. Sam was still silently crying.

"Attacked? By who?" *A voice, I heard a voice.* Agh, why couldn't she remember?

"We don't know, honey. Spud came running to the house acting crazy. I've never seen her like that. I followed her straight to you. When I saw you lying there, oh god, Charlie, there was so much blood, I thought you were dead."

Charlie shouted inside her head for her hand to move. Finally, her stubborn body listened. Shakily, she moved to take Emilie's hand that rested on the bed. "I'm okay, Em, I'm here." Emilie dropped to Charlie's chest and cried harder.

"I'll get the doctor," the nurse repeated. Sam stopped crying and dropped a kiss on her head, which was pounding like a motherfucker.

"Where's Anna?" Charlie asked.

"She's with Kim and Hélène at home. She couldn't fly, mate, she's been feeling bad."

"Okay. She's okay, right?"

"How are you asking about Anna when you're laid up in a hospital bed?" Sam laughed. "Anna's fine. Worried about you, but fine."

A tall, grey haired man swooped in like a tornado. "Charlie, good to see you awake. Let's do some tests and make

239

sure everything is okay with the old bean counter." Plucking a white pen out of his jacket, Dr Lanky began shining it in her eyes, asking her to follow his finger.

"Things look good. Your CT is clear now. You had some swelling that concerned us, but I think we're safe. You're going to have a headache for a while and your face will be sore, but your contusions are healing nicely. They just need a bit of time. The most painful part will be your ribs. Three of them cracked, I'm afraid. Honestly, though, Charlie, you were one lucky woman."

"I don't fucking feel lucky," Charlie growled. Her head was really hurting and her face felt swollen.

"Yeah, she's definitely okay, doctor. Her language skills are back to normal," Sam laughed. Emilie finally grinned.

"I've called Buddy, my police friend. He'll come and see you when you're feeling a little better," Emilie said, kissing her head.

"I can't remember anything," Charlie stuttered, looking at the doctor.

"It's normal after the head injury you suffered. It will take some time, but I'm confident you'll get your memories back. I can't say they will return in full, but hopefully enough for you to piece together what happened. I'll come back and check on you later. I expect you to be here for a few days, but then you can be released into the care of your friends."

"Girlfriend," Charlie stated, "Emilie's my girlfriend."

"Even better," the doctor winked.

"I'm going to go call Anna," Sam said, giving Charlie another kiss on the head.

"How do you feel?" Emilie asked quietly.

"My head hurts and my face feels big. Do I look bad?"

"You're gorgeous," Emilie said a little too fast.

240

Charlie grinned, but it hurt. "You're a shitty liar, honey. Can you show me? I want to see what I look like."

"Char, I'm not sure that's a good idea," Emilie said, looking uncomfortable.

"Please, baby," Charlie whined.

"Oh, for god's sake, how can you still pull your puppy dog eyes when you're all beat up?"

"It's a gift. Come on, show me."

Emilie walked over to a door in the corner of the room. Pulling it open, she disappeared into what Charlie presumed was a bathroom. A second later Emile appeared with a square mirror. "Here," she said, handing it over reluctantly. Slowly Charlie placed the mirror in front of her face.

"Jesus," she gasped. "I look like I've gone ten rounds with Mike Tyson."

"It won't take long to heal, baby."

"Will there be scars?" Charlie added. She could see a large area above her right eye that had been stitched and bandaged. Her entire face was a mix of purple, black bruises.

"Don't you worry about that, okay? Just concentrate on healing."

Charlie stared at her reflection a little longer. The eyes looking back at her were the same, but the face—the face in the mirror—was a stranger. Battered and bruised.

# Chapter 22

Emilie clenched her teeth together, determined not to let the latest wave of nausea get to her. It had been the same thing every day since she found Charlie lying in the woods covered in blood. No matter what Emilie did, she couldn't dispel the image from her mind.

Four days had passed since Spud had alerted Emilie to there being a problem. At first she thought her dog might have just been overzealous, too excited, but then she saw something in Spud's eyes. Emilie knew her dog and in that moment, as Spud barked, darting back and forth, Emilie knew something was very wrong.

It only took them a few minutes to reach the spot where Charlie lay lifeless. Thinking back to it, Emilie could feel her chest tighten as if it were happening in real time.

"Hey, hey, Emilie, breathe, come on," Sam said, kneeling in front of her. Charlie had woken up two days ago, but still Emilie couldn't find solace in that, not when she had a permanent horror film playing on repeat in her head. As soon as Charlie fell back to sleep, Emilie would rush out of the room to cry and hyperventilate.

"I... I..." Emilie gasped.

"Emilie, you're having a panic attack. You need to concentrate on your breathing."

It felt like hours were passing as she struggled for breath. What would she have done if Charlie had died? How could she have ever lived with herself? It was her fault, her crazy life that had put Charlie in the crosshairs.

"Emilie, Emilie, focus on my voice," Sam said gently. Emilie screwed her eyes shut, trying desperately to drown out her inner voice. *Focus on Sam and breathe.*

"I'm… I'm okay," she spluttered after inhaling deeply.

"I'm going to get the doctor," Sam stated. Emilie reached out to stop her, but Sam had already gone. She didn't need a doctor. Charlie needed the attention, not her.

"Emilie?" Dr Acton said calmly.

"I'm okay," she repeated.

"Let's pop into an exam room and I'll check you out."

"I said I'm fine," Emilie shot.

"I'm sure you are, but I can't just take your word for it. Please, come with me." Not having the energy to fight, Emilie followed the doctor into the exam room.

"Pop yourself on the bed." Following orders, Emilie sat as Dr Acton performed basic tests. "How are you feeling now?"

"Better, I just…" Emilie couldn't explain the crushing sense of dread she'd felt for the past ninety-six hours.

"I think you've had a panic attack. Have you suffered with them before?"

"Yes, when I was younger, but it's been years since I had one."

"Okay, I'd like to prescribe you something to help settle your anxiety. I'm also going to recommend you talk to a psychologist. You've experienced some trauma and your body is reacting."

"Charlie suffered the trauma," Emilie barked. No way was she going to play the victim when Charlie lay battered and bruised.

"Finding Charlie in that state will have left a mark on you, Emilie. Please, just think about it." Emilie closed her eyes and steadied her breath. Her chest was no longer feeling tight.

"When can I take her home?"

"Emilie—"

"I heard you. I'll look into a therapist. Charlie is the important one here, doctor. Please, when can I take her home?"

Understanding that pushing the subject further would be useless, Dr Acton sighed but answered. "I want to do one more scan this evening. If everything is still clear, I will allow her to leave tomorrow afternoon."

"You're sure? She doesn't need more time? She's only been awake for forty-eight hours."

"I'm sure. She's out of immediate danger, Emilie. A second scan isn't necessarily needed, but I'm being extra cautious. Honestly, she will probably heal better at home."

Emilie nodded, a seed of anxiety germinated in her stomach. Home, that should have been reassuring, but it wasn't. It was at *home* that Charlie was attacked. How could they stay there? Hell, Emilie hadn't been back there since. The thought of someone lurking in the woods was too much. Thank god Jess took Spud to her place.

"Hey, you doing better?" Sam asked when Emilie stepped back into Charlie's room. Charlie was out for the count again. Emilie took a second to look at her girlfriend. The bruises on her face were striking. It took all Emilie's strength not to break down again.

"I'm okay. The doctor wants me to see someone."

"Like a therapist?" Sam asks.

"Yeah."

"Will you?" Sam asked, looking at Emilie like she knew exactly what Emilie was planning, which was nothing. There was no way Emilie was going to waste time on herself when it was Charlie that needed looking after.

"Maybe," Emilie muttered, sitting herself down in the chair next to Charlie's bed.

"She'll make you go, Em, you know that." Sam stated matter-of-factly.

"Charlie doesn't need to worry about that. She needs to concentrate on healing."

"How do you think she's going to do that knowing you're suffering, too?"

"She doesn't need to know," Emilie snapped.

"What don't I need to know?" Charlie said sleepily.

"Nothing, honey," Emilie replied, smiling.

"The doc wants Emilie to see a therapist. She's started having panic attacks," Sam said, looking at Charlie. Balling her fist, Emilie shot Sam a death glare. "Get pissy all you want, Emilie, you're part of this family now, and that means you get friends that overstep when needed," Sam said, raising her eyebrow daring Emilie to argue.

"Sam, can you give us a minute?" Charlie asked, scooting herself into a sitting position. Sam nodded, leaned over, and kissed Charlie on the forehead. She then reached over and squeezed Emilie's shoulder.

"Babe—" Emilie began, but snapped her mouth closed when Charlie held up a hand.

"Emilie, I know you. I know what's zipping around that beautiful brain of yours and I'm telling you right now to stop. What happened is not your fault. The person who did this is at fault. I don't remember much, but I do remember the state you were in when I woke up. You were terrified." Emilie couldn't exactly argue. "If the doctor wants you to talk to someone, I want that, too. Don't you think I'll be chatting to someone after this? We can't move on if you're crippled with fear, babe."

245

"I'm not hurt though," Emilie whined.

"Not physically. Em, if this was the other way round, what would you be telling me to do?"

"That's not fair," Emilie said, pouting. Why did Charlie have to be so bloody reasonable?

Laughing and then wincing, Charlie grabbed Emilie's hand, bringing it to her mouth. "Em, please listen to Dr Lanky."

"Dr Lanky?" Emilie laughed.

"I don't actually know his name, just that he is freakishly tall, so yeah, Dr. Lanky," Charlie grinned. Even bashed up, that grin slayed Emilie.

"Alright, I'll listen to Dr *Acton*. He said I can take you home tomorrow if your scan is clear."

"Oh, thank fuck for that. I need a comfy bed with a fifty-inch TV," Charlie laughed. Emilie wished she could share Charlie's relief. Her phone buzzed in her pocket.

"It's Buddy. I've been waiting for him to call."

"Answer it then," Charlie said, rolling her eyes. Emilie didn't realise she was staring at the phone, motionless. Snapping herself out of her comatose state, she slid her finger across to answer.

"Hey, Bud."

"Hey, Em, any chance Charlie is ready for a visit? We need to take her statement."

"Hang on, I'll ask." Charlie was already nodding her head.

"I'm ready," she said confidently. To Emilie's knowledge, Charlie hadn't regained any memories yet.

"Yeah, swing by. She's due for release tomorrow."

"Okay, I'll be there in twenty. Do you need anything?"

"No, I think we're fi—"

"Decent coffee and a donut please," Charlie shouted. Buddy laughed down the phone before ending the call.

"Okay, he'll be here soon."

"Em, kiss me, please. You've been in the room for over thirty seconds and you haven't kissed me. I'm a little offended, if I'm being honest."

"Well, we wouldn't want that," Emilie scoffed playfully. No matter how shitty Emilie felt, the moment her lips met Charlie's, everything righted itself, even if it was temporary. Charlie soothed her raging emotions.

"Can I come back in now, without Emilie throwing stuff at me?" Sam laughed, peeking her head round the door.

"Yes, come in," Emilie smiled. It was strange having friends like Sam, Kim, Anna, and Hélène. These people really treated each other like family, and now they considered Emilie to be a part of that.

They sat chatting about everything and nothing, waiting for Buddy to arrive. Emilie sat praying for days that he would catch whoever did this to Charlie quickly, but so far, they had no leads. There was a light rap on the door as Buddy stepped into the room.

Buddy was in his early fifties. He was bald and built like a house. Nobody ever suspected him of being a detective, gym rat maybe, but not a police officer. His muscles bulged and his smile lit up any room he was in. Emilie had instantly felt safe with him when she'd gone through her crazy fan experience. Buddy looked tough, but when he spoke, he was caring, soft and steady. Everything a person needed when looking for comfort.

"Hey, everyone, I'm Buddy," He said, presenting his hand to Charlie, who shook it carefully. Emilie hated seeing the pain on her face as she tried to move.

"Buddy, this is Charlie and her best friend, Sam."

"Pleasure," Buddy said, tipping his head to Sam. "Charlie, do you feel able to chat?"

"Sure, but I really can't remember anything."

247

"That's okay. I just need to hear what you *can* remember."

Emilie hated having to go through the story again. Charlie had told her what she remembered when she first woke up, then she retold the story to Sam and the doctors. Each time, Emilie wanted to vomit. Sucking in a deep breath, Emilie steeled herself as Charlie recounted what she could.

"Okay, thanks for that, Charlie. I'll add your statement to the file. We recovered a bloody tree branch a few hundred metres away. We have your DNA from the clothes you were wearing. The test confirmed the blood on the branch is yours, Charlie."

"What does that mean? I mean, how does it help?" Emilie asked.

"To me, it signifies that the assailant wasn't planning the attack, it wasn't premeditated."

"Why do you say that?" Sam asked.

"I believe the attacker was watching Charlie, probably you too, Emilie. I think they overheard your conversation with Sam and snapped. I think they used what was available to them. If it was premeditated, I would have expected the weapon to have been something different. A baseball bat, gun even."

Emilie gasped at the thought of someone waiting for Charlie with a gun. "So now what?" Emilie cried. Tears falling down her face again.

"Babe, hey calm down," Charlie said soothingly.

"I'm sorry, Char, I'm so sorry," Emilie sobbed.

"Baby, please, it's not your fault."

"Charlie's right," Buddy added. "Emilie, it's only the fault of the person who attacked Charlie. I will find them. I can't promise it will be tomorrow, but I will get them."

"Where do we go from here?" Sam asked.

"We will have protection officers camped around Emilie's property. We still have a team scouring the area where the attack happened. I'm confident that the perpetrator isn't a professional. It's likely they left something behind and I plan to find it. We will keep you updated as much as possible."

"What about Lydia? You looked into her, right?" Emilie asked. Her sobbing was now a small whimper.

"I did. There isn't anything on the surface that's pointing to her. I have someone monitoring her, though."

"What do you mean? She's back in the UK, isn't she?" Emilie asked.

"No, she's still in Canada. She was scheduled to leave the day after the dinner party, but she never made her flight. I tracked her to Quebec City."

"Jess never said anything," Emilie commented.

"Maybe she doesn't know," Charlie added.

"Either way, so far, she hasn't left the city. She definitely wasn't in this area at the time of the attack, so I'm ruling her out as a suspect for that. I'm not discounting the notes," Buddy said quickly before Charlie or Emilie could interject.

"Thanks, Buddy." Emilie gave him a sincere smile. She knew he would do everything in his power to catch the bastard that did this.

"I'll call soon." With that, Buddy bid them farewell and left. The room was silent for a few minutes.

"Well, that was fun," Charlie chuckled.

"How are you laughing at any of this," Emilie grumbled.

"What else can I do, Em? I'm not going to lay here being scared. That gives power to the person who did this. Fuck that!"

"I'll call Anna and let her know I'm staying for a bit."

"No, you won't. Anna needs you home," Charlie shot.

"I think she'll understand," Sam joked.

"No, Sam, look, I'm doing fine. Em will look after me and I'll be happier knowing you are at home looking after your wife and baby. I promise to let you know what's going on."

249

"I don't like it," Sam moaned.

"Tough tits, Sammy, I'm the victim. You have to do what I say," Charlie grinned.

"You're an arsehole," Sam laughed.

"True, but I still want you to go home." Sam seemed to accept Charlie's demand, albeit reluctantly.

"I'll go book a flight and pack. You sure, Char?"

"Positive. Please, go home and give Anna and baby Charlie a kiss from me."

"Ha, mini Charlie, in your dreams, mate," Sam laughed.

"I had to try," Charlie smirked.

"I don't know how you two are acting so fucking normal," Emilie shouted. What the fuck was wrong with them? Couldn't they see how messed up the situation was?

Emilie was panting hard, her nerves were at breaking point again. She watched Charlie give Sam a subtle nod. Without a word, Sam left. "Talk to me, Em."

"Charlie, there is a crazy person out there who almost beat you to death, and you're acting like it's no big deal. It's a big fucking deal, Charlie. How can I take you back to the place it happened? It's not safe."

"Then let's go somewhere else. I don't need any specialised treatment, just rest and relaxation. We can do that from a hotel room."

"Hotels are too public. No, I need to get you away from everyone. Yes, I know where we can go." Emilie rambled. She was speaking to herself more than Charlie. A plan formulated in her mind. There was one place she could go that no one would find them. "Okay, it's okay. I have a plan. I'm going to go back to the house and pack. Lola will be outside your door the entire time."

"Em, can you just take a beat, you're kind of worrying me."

"Why? I'm okay. I just need to get you safe."

"Alright, but you're kind of acting manic. Could you just sit and calm yourself for a second?" That's when Emilie realised she'd left her chair by Charlie's side and was pacing as she planned. "When was the last time you slept?" Charlie asked.

Emilie had avoided closing her eyes as much as possible. Every time she tried to sleep, she was taken straight back to the forest and Charlie's body. "Um, I'm fine. I had a nap not too long ago."

"Bullshit, get in here," Charlie said, scooting over to the side.

"I'm not getting in bed with you, you need to rest," Emilie argued.

"Emilie Martin, so help me. Get your gorgeous arse in this bed now," Charlie demanded. A little perturbed by Charlie's tone and a little turned on if she were honest, Emilie tucked herself into Charlie's uninjured side. "Close your eyes and listen to my breathing," Charlie cooed. Was this woman a magician? Before Emilie could protest, her eyes shut against her will.

* * *

"Hello, sunshine," Charlie chirped, kissing Emilie on the side of the head. Emilie's vision was blurry with sleep. It took her a second to get her bearings. Charlie's arm pulled her tight, and that's when she remembered that she'd climbed into bed with her.

"What time is it?" Emilie bolted up from where she was nestled.

"Relax, you've been asleep for a few hours. You needed it, Em."

"No, I should have been organising," Emilie argued.

Charlie rolled her eyes. "I called Lola in and asked her to get some stuff for us. I didn't tell her why and she didn't ask. Apparently the house is swarming with police. Anyway, she has our bags ready for when I'm released." Emilie sighed. If she were honest, she felt a thousand times better after catching up on some sleep. Safe in Charlie's arms, she hadn't had her usual nightmare.

"Okay, how are you feeling?"

"Sore but okay. Did you see they shaved the back of my head?"

"Yeah, I was going to tell you but..."

"Ha, you were scared I was going to flip my lid. Everyone thinks I'm precious about my hair. I don't know why," Charlie commented.

"Because it's like the most gorgeous hair in the world and you've been growing it for your whole life."

"Well, I'm going to have to have it styled now. I can't go having a weird shaved patch on the back of my head."

"You need to wait until the cut is healed."

"Ooh, I can get an undercut," Charlie smiled.

"Yeah, that would be hot."

"How far up is the cut?" Charlie asked, sitting forward slightly so Emilie could look.

"Not too far up. You could have the rest of your neck shaved and that would work."

"I'll do neck and sides, but not too far up. I think I'll have a few inches off the top, but not loads."

Emilie was finding the conversation bizarre. Charlie really didn't look upset or scared, not for someone who'd been attacked by a raving lunatic, anyway. How was she this chill?

"You will be gorgeous." Emilie leaned in and kissed her head. If Charlie needed her to be calm, she'd try her level best.

# Chapter 23

"Freedom!" Charlie belted out the moment Emilie wheeled her through the automatic doors leading to the hospital staff parking garage.

"Shhh, for god's sake, we're trying to keep a low profile, Char," Emilie huffed. Charlie giggled because she enjoyed Emilie getting a little fiery. It was hot. Plus, nothing could dampen her good mood, not when she was finally busting out of the hospital. Okay, not busting out, she'd been released properly.

"Em, honey, cheer up, would you? I finally get to sleep in a comfortable bed with you beside me. No nurses waking me up at the arse crack of dawn to prod and poke me. We can have sex, baby, sex!! I've missed it so much."

"Charlie," Emilie hissed as they passed two nurses who grinned at Charlie's statement.

"I'm just excited," Charlie said, desperately trying not to laugh at Emilie's bright red face.

"Great, now the whole hospital will know what we get up to."

"Em, I'm sure people are aware you have sex. You're a superstar, not a nun."

"I don't go round airing my laundry for all to see, Charlie," Emilie huffed again.

"Alright, alright, don't get your knickers in a twist. I shall refrain from discussing our excellent and adventurous sex life in front of anyone." Charlie couldn't hold in her laughter any longer. Emilie slapped her hand over Charlie's mouth, trying to shut her up, but it was too late. Another hospital employee had overheard her last statement.

"Charliieee!"

"Sorry, babe."

"Ugh, let's get you into the car. I want to be on the road ASAP. We have a few hours to drive."

Emilie had been secretive with Charlie regarding where they were going to stay. Once Charlie had seen how upset and frantic Emilie was at the prospect of going back to the cabin, there was no question that they needed to get away for a while.

"Are you ready to tell me where we're going yet?"

"Nope, not until we're on the move. I have asked Lola to follow us for a bit, to make sure no one is pursuing us."

"Do you really think that's going to happen?"

"I never thought something like *this* would happen, but look at you. I know you think I'm being a little nuts right now, but I'd rather take precautions, Char." Charlie couldn't fault her, hell, if this had happened to Emilie, Charlie would have whisked her away to the most remote area on the planet until whoever did it was caught.

"Alright, I'll stop asking. Just a warning, I might be a pretty shit passenger. The meds knock me right out and they gave me a dose before leaving. I'll probably fall asleep on the journey." The pain medication was fantastic, much better than what was prescribed in the UK. Emilie wasn't happy about it. She'd already started concocting a plan to wean her off of it. Something about opioids and addiction.

"That's fine. You need to rest."

254

Charlie opened her eyes some time later. She had no clue as to the time or how long they'd been on the road. Soft music played through the car's speakers. Charlie heard Emilie singing to herself and that pulled a smile.

"Hey, you're awake, how you feeling, honey?"

"Stiff," Charlie replied. Her head wounds were far less painful than her cracked ribs. The doctor had told her they would be the hardest part of her recovery.

"Do you want me to pull over so you can stretch it out?"

Charlie peered through the car window. There wasn't a building in sight, only pine trees as far as the eye could see. "Where are we?"

"About half an hour away from our destination," Emilie chirped. Getting away had done wonders for Emilie's mood, Charlie could see the weight of her anxiety lift with every passing mile.

"Can you tell me where we're going now?"

"Yes, I got the all clear from Lola. No one is following us. So I have a house, and I do mean a house. It's a regular size, nothing fancy. I inherited it off of a friend when I was twenty. No one knows about it. Well, Buddy does, but that's only because I used this place when I was having problems with that fan. Anyway, it's completely off the radar. I kept it that way for a reason."

"You have a secret house?"

"Yes. I don't use it often, but when I need a place to disappear, I go there."

"And where is there?"

"Tadoussac. It's a famous town known for whale watching. You're going to love it, although we're too late into the winter to see whales, but the town itself is awesome."

"If it's famous, how can we be there without you being recognised?"

"Costumes, honey. We're going to play dress up." Charlie's clit pulsed. It wasn't the right time to be getting horny, but hell, the thought of Emilie dressed up was hot. "Get your head out of the gutter. I can see you getting turned on from over here." Emilie laughed.

"Hey, you mentioned dress up," Charlie mumbled.

"I promise, the costumes are not in the least bit sexy, I'm afraid. I have a couple of great wigs. I use coloured contacts and bulk out my clothing a bit."

"Do I need to dress up?"

"No, babe, you're fine. We've been pretty lucky in that the press hasn't got wind of the attack, well, for now. If that happens, we may need to be a little more careful when out in public."

"To be honest, Em, I think I could do with a few days hidden away. My face is enough to give the local kids nightmares so until I look semi-me again, can we just hunker down with movies?"

"You got it, honey. Whatever you need, okay? I've told Buddy where we will be, just in case."

Charlie nodded. "So, who was the friend that left you a house?"

"It was actually my childhood neighbour. I was really close to her. She was like another grandma. Elsie was her name. She didn't have her own kids. She also didn't like the way my parents treated me. They never found out that Elsie left me everything in her will, thank god. This house was her summer vacation place."

"Well, thank you Elsie. I'm glad you had someone other than your uncle trying to help you."

* * *

256

The house they pulled up to wasn't what Charlie was expecting. Emilie had said it was just a regular house, but Charlie couldn't help but think that maybe Emilie's idea of regular was probably far beyond other people's idea of regular. Charlie was wrong. The house was a small white one-story. A small porch wrapped around the entire building. The location of the house was residential, but the building was set back from the road. It looked in good shape. The outside could have benefited from a fresh coat of paint though.

As they got out of the car, Charlie inhaled as deeply as her cracked ribs would allow. The fresh air filled her from head to toe. "Wow, Em, this is really cute."

"It only has one bedroom, but I think we'll survive," she grinned. "It isn't flashy. Everything inside is original. I updated the plumbing and electricity but I haven't got round to doing anything else. Actually, I feel weird about changing it. Everything inside reminds me of Elsie."

"That's really nice, Em. Keep it as you want. You don't have to change anything at all. As long as it has a shower and a TV, I'm happy."

Charlie hobbled to the front door as Emilie grabbed their bags. The smell of cinnamon smacked Charlie in the face as soon as the door opened. "Why does it smell like a McDonald's apple pie in here?" Charlie chuckled.

"Elsie had a thing for candles. Seriously, I could open a shop with the amount she had stored in her closet."

"It's making me hungry," Charlie laughed. They stepped into the house, and Charlie took a second to look around. It was clear that an older woman had lived there. Most of the furniture looked antique.

"So, what do you think?"

"It's cozy. A great place to recuperate."

"Speaking of, let's get you settled on the couch. I'm afraid your enthusiasm over reclaiming our sex life is a little premature, Char. Those ribs are going to take time."

"I can be on the bottom," Charlie argued. Days without touching Emilie were proving to be more painful than her injuries.

"Settle down, tiger. All in good time. I promise we'll have a night of passion as soon as you're ready."

"I am ready," Charlie sulked.

"Charlie, stop pouting, you baby. Listen, you be a good patient, do as you're told, and I promise I will do whatever you want in bed when the time comes."

"Okay," Charlie shot, her face breaking out into a grin.

In reality, there was no way Charlie could partake in a night of passion. Her body ached from face to feet. Every time she moved an inch in the wrong direction, her ribs screamed at her. Would they really have to wait weeks to touch each other again? Charlie rolled her eyes at her own misery.

The next few days passed with Charlie swimming in and out of consciousness. When she woke up from her frequent naps, Emilie was always close by, either reading, writing, or listening to music through her headphones. After nearly two weeks of them hiding in the little house, Charlie was finally feeling like herself again. She was still stiff after waking up and she had to be careful with her movements, but otherwise she could get up and walk about a lot easier.

Standing in front of the bathroom mirror, she surveyed her face. The bruising had almost disappeared. Feeling around the back of her neck, she noted the cut was scabbed over. It no longer hurt.

There had been no significant breakthroughs in the case, which wasn't a surprise. The only thing Buddy had to go on was a blood-soaked tree branch and a set of footprints they had

258

found close by. Buddy thought the prints were too small to be a man, which, in Charlie's eyes, gave credibility to her theory that Lydia was behind it all.

"Hey, how about a little walk down to the bay?" Emilie asked, sitting down on the couch with a cup of tea and a biscuit. Charlie smiled. She loved that Emilie was a tea monster. Charlie also loved that Emilie knew how to pair her biscuits with her tea. Not everyone understood the delicate relationship between biscuit type and tea.

When they were in school, Charlie had had to have a lengthy discussion with an American student who was dipping her Hob Nob into a cup of green tea. Emilie had laughed her ass off as Charlie tried to explain why pairing that biscuit and tea was an aberration. Thankfully, Charlie had never had to have that kind of talk with Emilie. Their relationship was safe.

"Sounds like a plan. I could do with seeing the outside world again. Has anything changed? Are robots the superior race yet?"

"You dork, it's been two weeks and you've been out in the garden."

"Wow, the garden. I need to see other people, see the fjord or whatever it's called. Ooh, have a beer in the local microbrewery."

"How the hell do you know about that?" Emilie laughed.

"Well, my darling, in between naps and TV binging, I have used Mr Google to research the area. I'm a bit gutted that we won't see any whales, but I'll get over it. The surrounding area looks awesome. When I'm one hundred percent better, we can walk the trails."

"Colour me impressed, Charlie Baxter. You've gone from screaming about bears to planning hiking trips in just a few weeks."

"What can I say? I'm an onion."

"What?" Emilie cackled.

"I have layers, some I didn't even realise I had myself. But peel one away and, hey presto, there's something new to learn about me."

"God, I love you," Emilie laughed and then froze. They hadn't said the words yet. They'd confessed their love as teenagers but not as adults, which in retrospect was stupid. After everything they had gone through together, the words should have been spoken weeks ago. Charlie bit her lip as she watched Emilie imitate a deer in headlights.

"I love you too, Em, surely you know that."

"Well, I hoped, but I didn't want to presume," Emilie mumbled.

"Stop looking so worried. It's always been you, Em, always. Come here." Charlie opened her arms and waited for Emilie to move into her. The kiss started out softly. As usual, Charlie lost herself in Emilie. It didn't take long for the kiss to deepen. They still hadn't had sex, and now Charlie was practically crawling out of her skin with want. *Please don't stop this, Emilie, not again.*

Charlie had tried to initiate sex on several occasions, but Emilie always pulled away when things were about to escalate. At first Charlie understood she needed a little more time to heal, but then the last two times when Charlie had voiced out loud she was ready Emilie had still stopped them taking it further.

"Em, I want you," Charlie breathed against Emilie's lips.

"Charlie, I — "

"Please, Emilie, please, don't shut this down." Charlie didn't like that she was begging, but that was the point she was at. Feeling Emilie hesitate for a second, Charlie almost cheered out loud when she felt Emilie's tongue invade her mouth with an urgency that befitted the circumstance.

Charlie ran her hands through Emilie's hair. Emilie moved to mirror her actions, but stopped when she felt the cut at the back of Charlie's head. Knowing that it would likely make Emilie hesitate again, Charlie pulled Emilie on to her lap so she was straddling Charlie's thighs. Letting her hands roam, Charlie mapped Emilie's curves with her fingers. When she reached the bottom of Emilie's shirt, she surged on, not permitting Emilie to overthink.

Emilie lifted her arms, allowing the shirt to be tugged off. Charlie smiled when Emilie's breasts spilled out. *No bra, thank fuck.* "I'm okay, Em. You won't hurt me."

"Are you sure," Emilie panted.

"I promise," Charlie replied. It wasn't hard to understand why Emilie had been reticent. She knew Emilie was petrified of Charlie hurting anymore and that she still carried unwarranted guilt over the attack. Charlie hoped their intimacy could erase those thoughts from Emilie's head once and for all.

"Trousers off, Em, I want you to ride me." Charlie released Emilie's body as she hopped off the couch, pulling off her trousers. Charlie's heart was drumming wildly. Emilie's body was heavenly.

"What about you? You're wearing a lot of clothes," Emilie purred.

"I am. Why don't you do something about that?"

Charlie sat back and waited. She wanted Emilie to be fully in the moment with her. Slowly, Emilie sank to her knees and began pulling at Charlie's joggers.

"You're not wearing any underwear?" Emilie sighed happily. "I love that my girlfriend has such affection for going commando."

261

"I'm glad it pleases you. Now let me do something else that will please you even more. Hop on." Charlie patted her lap. Emilie grinned and re-took her position on Charlie. Kissing Emilie's neck, Charlie palmed her breasts. They were, after all, magnificent. She smiled when Emilie's nipples reacted instantaneously. Rolling and pinching one nipple, Charlie bent her mouth down to the other, luxuriating in the soft skin as it touched her lips. Hungrily, she sucked in the peaked bud and lavished it with licks and bites. Emilie was gyrating above, her hips pressing down, trying desperately to find some friction.

"I'm so turned on," Emilie hissed. "Charlie, I need your fingers." Charlie didn't miss a beat. The hand that was pinching Emilie's nipple slipped down between them. Coating her hand in Emilie's excitement, Charlie slipped two fingers inside with ease.

"I love your pussy. My god!" Charlie growled. Easing a third finger in, she pumped her hand. Emilie's gasps spurred her on. "Can you take one more?" Charlie whispered into Emilie's neck.

"Yes," Emilie moaned.

Charlie slid a fourth finger in. She waited a beat before moving, allowing Emilie's body to adjust. "Ride me, honey." Emilie lifted herself a little before slamming down on Charlie's hand. There was nothing soft about it. Emilie was punishing Charlie's wrist, but she didn't care. The sight of Emilie looking so wild and out of control was worth every cramp and strain.

Sliding her free arm around Emilie's back, she gripped Emilie's hip, steadying the movement. Emilie ran both hands through Charlie's hair, forgetting about her earlier hesitation and the cut. Charlie let out a growl as Emilie pulled at her hair, her head rolling back in pleasure. All the time, Emilie continued to pound down on Charlie's hand. Charlie could feel Emilie's pussy tighten. She felt the gush of liquid as Emilie

262

screamed her pleasure into the room. "Yes, Charlie, Yes, Jesus don't stop."

Charlie doubled her efforts. Leaning her head against Emilie's chest, she gritted her teeth as her wrist took a beating. Emilie's whole body convulsed. Charlie bit into Emilie's skin as she came undone. When she felt Emilie slow her undulations, Charlie leaned back and captured Emilie's mouth.

"Holy shit," Emilie breathed into Charlie's mouth. "I think I gushed on you," she added.

"Yes, you did, and it was so goddamn hot," Charlie stated proudly.

"That was so intense. The orgasm just kept going. God, Charlie, it has never been this good with anyone."

"That's because *we* are made to do this, Em. Me and you."

"I want to make you feel just as good, Charlie. What do you want?"

"Ah, yes, I remember you saying you would do anything," Charlie smirked.

"Baby, after that explosion, I'll give you whatever you need."

"Good. Go and get our little friend. I feel like being bent over a table."

"How about I fuck you from behind on the sofa? It has a little more cushioning, babe." Charlie rolled her eyes. Obviously Emilie wasn't *completely* over fussing.

# Chapter 24

The pained moan coming from Charlie woke Emilie up with a start. "What's wrong?" she asked urgently.

"Nothing, I'm just stretching."

"Are you sure, you sound in pain," Emilie pushed. The last thing she wanted was for Charlie to overdo it and spoil her recovery. Maybe having sex wasn't such a good idea in retrospect. Damn it, they should have waited. Emilie knew it had been too soon. Goddamn her libido.

"Babe, you gave me four orgasms with a strap-on. Of course I need to stretch it out," Charlie laughed.

"We should have waited. Charlie, you weren't ready."

"Stop, Emilie. I know you're worried, but you're ruining my post orgasm rush. I know my body and I was ready. My muscles are tight, but nothing out of the ordinary. We didn't get too adventurous and let's be honest, you did all the hard work. I just bent over and enjoyed myself."

"What a romantic way to describe our lovemaking," Emilie laughed, her body relaxing a little. Emilie knew she had to let go of her worries. It was proving harder than she imagined, though. Everything felt out of her control. She couldn't do a thing about what had happened to Charlie, so she was latching on to what she could do, and that was helping her get better.

The problem was that she was overthinking, over analysing and over worrying. Charlie had voiced her irritation on several occasions. Two weeks had passed and Emilie could see Charlie was getting better by the second, but she couldn't stop herself from fussing and fretting.

"As soon as I have the energy to move, I'll jump in the shower. That will relax my aches and pains, okay?"

"Alright. Do you still want to take a walk? We have a couple of hours until sunset. We could walk slowly down to the bay. There is a wonderful little nature path that leads to the Fjord."

"Sounds perfect. Can we stop in and have a beer?"

"Sure. I'll get my disguise on. I don't think there will be a problem. Most of the tourists are gone and won't be back for a few weeks, but I'd like to be cautious."

"Sure thing, love. Right, come on, let's hop to it."

Emilie donned her disguise and waited for Charlie. A small smile played on her lips because she knew Charlie was going to laugh her ass off when she saw what she was wearing. Sure enough, Charlie rounded the corner, stopped, looked Emilie up and down, and then doubled over in hysterical laughter.

"E-em, you... you can't be serious?" she spluttered, tears rolling down her face.

"Of course I am."

"Babe, you look like one of the identities Melissa McCarthy is given in *Spy*. Where the fuck did you get that wig? Oh, Jesus, is that a howling wolf fleece jacket?"

Emilie felt her laughter bubble up. Charlie's whole body was shaking, causing Emilie to laugh along. "No one will recognise me like this. I'll just be sweet Dory Blatch from nowhere USA. On my holidays in my Winnebago."

265

"Sweet Jesus, I can't breathe," Charlie choked. Emilie was in full hysterics now, the pair of them crying with laughter.

"Come on, sweetie, we have a walk to take." Emilie wiped under her eyes and straightened her clothes.

"Have you padded your clothes out?" Charlie asked, wide-eyed. Emilie had indeed padded herself out. Not dramatically, but she'd added a bit of a love pouch around her middle.

"Yup. Hey, get used to it, lady. The moment I'm not forced to look like a supermodel on the stage, I will be pigging out. Do you know how much I miss donuts?"

"Hey, baby, have at it. Eat what you want. You're gorgeous." Charlie stated.

Slowly, they made their way down the street towards the main part of town. They would have to take it even slower on the way back as it was all uphill. Emilie kept a watchful eye on Charlie. So far, so good. Emilie nodded to a break in the trees that allowed them to see the bay. It was a wondrous sight. The water was completely still. The sun was starting its descent over the mountains. Emilie stood and watched Charlie as her face lit up, her eyes reflecting the winter light.

"Wow, Em, it's beautiful."

"Come on, it gets better from the shoreline. You okay to walk still?"

"I'm fine, honest. I think this is really doing me some good. My legs needed working more."

Arm in arm, they continued their steady amble down to the decked promenade that overlooked the beach and water. Emilie pulled Charlie along, wanting to do the nature trail before they lost the light. It took them double the time but Emilie was anxious that the rocky trail would prove too much for Charlie if they rushed. Finally, they stepped out of the wooded area and onto the decking that ran the length of the fjords' peak.

"Wow," Charlie whispered. "This is magnificent." Emilie remained silent. They listened to the water gently lapping over the rocks... the birds. They stood gazing over to the mountains that reflected flawlessly off the water's surface. "We have to come back here, Em, I want to see whales."

"Definitely. Over there—"Emilie pointed inland up the fjord, " —is where the Beluga whales mate. There is an outlook point in the National Forest. I've never been. I would love to do that with you."

"Yes, yes, yes. Ah, I'm frustrated I'm not up to doing the hikes around here." Charlies growled, her eyebrows furrowing.

"Hey, come on. No grumps, okay. We will come back on holiday and do all of that. Now, shall we walk to the micro-brewery?"

"Yes, beer, that's what will make this day perfect," Charlie grinned.

They set off at a snail's pace towards the town. The micro-brewery was on the road that ran along the bay. "Grab a table and I'll get us some menus," Emilie said, ushering Charlie to sit at the table by the window. What could be better than a local beer overlooking the bay as the sun set?

"They have a lot of choices," Charlie said, indicating the chalkboard above the bar.

"You can order a five, half pint board. That way, you can taste several beers at once."

"Now that is a grand idea, Em. I knew I loved you for a reason."

So far, no one had batted an eye at Emilie. Either they saw through her disguise and didn't care or they had no clue that an international superstar was sitting in their brewery having a quiet drink with her girlfriend.

The brewery's bar was small. A handful of tall tables littered the floor. Around half of them were occupied by locals.

It was the first time in years that Emilie had been able to just sit and relax with a drink in public. Okay, so she had to dress up for it, but that didn't matter. Actually, in the frigid temperatures, she was quite happy to have the added layers.

Well into their third drink, Emilie noticed Charlie looking out the window. Her gaze wasn't that of awe and wonder, it was troubled. "Hey, what's up?"

"Nothing," Charlie replied quickly, but Emilie didn't believe her. Charlie was still surveying something outside. Emilie turned her head to look.

"No, don't look, Em," Charlie said rapidly.

"What is going on?"

"I'm sure I've seen the same woman walk by like four times. She keeps looking over. I caught her eye, and she scurried off. Maybe it's nothing?"

"What did she look like?"

"Well, hard to tell. She had a bobble hat on, scarf and a big ass coat."

Emilie so desperately wanted to look, but she refrained. It was likely that they were being a little paranoid. Nobody knew where they were. It was to be expected that they both might be a little jumpy. "Shall we head back to the house? It's dark and we have a bit of a hill to climb."

"Yeah, come on, let's get back. We have some cuddling to do."

Even though Charlie was acting completely normal, Emilie saw her worry. They settled the bill and headed out. Their route home was simple. They only had to follow two roads. It was the uphill part that sucked.

The walk back was relatively silent. The panic they had both suffered in the brewery may have been unwarranted, but it had left its mark. Emilie didn't know what to say. Her nerves were on edge, but she didn't want to make it about her. Charlie

268

was the one that had a target on her back. She could only imagine how she must be feeling.

The loud roar of a car engine shattered the night's peace. Whirling round, Emilie caught sight of the car's headlights approaching them at speed. Screaming Charlie's name, she lunged for her girlfriend, who had been walking on the path closest to the road. Grabbing hold of Charlie's coat, Emilie tugged her hard away from the road as the car swerved towards her. They fell into a garden. The cars tyre's squealed as it raced off.

"Charlie, are you okay?" Emilie hauled Charlie to her feet, patting her body and face, checking for injuries. Charlie was pale. All the blood had left her face, leaving her looking haunted.

"Em, call Buddy. I think they found me," she choked out. Emilie watched as Charlie doubled over and vomited.

* * *

"Are all the doors and windows locked?" Charlie called from the kitchen.

"Yes, I double-checked. Buddy just sent me a text. He's ten minutes out. Lola is not far behind." There was a flaw in Emilie's brilliant plan to hide away, with no one knowing where they were. She wanted to kick herself for leaving them so vulnerable. Why hadn't she asked Lola to stay close by? How the hell had they been found?

Suddenly, the silence of the night was far too loud. Every creak of the house sent spikes of fear through Emilie's body. Charlie wouldn't sit still. She had been pacing through the house since they'd returned. The only visible sign of their altercation with the car was a small graze on Charlie's palm where she'd braced after Emilie pulled her away from the curb.

"Charlie, can you sit down? You're making me nervous."

"Emilie, I can't sit down. I'm freaking out a bit, to be honest. I hate that we're trapped here."

Emilie took some calming breaths, no matter how scared she felt. She had to be strong for Charlie. "I know you're scared, Char, but we are okay. Everything is locked. Buddy contacted the local police to send a car round. No one is getting to us." Emilie repeated the sentence in her head several times, hoping that she could believe her own words.

"Did you get a look at the car?" Charlie asked. Her pacing had slowed, but she was still moving about.

"No, just that it was a dark colour."

"Damn," Charlie whispered. "And Buddy is sure that Lydia is still in the city?"

"Yep, it's the first thing he checked. She hasn't left the city once. Whoever this is, it's not her."

"What about Jack? He's pissed at me."

"His footprints are too big for the ones found. Buddy checked that, too."

"Then who the fuck is it?" Charlie screamed, her face red with anger. Emilie flinched. The stress of the situation was becoming untenable for them both. The waiting around was awful, like they were just sitting there waiting for this unhinged psycho to come and find them again.

"Charlie, honey, please," Emilie said calmly. "Buddy will be here soon. We will get this sorted."

"When? We could be hiding for months if they don't find this nut job. Emilie, I have a fucking life in England, a career." The words were true, but they cut deep. It was the first time that Emilie saw the cracks in their relationship. A relationship that was in its infancy. Of course, Charlie would have to go home soon. Emilie was well aware they had things to sort out, but she wasn't sure they could do that under these circumstances. Would Charlie come to resent her? It was possible. Who the hell wanted to deal with this bullshit?

"Please, Charlie, I don't know what to say."

"There is nothing to say, Em," Charlie replied hotly. "I'm stuck in this nightmare and there is nothing you or I can do."

Emilie felt the hot sting of tears welling in her eyes. Her rational brain was telling her that Charlie was scared and lashing out. Her emotional side was telling her she was being selfish by wanting a life with Charlie. Even if she cut her work life back, Emilie would always be a star. She would always be in the public eye.

Until now, she never thought that would be a problem with Charlie. She thought they were too strong, they could weather any storm. Now, though, as she looked into Charlie's scared and pained eyes, she could see that it was just a dream, nothing more than a fantasy.

A loud crash echoed through the house from the bathroom. Emilie froze. Her heart rate was through the roof. Instinctively, she looked at Charlie. Instead of panicking, Charlie was snarling. Something had taken over her features. "I will not be ruled by this motherfucker," she growled through her teeth.

"Charlie," Emilie whispered, but it was no use. Charlie was stalking towards the bathroom door. Emilie's heart was in her throat. What the hell should she do? She couldn't let Charlie face a maniac. They could be armed. If anything happened to her, Emilie knew she would never forgive herself.

Standing from her seat on the couch, Emilie tiptoed towards Charlie, who was leaning against the wall flush to the bathroom door. Charlie turned to Emilie, raising her finger to her mouth, telling her to be quiet. Emilie wanted to roll her eyes at the command. Did Charlie think she was going to start a conversation, maybe sing a little? Of course not. She had no intention of making a sound.

Emilie listened intensely. Since the crash, there had been no other sounds from the room. Charlie turned to look at her, her mouth open as if she was about to speak. Instead, her eyes went wide, looking over Emilie's shoulder. Whipping her head round, Emilie gasped as a masked body ran at her, knife in hand. Sheer panic overtook every muscle in her body. The world slowed down as blood pumped in her ears, deafening her. Was this how she was going to die? No, it wasn't because the masked assailant didn't have their eyes on Emilie. No, they were trained on the person behind her. Charlie. *Oh God, no!*

Everything happened in an instant. The moment Emilie realised Charlie was about to be hurt again, her body took over. Launching herself as fast and as hard as she could, Emilie slammed her body into the attacker. They fell to the ground. Emilie heard Charlie scream her name, but she couldn't focus on that. The body underneath her was stirring from the shock of being body tackled. The knife had slipped from their hand. Reaching out, Emilie tried to grab it, but she was stopped. A hand was wrapped around her wrist, pulling it away from the knife.

Without warning, Emilie felt herself being dragged backward. The hands around her waist gripped tightly. Charlie was pulling her away from danger. What Emilie didn't bank on was that Charlie then threw herself at the person lying on the ground who was now scrambling to get the knife.

"Not so fast, arsehole," Charlie shouted, pounding her knee straight into the crotch of the assailant. A shrill scream pierced the air. Emilie looked on as Charlie lost all modicum of restraint. Her fists landed blow after blow. If Charlie's body was hurting, she wasn't showing any signs of it.

Red and blue flashing lights lit up the hallway through the front door window. Throwing herself forward, Emilie pulled at the door frantically. It took her a few moments to calm herself enough to unlock and open it. "Help, help," she screamed at anyone who was listening. Three officers rushed towards her. Buddy and Lola jumped out of their cars before they'd stopped moving. Emilie turned to go back inside. She had to see Charlie. Strong hands grabbed her, pulling her back to the garden. Shouts came from the house.

"Charlie, Charlie!" she screamed. She didn't care how loud she was, she had to make sure Charlie was okay.

"Em, Emilie, look at me," Lola said. Grabbing her head, Lola tried to get Emilie to focus on her face. "Charlie will be fine."

"There was a knife, and... and Charlie, she pulled me away."

"Okay, it's okay. Come on, let the police do their work."

Allowing Lola to drag her away, Emilie found herself sat in the back of an ambulance. The paramedic checked her out. There was a noise from the house. Emilie strained to see. When Charlie's eyes appeared like a beacon in the dark, nothing and no one was going to stop Emilie from getting to her. Pushing past everyone, Emilie flew across the garden and into the open arms of Charlie.

"I'm okay, I'm okay," Charlie whispered in her ear. Emilie sobbed... Twice she had come close to losing the most important thing in her life. Never again. Emilie would give it all up. The fame, the money, all of it could go to hell if it meant she would have to live a second without Charlie Baxter.

"I love you, I love you," she cried into Charlie's hair. A police officer came and escorted them to the same ambulance where Emilie had been sitting moments before. Loud shouting emanated from the house. Emilie turned to look. Her breath hitched when she saw the woman who'd attacked Charlie being dragged out in handcuffs.

# Chapter 25

The human body is a wondrous thing. Its ability to respond intuitively to its surroundings is miraculous. Watching a masked psycho running towards her had caused Charlie's body to flood her system with adrenaline. The moment Emilie had body slammed the attacker to the floor, it was as if Charlie's body became a separate entity to her mind. Her legs carried her over to the pile of arms and legs writhing around on the floor. Her arms had automatically wrapped themselves around Emilie, dragging her away from danger.

Once Charlie had put distance between Emilie and the nut job on the floor, she'd seen red. Charlie was a calm, peaceful person. She'd never seen the point of losing it. Of course it happened sometimes. She was only human. But as she stood there looking down at the person on the floor, all the fear and panic that the attacker had caused her moments ago — plus the physical pain she'd endured — collected in a tight ball in her chest. Transforming into unhinged rage.

The attacker, or Arsehole Supreme, as Charlie liked to call them, had tried to grab the knife that had fallen on the floor. Once again, Charlie's body reacted automatically, driving her forward. Well, driving her knee straight into the Arsehole Supreme's crotch.

There was no way she was going to let the person get up off the floor, not whilst Emilie was close by. Charlie would do anything to make sure Emilie had a chance to get out of the house. Sure, the attacker had been there for Charlie; but who was to say that Arsehole Supreme wouldn't turn their attention to the woman that they were obviously obsessed with?

The next thing she recalled was being surrounded by police officers, dragging her off the person on the floor. Charlie's mind snapped out of her anger-induced haze and instantly focused on finding Emilie. When she'd exited the house, there were people buzzing around everywhere. The whole neighbourhood seemed to be alive with red and blue lights. A second passed before she noticed Emilie pushing through the throng of police and paramedics.

With Emilie in her arms, Charlie had let some of her adrenaline and anger drain away. Knowing Emilie was okay was all she needed. They'd been ushered to the back of a waiting ambulance. Charlie hadn't noticed the minor cut on her arm. The paramedic made quick work of cleaning it and slapping on a plaster.

Charlie's focus was on Emilie and the look of shock etched on her face as the person who attacked them was led out the house in handcuffs. Emilie's face had drained of all colour.

"Em?" Charlie called as she watched Emilie stagger towards the police officers restraining the Arsehole Supreme. Whoever this person was, Emilie clearly knew them well.

* * *

"How? How is this possible, Buddy?"

"I don't know, Emilie, as far as I was aware she was locked up in California. Her release date isn't for another eighteen months."

Emilie could feel her body shake. Margo Pike had terrorized Emilie for months. She was the reason Emilie knew Buddy.

"Em, who is that?" Charlie asked from behind. Emilie was paralyzed. Margo was looking directly at her, a smile playing on her lips. "Em?"

"She's, she's—"

"Margo Pike was the crazed fan that Emilie had a problem with seven years ago. As far as we were aware, Ms Pike was serving an eight-year sentence in California for an unrelated incident."

"Clearly not, Buddy," Charlie shot. "Why didn't someone warn Emilie when this Margo bitch was released?"

"Charlie, calm down," Emilie said softly. Charlie's rising anger had been enough to break Emilie out of her fear-induced paralysis. "What happens now, Buddy?"

"Now we take you to the police station for your statements. Margo will be placed in holding until I can arrange to have her transferred to Quebec City."

"Emilie, Charlie, come on, I'll take you to the station," Lola said, making Emilie jump.

Feeling Charlie's arms around her shoulders, Emilie tried to relax. If she kept up this level of anxiety, she was going to have a heart attack or develop an ulcer. "Come on," Charlie whispered, moving them both towards Lola's jacked up SUV.

The ride to the station was short. Walking through the main doors, Emilie and Charlie were directed to Buddy, who waited for them at an empty desk. The room was small, with only four desks sitting back to back. Each one had piles of paperwork and files on them. So far, Emilie had only seen one other police officer.

Movement at the back of the room drew Emilie's attention. Margo stood at the bars of the holding cell, smiling widely at her. A shiver ran the length of Emilie's body.

"This way, Emilie," Buddy said, leading her away. The office she was put in was just as uninspiring as the main room. "Okay, Emilie. I'm going to take your statement whilst Officer York takes Charlie's in the room next door. Once I have everything from you, I'm going to interview Margo."

"Okay," Emilie answered automatically.

"Alright, take it from the top. When did you notice something was wrong?"

Emilie took a deep breath before recalling their evening in Tadoussac. By the time she had finished describing the attack in the house, Emilie was completely drained.

"That's everything," she commented, tears stinging her eyes. Reliving the attack was harrowing. Emilie held on tight to the edge of her chair, trying to ground herself. The signs of a panic attack felt dangerously close to becoming a reality. She couldn't break down, not now. Charlie needed her and she wouldn't let Margo win, not again.

"You did great, Emilie. I'm going to interview Margo now. Once Charlie is done, you can have Lola take you back to the cabin. I asked an officer to grab your belongings from the house in Tadoussac so they should be waiting for you outside. As soon as I know more, I'll contact you, okay?"

"Thank you, Buddy."

\* \* \*

Charlie paced the ten steps it took to reach the end of the shitty office she'd been dumped in. "Where the fuck is this Officer York?" she grumbled out loud. All Charlie wanted to do was scoop Emilie up into her arms and run away from it all.

Peeking through the broken aluminium blind that hung from the office door, Charlie saw a young woman in a police officer's uniform walk her way. "About bloody time," she mumbled to herself.

"Sorry for the wait, we're not really equipped for this kind of thing," Officer York giggled.

"What? You're not equipped for police work?" Charlie questioned.

"Oh, no, of course we are. It's just we don't have big things like this happen." Charlie refrained from making any more remarks she wanted to get this over and done with as fast as possible. "So let's get to it, shall we? From the top."

Charlie began at the brewery, telling Officer York about the woman she'd seen walking past several times.

"Can you identify the woman you saw as the suspect arrested in the house?"

"Nope, she was wearing a wool hat and a scarf that masked her face." Officer York nodded and made a note. "After that, we got a little spooked, so decided to call it a night. As we walked back, a car swerved towards us. Emilie had to pull me out of the way."

"Did you get a model or licence plate?"

"No, it all happened too fast."

"What about the driver? Did you get a look?"

"Nope, didn't have time to stop and look, you know, because we were trying to avoid getting mowed over."

"Then what?"

"We got home. Locked all the doors and windows. Emilie called Buddy. As we waited, there was a crash in the bathroom. It sounded like the window had been caved in. I went to listen. I stood by the bathroom door."

"Did you hear anything else?"

279

"No, everything went quiet. Emilie came up behind me. We waited but there was no movement. When I turned around to tell her to go back to the living room, I saw a masked person down the hall behind her, holding a knife."

"And what did the masked assailant do?" Charlie had to bite her lip from voicing the sarcastic comment floating around her head.

"They lunged towards me but Emilie tackled them. They ended up on the ground together. The knife fell out of the attacker's hand. I pulled Emilie away and then I wrestled the attacker on the floor. I didn't want them getting up and hurting Emilie. Then you guys came in and took over."

"Is there anything else you can remember?"

"Nope, that's the top and bottom of it."

"Have you ever met Ms Pike? Seen her around?"

"Never. I only found out who she was when Buddy explained."

"Great, okay then, that's it. I'll give this to Buddy and he will take it from there. You can go now." Officer York smiled. Charlie returned the smile to be polite. All she wanted to do was get the hell out of there.

* * *

Emilie rushed to Charlie as soon as she saw her exit the office with a young police officer in tow. "Charlie," she sobbed, throwing her arms around Charlie's shoulders.

"It's alright, Emilie, it's done." Charlie reassured. Emilie wasn't convinced. Something still felt off.

"Let's go, you two, the car's packed and waiting. I'm driving us straight back to the cabin," Lola interrupted.

The car journey was a silent affair. Emilie had stayed tucked into Charlie's side the entire journey. They were about fifteen minutes from their destination when Charlie shifted in her seat. Emilie sat up. "Can you tell me what happened with this Margo woman?"

Emilie closed her eyes for a moment. She really thought she'd left all that behind her. "Margo was or is a super fan. Seven years ago, I started receiving fan mail from her. Nothing out of the ordinary to begin with. Then she wrote to me saying that she'd had a dream. One that told her she needed to be with me. Not romantically. Her dream told her I was her sister, and she had to be with me, that it was her duty to protect me. I ignored it at first, but then weird things started happening.

"She was stalking me. Somehow she gained access to my private rooms in the hotels I was staying at during my time on tour. She would leave me things. Then she started getting really possessive, she started sending threats. She said I was hers and that one day we would be together.

"Buddy was the officer in charge of the case. It took a few weeks, but eventually, he caught Margo. She ended up serving a few months in jail. From what Buddy told me, it wasn't the first time she'd been in trouble. Her criminal record was quite thick. Buddy kept track of her for a while after she got out, but she was soon back inside again. She wasn't due for release anytime soon, which is why Buddy didn't connect her to this."

"Jesus, Em. I can't believe you had to go through all that."

"Yeah, it wasn't the best time." Emilie fiddled with her cuff. Should she voice what was niggling at her? "I just…"

"What?"

"Something doesn't add up." Emilie had been churning over everything from the second she saw Margo being escorted out of the house in handcuffs. The attack in the woods, the car swerving towards Charlie and then the subsequent attack in

281

the house was Margo. Emilie didn't need Buddy to confirm that for her to know it was true. What didn't make sense were the notes. Well, the note to Sam and Anna, to be precise. It was too familiar. Charlie's friends had only been in Canada for a couple of days. They hadn't really been out in public a lot, well not enough for Margo to work out that Sam was Charlie's best friend. So if the notes didn't come from Margo, then who sent them?

"In what way? The woman was caught red handed, love."

"I know that. It's just the notes. They don't fit."

"What, you think there is someone else involved?"

"Maybe, I don't know. I'm probably just being paranoid. I'll wait for Buddy to fill me in."

* * *

Charlie didn't think Emilie was being paranoid. The notes didn't connect to Margo. Charlie was sure of it. Whoever wrote the second note knew where to strike, and that could only have happened if the person had intimate knowledge of Charlie's friendship group.

By the time they got back to the cabin, Charlie was filled with restless energy. What were they supposed to do now? The last thing Charlie wanted was to stay in the cabin. Too much had happened there. Would Emilie go away with her if she asked? Only one way to find out, she supposed.

"Em, would you consider coming back to the UK with me?"

"When, now?"

"Yes. If Buddy says it's okay. I want you away from here, Em, just for a little while. We can go back to the manor or your cottage. I really don't care as long as we're together and safe."

"If that's what you want, then of course I'll go with you. I think we could both do with a little calm."

Charlie breathed easily for the first time in weeks. "Call Buddy, double-check it's okay for us to go. I'm going to call Sam and let her know. She's going to lose her shit when I tell her what's happened, but I think it will help her calm down if she knows we are coming home."

Emilie took herself to the kitchen to grab her phone, leaving Charlie with the unenviable task of calling her best friend. The last thing she wanted was to pile on any additional stress. Sam was already wound tighter than a coiled spring over Anna. The phone rang twice before it was answered.

"Hi, Charlie, Sam is just in the shower," Anna said. She sounded tired.

"Hey you, how are you feeling?"

"Tired. It's ridiculous. I can't move more than ten metres before I need to sit down." Anna grumbled.

"You just take it easy. Jesus, Anna, you're like growing a whole person in your body. Rest up, love."

"I am, honestly. I wish your best friend would be as calm as you. She's buzzing around like I'm going to drop the baby at any minute."

Charlie laughed. She knew Sam was going to be a worry wart. "It's only because she adores you. I've never seen her so excited."

A contented sigh filtered through the phone. "I know. I just want her to enjoy this with me, though."

"Do you want me to talk to her?"

"Yes, please, she might listen to you. Anyway, how are you? Healing okay?"

Charlie worried her bottom lip. She was expecting to speak to Sam, but maybe telling Anna first was a good thing. "So there's been a bit of a situation."

"Okay, care to elaborate?"

"I will, but I need you to promise to not get worked up. I'm already expecting Sam to fly off the handle. I need you to be the calm one."

"I'll try."

Sucking in a breath, Charlie launched into the story. She was selective with the details, no need to scare the crap out of everyone. "So, now we're back at the cabin. I think it's better if I bring Emilie over to the UK."

"*Mon Dieu*," Anna rasped.

"Yeah, it's been intense."

"Just get yourselves home. I'll talk to Sam. Don't worry, she'll just be happy you're safe."

"Thanks, Anna. Give the little peanut a kiss from their favourite aunt. I'll call soon."

Okay, that was the hard part done, kind of. Letting Anna break the news to Sam was a little cowardly, but after the past few days, Charlie reasoned she'd earned the right to be chicken shit this time round.

* * *

Emilie was going to have to relay what Buddy had just told her. Couldn't she get five minutes of peace before more shit got piled on?

Charlie suggesting they head to the UK was a great idea. As much as Emilie loved her cabin, it only chilled her to the bone now. Memories of Charlie's seemingly lifeless body just outside her door had tarnished her home. Spud would be okay with Jess for a little while. If Emilie stayed in the UK for any length of time, she would arrange for her to be sent over.

So, she needed to talk to Charlie, but she didn't want to do it now. In fact, she'd wait until they were safely on the way to the airfield. Maybe until they were on the jet.

As soon as she'd got the okay from Buddy, Emilie organised her private jet to be ready to go within the hour. "Okay, honey, Buddy gave us the green light. I'm going to pack. I'd like for us to be gone sooner rather than later. Can you call Jess, ask if she can keep Spud?"

"Sure thing. Everything go okay with Buddy? Any new updates?"

"He's only just finished with Margo. He will call when we arrive in the UK." Emilie hated lying, well, lying by omission. It's just that when Charlie learned the truth, she was going to go apoplectic.

"Sure, everything is cool?" Charlie asked, squinting her eyes. Emilie was so bad at lying.

"Fine, come on, let's get going." Not waiting for Charlie to respond, Emilie bounded up the stairs, grabbed her suitcase, and began packing.

Lola was humming gently to herself as she drove Emilie and Charlie to the airfield. Thankfully, Lola was more than happy to accompany them to Charlie's house. It was on Charlie's request that Emilie asked her bodyguard to come along. Lola was pumped, she'd never been to the UK before.

"Two minutes away, folks," Lola called. Emilie sat holding Charlie's hand, her thumb stroking rhythmically on her skin. The hangar came into view. Emilie was so thankful she had a private jet. The last thing they needed was to fight their way through Quebec's major airport. The press would be everywhere. Emilie wasn't naïve enough to think the recent attack on her and Charlie wouldn't have leaked by now. Emilie could picture the swarm of paparazzi that was probably staking out the airport just in case Emilie showed up. They'd seen a few reporter vans in the area near the cabin as they drove away.

Lola pulled the car to a stop, got out, and opened the door for Emilie. Tyres squealing in the distance gave Lola a reason to shove Emilie back inside the car.

"What the hell?" Charlie barked. Emilie had fallen on her lap, which in normal circumstances would have been great. Emilie sat herself up and peered out of the car window. To her utter horror, she saw Lydia hauling herself out of the car that had come to a stop close to the jet.

"Shit," Emilie hissed.

"What's going on?" Charlie asked, craning her neck to look out the window. "Emilie, why is Lydia here?"

"I was going to tell you on the plane," Emilie said, her voice nearly at a whisper. Argh, she thought they had time to get away before Lydia caught up.

Before Emilie could register another thought, Charlie climbed into the driver's seat and opened the door. Lola should have known a locked rear passenger door wouldn't stop a tenacious Charlie Baxter.

"Charlie, stop!" Emilie called, climbing out after her.

"Lydia, what's going on?" Charlie asked calmly. Emilie watched Charlie approach the woman — who looked unhinged — slowly, with her palms up.

"Charlie, get back in the car," Lola barked.

"Nope, not this time. Lydia?"

"You!" Lydia screamed, pointing her finger at Charlie. Her face was red with anger. "You're a fucking parasite, Charlotte! Nothing I do gets rid of you, does it." Lydia was bellowing, gesticulating wildly. All the time, Charlie stood still, never flinching. "You are not good enough for her. You never

286

were. What do I have to do, hmm?" At this point, it looked as if Lydia was talking to herself as she paced back and forth in front of them. Her hands grabbing at her own hair. Emilie winced. Lydia was going to injure herself at this rate.

"Lydia," Emilie said loudly. Lydia's gaze snapped to hers. "Lydia, please calm down."

"Why won't you see what a fucking virus she is? Look how well you did when I got rid of her the first time. Emilie, I'm the one who looks out for you. I always have, not her. She just distracts you, takes you away from your music."

"It *was* you back then," Charlie growled. "I knew it."

"I did what needed to be done!" Lydia screamed. "Emilie is a goddess. All you ever did was take her away from me. She was my friend, Charlotte, mine! I was the one she was supposed to be with, not you. Why couldn't you just stay away?"

Emilie saw Lydia reach around to her back. Did she have a weapon? Fear screamed its way through Emilie's mind. She had to do something.

"Lydia, please. I understand why you did it, I do really. I was just about to put Charlie on a plane to go home. I'm staying here with you." Emilie didn't know what else to do. Lydia was raging and Emilie could see she was walking a fine line. At any minute, Lydia could snap.

"You're lying," Lydia replied, but there was a sliver of hope in her voice.

"I'm not, I swear. Charlie tell her." Emilie prayed Charlie would play along.

"It's true. We're done." Fuck, Emilie hated hearing those words come out of Charlie's mouth.

"You're leaving for good?" Lydia barked, her face transforming from pure rage to delight.

287

"Yup, you win, Lydia, she's all yours." God, Emilie wanted to vomit.

Lydia slowed her pacing. She was no longer reaching for whatever she had behind her back. "I knew you'd see sense, Emilie. All she does is bring you trouble. If it wasn't for Charlie, Margo would never have gotten involved. See, I'm saving you." Emilie had to bite her tongue. Buddy had relayed what Margo confessed back to Emilie over the phone.

Lydia had apparently contacted Margo six months ago. Writing to her in prison. The timing made sense. That was when Mr Eccleton had first approached Emilie about the Pickerton Ball. Stupidly Emilie had confided in Jess and Lydia that going to the ball could mean she would see Charlie again.

By the looks of it, that had been what set Lydia off. She'd contacted Margo, forming one hell of a fucked up alliance. According to Margo, when it was clear that Emilie was bringing Charlie back to Canada, Lydia had convinced her that Charlie was a threat that needed to be eliminated. Margo also denied sending the two notes.

It all sounded so farfetched, but Buddy confirmed Margo's story. Margo provided letters and emails sent from Lydia.

"I appreciate you looking out for me, Lyds." Emilie smiled, which was hurting her soul right now. In the corner of her eye, Emilie saw Lola move. With Lydia distracted by Emilie, Lola had time to eject her Taser and drop Lydia to the floor in a writhing mess. Her body jerking erratically from the pulses of electricity surging through her nervous system.

"Charlie," Emilie called, rushing to her side.

"We're good, Em," Charlie responded, still staring at Lydia on the floor. Lola was on top of her, securing her hands.

"I'm sorry —"

"Stop," Charlie said, finally looking away from Lydia and into Emilie's eyes. "I think we've both said enough sorries to last a lifetime."

"I know but—"

"But nothing. Emilie, nothing Lydia said is a surprise. Well, maybe it is a surprise because, well shit, she fully lost the plot. What I mean is that me and you already forgave our past selves, right? I don't want us constantly rehashing this," Charlie said, waving her hand towards Lydia. "Enough is enough, Em. We have to let it go. Lydia will deal with the consequences. I hope she gets the help she needs. I really do. Buddy will sort all that. I just want us to get on that jet and fly away. We have so much to look forward to and I'm *sick* of looking back. It's done. I love you, Emilie, and you love me. That's it."

What could she say to that? Yes, bad things had happened to them and they would need to process it, but hell, Charlie was right. They'd waited long enough to start their lives together.

Emilie cupped Charlie's face. "I'm so glad you're back in my life. I love you, Charlie Baxter. I want to keep your heart safe with mine for the rest of my days. Will you let me?"

"Always, Emilie."

# Epilogue

"Oh. My. God! I cannot believe I'm backstage at an Emilie Martin concert," Kim squealed, causing everyone around her to laugh. Charlie grinned at her friend's excitement.

"You know your friends with her, right?" Anna laughed from her chair. Charlie couldn't believe how big she was now. Sam and Anna had wasted no time getting pregnant for the second time. Millie was such a good kid they'd wanted her to have a sibling ASAP.

"I know that, but this... this is different. I mean, look at her up there! She's awesome." Kim said, swooning. Charlie caught Hélène's eye roll.

"You are ridiculous," Hélène chuckled.

"Well, you married me like this," Kim laughed, kissing Hélène soundly on the lips. "Oh listen, Emilie's about to sing 'Timeless'."

Charlie's heart was going at the rate of a hummingbird's wing. No one—not even Sam—knew about her plans. Scratch that, there were a couple of exceptions, and they were Jess who Charlie had become really good friends with over the last two years—Jess had helped her set it up—and a couple of crew members who were in on it too and sworn to secrecy.

"I'll be back in a minute," Charlie shouted over the noise of the crowd. Emilie's new release, "Timeless," had topped the charts immediately and had stayed there for weeks. Sam shot

Charlie a look. Her best friend could sense there was something going on.

Running as fast as she could, Charlie made it to the top of the construction platform at the back of the stage. Everything had to be timed perfectly. Slipping on to the platform that held her grand piano, Charlie let the safety guy clip her in. Listening to Emilie sing, Charlie began her countdown. She hoped Emilie wouldn't be mad at the interruption.

The natural lull in the song appeared at the end of the first verse, and that was Charlie's cue. Pressing her fingers over the keys, Charlie played. The piano gently lowered and Charlie had to stop herself from laughing when she saw pure shock written across Emilie's face.

This was the first time Charlie had ever joined Emilie on stage. They only played together at home. Charlie loved the piano, but her career and passion was photography. Tonight, though, was about her and Emilie and, hopefully, the start of something new.

Finally, the piano reached the stage floor. Charlie was completely immersed in Emilie's eyes, who had stopped singing and was turned in her direction, her back to the crowd, jaw to the floor. The crowd was going nuts.

It hadn't taken long for their relationship to hit the press, not after the story broke about Lydia and Margo. Something they'd put firmly in the past.

Charlie had to lay low for a while. The press hounded them both, but they took an exceptional interest in Charlie. Finding out that Charlie and Emilie had been together in school and then the breakup provided the tabloids with the heart-wrenching love story they craved. Not to mention that Charlie was the elusive Charlotte Munroe. That had upped the interest in Charlie tenfold.

Thankfully, Emilie had helped guide Charlie through her new reality. There had been times when Charlie worried the pressure of Emilie's stardom would cause them stress, but it actually brought them closer together.

The reaction from Emilie's fans towards Charlie had been overwhelming. They treated her like *she* was a superstar in her own right, which baffled Charlie no end. S.C. Photography had become so successful because of Charlie's new fame that she'd had to talk to Sam about hiring a bunch of new photographers.

Charlie could now pick and choose her projects, which was a godsend, especially when Emilie decided to tour again after an extended break. Emilie had hired a new manager who was wonderful. Charlie knew Emilie was much happier now she got to do what she wanted without the pressure that Jack had put on her constantly.

Tonight was Emilie's final show and the perfect place for Charlie to surprise her. Taking a calming breath, Charlie sang the second verse. She could see tears brimming in Emilie's eyes. In her peripheral vision, she saw Sam, Anna, Kim and Hélène beaming, as was Jess, who stood to the right of the piano.

Charlie poured every ounce of love she had for Emilie into the song. The song *they* had written together six months ago. The crowd was getting louder, but Charlie easily muted them as she played and sang. The only person in the stadium she tuned into was Emilie.

Considering she'd hijacked Emilie's concert, Charlie wasn't worried now that Emilie would be upset. The final few notes of "Timeless" echoed through the stadium. Emilie hadn't moved a muscle, which Charlie was thankful for because she would seriously mess the plan if she did.

The crowd took a lifetime to settle down, but eventually an anticipatory silence fell. Charlie was breathing heavily and not just because she'd sang whilst playing. This was the moment.

"Emilie," Charlie said, a little surprised to hear her voice ring out across the vast arena so loudly. Charlie held her breath. Saying Emilie's name was Spud's cue. God, she hoped their weeks of training stuck. It had been difficult to train Spud to sit at Emilie's side without Emilie catching on.

Sure enough, from stage left, Charlie grinned to see her furry best friend — who had the cutest doggy ear defenders on — trot out with a small basket in her mouth. Like the best girl she was, Spud sat at Emilie's side, waiting. It took Emilie a second to register that something was happening. It was probably the huge gasp from the crowd that finally snatched her attention away from Charlie's eyes.

Charlie chuckled when Emilie missed Spud sitting there. Instead she looked over her shoulder at the crowd with confusion plastered all over her face. Finally, Emilie brought her gaze back to the stage and looked down. "Holy shit," could be heard through her microphone, causing the crowd to whistle.

"Emilie Martin," Charlie began. Emilie snapped her wet eyes from Spud back to Charlie. "Will you marry me?" The crowd lost their shit completely. Charlie wished *she* had ear defenders. The time between Charlie asking and Emilie's reaction felt like forever. But when she saw Emilie drop her mic and run towards her, Charlie had her answer. Quickly unhooking herself from the safety line, Charlie jumped from the piano platform and swept Emilie up into her arms.

"Yes," Emilie whispered in her ear.

Sobs ripped through them as they embraced fiercely. It was only when the chants of "kiss her, kiss her" got to a fever pitch that they put a bit of space between them. Charlie captured Emilie's lips. Soaking in every morsel of love radiating from her.

"I love you," Charlie whispered against Emilie's lips. Emilie dove back in, crushing their mouths together again. A sudden thought hit Charlie. *Spud!* Her canine sidekick was still sitting diligently in place, as instructed. Breaking away from Emilie, Charlie called her name. Spud sprang into action, running over with the basket still between her teeth.

"Good girl, Spud," Charlie cooed, rubbing her head before taking the ring box off the little cushion nestled in the basket. "Off you go," she added, which was Spud's command to leave the stage. She'd done so well that Charlie could only laugh when Spud ignored her completely, thumped her tail on the floor before zooming off around the stage to the pure delight of the crowd and band members.

Charlie dropped to her knee and looked up into Emilie's eyes. "It was always you, Em, always." Gently taking Emilie's hand, Charlie slipped on the sapphire ring she'd spent weeks agonising over. It fit perfectly.

\* \* \*

Emilie's heart was still thudding like a bass drum as she pulled Charlie up after she'd slipped the most gorgeous ring on her finger. This was all so unreal. It was already an emotionally charged night. The last concert of a tour was like that. Together with the band, she'd put everything she had into the show. "Timeless" was the last song, and she'd been looking forward to performing it. After all, it was about her love for Charlie and she could never get enough of that.

When the sound of a piano had begun just before the second verse, Emilie thought she was imagining it at first. They'd written the song together with Charlie playing the melody on her piano, so naturally Emilie believed she was so lost in the music on stage she was imagining Charlie playing.

294

Then it hit her that no, in fact, she wasn't imagining anything because there was a goddamn grand piano descending from the heavens with Charlie attached to it. All cognitive functions had ceased to work after that. Emilie was just a passenger along for the ride as her body froze in place, watching the wonder that was her girlfriend sing their song to her on stage in front of thousands.

When the song was over and Charlie spoke her name, Emilie was so stunned that she still hadn't been able to move. It was only after the crowd grew so loud that her brain kicked in again. She knew something was happening. Peering down to see Spud sitting by her side holding a little basket with a ring box inside had almost caused her to pass out. Then Charlie had spoken those four words.

Emilie knew they would marry. That had never been in question. She hadn't wanted to rush Charlie, though. The change in lifestyle for Charlie was huge, and Emilie was scared deep down that she would find it all too much. Her worries were, of course, for nothing because time and again Charlie had shown her how devoted to them she was.

The thunderous applause from the audience brought them out of their bubble. Turning to the whistles and shouts, Emilie couldn't stop her laugh breaking free. Grabbing Charlie's hand, she walked them closer to the edge of the stage and took a little bow. Charlie laughed and did the same. Shrieks from the side of the stage grew louder as Kim, followed by Hélène, Sam and much slower Anna, crossed the stage to embrace them.

"I told her not to run out here," Hélène laughed.

"I'm sorry," Kim cried, "I just had to hug you both. Charlie, that was… wow."

"I'm so happy for you both." Sam had to shout to be heard. The group smashed together in one big family hug.

295

"I need to pee," Anna moaned after a few seconds. Emilie threw her head back, laughing along with the rest of them as Anna struggled free, waddling away to find the nearest loo waving at the crowd as she went.

"I think your fans would like to hear from you," Charlie whispered in her ear. Emilie would never tire of the electricity that thrummed through her body when Charlie spoke.

Pulling herself away from the rest of the group, Emilie turned to her fans. Picking up the mic she'd dropped, she steadied her breath, ready to address her fans that were still going batshit crazy.

"Well," Emilie started and then laughed. "This was a surprise." The crowd whistled louder. "Sorry for the interruption there, folks," she laughed again. "How about we have one more song?" Emilie didn't need an answer. The arena was vibrating with applause. Stepping up to Jess, Emilie gave her a quick peck on the cheek, whispering, "Thank you," before picking up her guitar. Jess was the only one that could have helped Charlie pull off a proposal like that on stage.

A crew member rushed on stage with a mic stand and stool. Charlie went to leave the stage with her friends, but Emilie stopped them. This was their moment, and she wanted her family to be a part of it. There was only one song that she could play. The melody that had kept her mind calm before a show for twenty years. A song that imbued everything Emilie ever felt for Charlotte Munroe all those years ago and the sheer elation she held in her heart now for Charlie Baxter.

"This is for you, my love," Emilie said softly into the microphone, looking towards Charlie. She strummed the first chord to "Losing My Head Over You" and then she sang. No longer did she drown in the memories of losing the girl she loved. Tonight she sang, swimming in the love and promise of their future.

296

# Afterword

Thank you so much for reading my book. I hope you liked reading it as much as enjoyed writing it! Please spare a few seconds to add a review on Amazon and/or Goodreads. Even just a star review without a comment helps Indie authors so much!

Sign up to receive my monthly newsletter. Just visit my website and enter your email address.

www.alysonroot.com/sign-up

# Acknowledgement

A massive thankyou to my wife Angelique and all my family for being so supportive. Once again, I have to give Monna a shout out! You are a godsend.

# About Author

Alyson was born and raised in the heart of England. She moved to Paris in 2015 when she met her wife. Together they moved to the west of France where they now live with their two dogs and pet bird. Alyson spends her time running a small campsite and holiday home. During her off time, she loves to read lesbian romance books, write and Scuba Dive.

# Praise For Author

## A Dance Towards Forever

"This is my first Alyson Root book and F/F book. I actually really enjoyed it. The story was funny and sweet and at a few moments had me wanting to strangle Kim, Helen and Greg. I liked that she used common problems in relationships like education, careers, family, friendships and addiction. It really makes the story more relatable. I am definitely looking forward to reading Sam and Anna's story and more books."

Goodreads review

## Diving Into Her

"This story is so well written with enough anxiety to sink a ship, beautiful love to fill the sails of a large schooner, and confused lovers scared of their own passion to break hearts! The characters are well developed, each one needed to fill the story. The writing style is perfect for this story. I strongly suggest you purchase this, keep it on your reread often shelf, just like I am doing!."

Amazon Review

# Books in Series

.

## The French Connection Series Book 1

## A Dance Towards Forever

There are three things that Sam Chambers knows to be fact. One, her heart is broken, two, her career is sinking, and three, she hasn't a clue how to turn any of it around.

When her new boss John Spencer shakes things up at the photography company she works for, the last thing she expects is to be sent to Paris on a career changing project. Unbeknown to Sam, the brief glimpse of a dark-haired beauty at St Pancras is about to tip her world upside down.

Anna Holland has the life she worked hard for. She's successful, she lives in the city of love and she is in a steady relationship with a nice guy. The problem? Her nights are filled with the vision of a red-haired woman. Nothing makes sense when the woman of her dreams shows up in Paris and her office.

Together, they start a journey of exquisite discovery. Is there something more to their chance meeting? The unfathomable connection between them would suggest so.

**Available to buy on Amazon.**

**The French Connection Series Book 2**

## Diving Into Her

Kim Richmond is a 5'0" sassy blonde bombshell with a love of vintage dresses and killer heels. She is also a woman on the edge of losing her mind after her boyfriend cancels their holiday again. Accepting a two-week trip to the south of France courtesy of her best friend is the just what she needs. Staying at the five-star luxury Sapphire Hotel and Spa is like a dream come true. That is, until it all comes crashing down.

Helene DuBois has been dumped again! The cosmos really has it out for her, well that's how she sees it. There's only one thing for it, she needs a holiday. A break away from her messy life. Sun, sea, scuba diving and absolutely NO women. A trip to Saint Tropez should do the trick. Rest and relaxation with no drama, perfect! What could go wrong? Seeing Kim Richmond sobbing in the hotel lobby would be one clue. Offering to share her suite with the blonde beauty would be the second.

**Available to buy on Amazon.**

Printed in Great Britain
by Amazon

37669285R00175